THE STORY GRID

What Good Editors Know

SHAWN COYNE

THE STORY GRID

What Good Editors Know

SHAWN COYNE

Black Irish Entertainment LLC

NEW YORK LOS ANGELES

BLACK IRISH ENTERTAINMENT LLC

ANSONIA STATION

POST OFFICE BOX 237203

NEW YORK, NY 10023-7203

COVER DESIGN BY MAGNUS REX

EDITED BY STEVEN PRESSFIELD

FIRST BLACK IRISH ENTERTAINMENT EDITION APRIL 2015

FOR INFORMATION ABOUT SPECIAL DISCOUNTS FOR BULK PURCHASES,

PLEASE VISIT WWW.BLACKIRISHBOOKS.COM

ISBN: 978-1-936891-35-1

EBOOK ISBN: 978-1-936891-36-8

PRINTED IN THE UNITED STATES OF AMERICA

1 2 3 4 5 6 7 8 9 10

For Bibb, Bleecker, Waverly and Crosby

Contents

Preface

FOR THE RAMEN NOODLE EATERS

In the days, months and years to come, it is my intention to map out *Story Grid*s for as many novels (and some key nonfiction works) as possible. You can follow my work at www.storygrid.com and get free access to everything I do.

No joke. It's free.

Would I prefer that you buy this expensive textbook instead? Pay even more to view or attend lectures? Hire me for an outrageous sum to give you personal tips?

Well, sure I would.

But, here's the thing:

When I started out, there were very few people in book publishing who shared what they knew. Almost no one would. So I had to learn 99.9% of what I know and what I write about in this book myself. It took me twenty-two years to do that. And three years to write this book.

I can only wonder what I would have been able to do if I were given access to this information all those years ago. For Free!

I was broke back then. I walked a lot of times to work because I didn't want to spend the subway fare to get there. And I spent practically every weekend at my desk at the publishing office because where I lived was…dark, dank and depressing. Plus it had no air conditioning in the summer and poor heat in the winter.

But I would have done the same thing even if I had lived in the penthouse of Trump Tower.

I love what I do and I'm not complaining about my life's path or work. I just think it would have been incredible if there were something like *The Story Grid* available to me back then.

So if you're that man or woman eating ramen noodles every night and staying every waking hour at the office trying to figure out how to write a great Story or edit a great Story, go to www.storygrid.com and dive into the archives. You'll get everything you need there. And after you've sold your novel or gotten that big job, buy a copy of this book and give it to someone like you were...before you made it big or even just big enough. And continue the conversation.

Stories are the most important thing we humans can create.

We need more Story nerds! As one to another, I hope you get something out of this book to make your work better.

Shawn Coyne
New York
March 2015

Introduction

BECOMING OUR OWN EDITORS

It was the great Maxwell Perkins, if I'm not mistaken, who told Hemingway to get rid of the first two chapters of *The Sun Also Rises*. Hemingway did. The book made him famous.

Perkins got Thomas Wolfe to cut ninety thousand words from *Look Homeward, Angel.* He whipped twenty shoeboxes of raw manuscript into *Of Time and the River.*

Do you know what an editor does? I don't either. All I know is it's make-or-break, do-or-die, indispensable, can't-do-without, gotta-have-it.

But there's one problem:

Editors don't exist any more, at least not in the grand Old School sense.

These days if you're lucky enough to get your book picked up by a major publisher, you may get taken to lunch by your editor. You may receive a few consultatory e-mails. You may even get a three-page memo of "notes."

But you will not get Maxwell Perkins.

If you're indie-publishing or self-publishing, you'll get no editor at all.

It's a hard fact of the twenty-first-century book biz that the writer, for all intents and purposes, has to be her own editor.

You and I are expected to deliver a Story that works, a manuscript that's flawless, a book that's ready for the printer.

That's editing. (Or, more accurately, self-editing.)

But what *is* editing?

Is it correcting grammar? Spell-checking? Syntax tweaking?

When I was working on my third book, *Tides of War*, Shawn Coyne was my editor at Doubleday in New York. He read the manuscript (which was almost nine hundred pages long). He studied it. He lived with it. Then he got on a plane and flew out to Los Angeles, where I live. Shawn stayed with me for three days. He worked with me around the clock, explaining what was working in the Story and what wasn't and why—and, more importantly, showing me what I needed to do to fix it. He left me with a twenty-six-page single-spaced memo. I still have it.

It took me four more drafts and nine months before Shawn accepted the manuscript.

That's editing.

Over a twenty-five-year career as editor, publisher, agent, manager and writer, Shawn has been part of more than 350 books, 97 of which have become national bestsellers in North America. Books he has edited or published have sold over fifteen million copies. But until I began working with Shawn as a partner in our own small publishing company, I had no idea of the depth of an editor's contribution.

A great editor sees the Story globally and microscopically at the same time. He has x-ray vision. He looks down from thirty thousand feet. A great editor can break down a narrative into themes, concepts, acts, sequences, scenes, lines, beats. A great editor has studied narrative from Homer to Shakespeare to Quentin Tarantino. He can tell you what needs fixing, and he can tell you how to fix it.

How many editors of that caliber are working today? I'm guessing now. A dozen? Two? No more.

But what about us, the writers? How many novels have we written that are near-brilliant, almost-great, wildly-promising-but-not-quite-fulfilled? What's missing? What did we get wrong?

What's missing is editing. Story analysis. Concept, character, and narrative breakdown.

But how do you learn editing? They don't teach it at Harvard and they don't school you at Random House.

A great editor has to teach himself. He learns through experience, through manuscript after manuscript and book after book.

A great editor develops a system, a philosophy. He distills the arcane and the academic into a working model that's clear, practical, and usable.

Shawn did that.

He calls his method *The Story Grid*.

It took me twenty-two years [Shawn writes] to figure out The Story Grid was not something that any other book editor I knew used. After innumerable lunch and drink dates, I found out that they didn't create their own method to evaluate work by studying Story structure. And they thought I was kind of a nerd for doing that myself.

The writer is allowed to be crazy. She's permitted to wing it, to plunge ahead on instinct, to follow her Muse and let her Story rip. But it's the editor who has to take that Story and make it work.

A great editor has to fathom the narrative's underlying design (of which the artist is often blissfully unaware), and if there is no design, he has to draw one forth from the existing material. He has to chart the Story's movements, conflicts, themes and counter-themes, its values and the valences of those values. He's the mechanic. He's the surgeon. His left brain makes the artist's right brain work.

Who is the editor today?

He's you.

You have to master the editor's skills. You have to know how to break down your own Story, before you begin (hopefully) and after you're done (if necessary). Art is not enough. Genius is not enough. Editing and Story analysis are not some extra goodies affixed at the end of the banging-out-the-pages work; they are the heart and soul of Storytelling. You, the writer, have to know them.

How do you learn?

The book in your hand is the place to start.

Steven Pressfield
Los Angeles
March 2015

THE STORY GRID

PART ONE

WHO I AM AND WHY I AM HERE

1

WHAT I DO

When a person meets me for the first time and learns that I make my living as a literary editor, the first question he invariably asks is:

"What exactly is it that you do?"

This book is the long answer.

The short answer is this:

When a manuscript that intrigues me arrives, I read it. I don't take notes. I just read it. If I finish the entire book— twenty-four times out of twenty-five, I'll abandon it early on as the obvious work of an amateur—I will start to think seriously about its publishability. Does it work? Will it sell?

My editorial juices have started flowing now. Already I'm beginning to analyze and break down the manuscript's narrative. My decades of experience are telling me where, more or less, the Story is working and where it's not.

So far my process is identical to that of every other professional editor. But now, at this stage, I'll do something that no one else does.

I will run the manuscript through *The Story Grid*.

I'll do this as deeply as necessary and as many times as required to identify the problems, to evolve suggested solutions, to hone the Story and shape it and elevate it to the highest level of Storytelling craft.

Over a twenty-five-year career as an editor and independent publisher (as well as a writer, agent and manager) I've used this method to bring hundreds of works from raw manuscripts into A-level published fiction and nonfiction. Books that I have edited and published have grossed more than one hundred million dollars. But more importantly, these books have changed people. They've changed the lives of readers and they've revolutionized the lives of the writers who authored them.

The Story Grid is a tool. It's a technique. It can't make something out of nothing, but it can make something out of almost-something, out of not-quite-something, out of two-inches-away-from-something.

And it can inspire a work from idea to first draft.

What *The Story Grid* offers is a way for you, the writer, to evaluate whether or not your Story is working at the level of a publishable professional. If it is, *The Story Grid* will make it even better. If it isn't, *The Story Grid* will show you where and why it isn't working—and how to fix what's broken.

What follows is how you can become your own editor.

2

WHAT IS *THE STORY GRID?*

The Story Grid is a tool I've developed as an editor to analyze and provide helpful editorial comments. It's like a CT scan that takes a photo of the global Story and tells me what is working, what's not, and what must be done to fix it. When I show *The Story Grid* to writers, they love it because it allows them to break down the component parts of their novels (or narrative nonfiction) to see where their Storytelling went off track. Identifying the problems in a Story is almost as difficult as the writing of the Story itself (maybe even more difficult).

The Story Grid is a tool with many applications:

1. It will tell the writer if a Story "works" or "doesn't work."
2. It pinpoints problems but does not emotionally abuse the writer, revealing exactly where a Story (not the person creating the Story...the Story) has failed.
3. It will tell the writer the specific work necessary to fix that Story's problems.
4. It is a tool to re-envision and resuscitate a seemingly irredeemable pile of paper stuck in an attic drawer.
5. It is a tool that can inspire an original creation.

3

WHERE DID *THE STORY GRID* COME FROM?

When I began my editorial career at one of the major New York publishing houses, there was no systematic process to learn how to edit a Story. That is, how to read a Story, diagnose its strengths and vulnerabilities, and then help the creator heighten the highs and eliminate the lows.

There was no training program at the publishing houses.

There was no course in college or in graduate school.

You couldn't sign up for Editing 101.

While there were (and still are) hoity toity finishing schools for recent college grads to matriculate through in order to secure an entry-level position in the field, these summer programs were more attuned to the business side of publishing than to the art.

The assumption was (and still is) that the capacity to edit a Story is a mystical combination of intellectual rigor (one must be well-read and well-schooled in comparative literature, the classics etc.) and an intuitive *je ne sais quoi*, a flawless internal Geiger counter that can magically sort radioactive literary or commercial works out of the inert rubble piles where they are hidden.

To learn the editorial craft, one had to apprentice. One would sit in the presence of and serve someone who had the magical editorial hand, and by osmosis, the mentor's skills would pass on to the neophyte. Like a cobbler or a blacksmith, one learned how to do by watching someone else do it well and then applying the lessons from those observations in one's own work. Under the tutelage of an expert who would redirect the pupil when he went off course, editors were made. This is the way it has worked for decades, even centuries.

But apprenticeship as vocational training is highly dependent upon the "master" role in the relationship. And unfortunately the editing masters of my era, and even more so today, are overwhelmed with the business of book publishing. They just didn't have an hour a day or an hour a week for that matter to devote to training editorial assistants. Their time was spent finding books that the company could publish successfully, reading submissions and competing with likeminded editors at other publishing houses for the best properties. And when they weren't hustling acquisitions, they had to attend meeting after meeting and prepare thousands of words of editorial copy to sell the books into the marketplace.

So what separated the good editors from the great editors? And how could I find a way to put myself in the latter category?

There are amazing editors out there who have a knack for finding the Story that will become the next big thing. And there are extremely charismatic editors who can dazzle sales forces and book reviewers in ways that make their projects reach the widest possible audience. But the ones I admire most are what I would call the "Hail Mary" editors. These are the ones that publishers call in when a project is in deep trouble. These editors can take a book that almost works or is even sometimes a complete disaster and retool it with the author in such a way that it not just works, but oftentimes it reaches frontlist bestsellerdom and then backlist nirvana.

Frontlist sales come at the front, those that result from the initial splash of publication, the reviews by the big newspapers, the ad campaigns, the marketing programs etc. Backlist sales are titles that come quietly day after day, month after month and year after year, from word of mouth recommendation, from one reader to another. Backlist classics build publishing houses.

Hail Mary editors help create the classics.

This is the kind of editor I set out to be.

All I had to do was learn how to Edit with a capital *E*. And then hone my skills to razor sharpness. There was only one problem. There was no book called *How to Edit*. I'd have to figure it out myself.

The result of this decades-long exploration is *The Story Grid*. It came out of my life's work and is my attempt to create that *How to Edit* book that I needed way back when…

4

THE AUTODIDACT'S DILEMMA

Faced with the reality that the editors with whom I was apprenticing (very respected, very talented, and very generous) did not have the time or the textbooks necessary to teach me how to Edit, I set out to teach myself. The primary dilemma we face with a task that is foreign to us is *"where do I begin?"*

Where you begin is a personal choice and as long as it pushes you to dive deeper into or zoom out from a particular discipline, it matters little if you start at the sentence-by-sentence editorial level or the global Big Picture elevation. As someone with a science background, I like to begin at the top of the mountain (a grand hypothesis) and chip my way down to sea level (a series of experiments to test the hypothesis) and eventually into the basements and subbasements (the tactical approach to setting up the experiments themselves).

Knowing that editing was dependent upon understanding Story, the first question I asked myself was:

"What is the primary divide in the long form Story business?"

If you were to create a flow chart of how book publishing works with a box at the top that says STORY IN BOOK FORM, what would be directly underneath? How many secondary classifications would there be?

This turned out to be a simple question to answer.

There are two categories in book publishing, like yin and yang, light and dark, wet and dry. There is "literary" and "commercial." The divide seems ridiculous of course, akin to the old chicken and egg debate. Obviously, what is literary must be commercial too and what is commercial is also literary. But these two global designations define the two cultures of book publishing. As a practical matter, it's crucial to understand exactly what each is and why there is a distinction in the first place.

STORY IN BOOK FORM

LITERARY **COMMERCIAL**

5

LITERARY AND COMMERCIAL

If you are a writer, an editor or a publisher in traditional trade book publishing, you have to decide which of these two cultures you want to align yourself with.

The literary culture is represented by publishers like Alfred A. Knopf, Farrar Straus and Giroux, Scribner, Random House, Riverhead, Penguin Press and a number of other houses both independent and corporate owned. These houses are known for the high end literary stuff—Cormac McCarthy, Robert Caro, Toni Morrison, Jonathan Franzen, Anne Lamott, Richard Powers, Zadie Smith, Don DeLillo, Thomas Pynchon, etc. Young English Lit grad editorial assistant wannabes long to land a job at one of these houses. Working at these shops grants entrée to *Paris Review* parties and publishing street cred that says, "I'm in it for the right reasons…to nurture tomorrow's great American novelists." Acquiring a writer who ends up on *The New Yorker*'s 20 under 40 can get you a promotion. A rave in *The New York Review of Books* or *The Atlantic* puts a swagger in your step.

On the other side of the street is the "commercial" culture, often referred to as Genre fiction (even though every great Story abides by Genre conventions) and in the case of nonfiction, "Merch" like self-help, how-to, celebrity biography, etc. Future editors in the commercial arena are the nerds you see reading *The Hobbit, The Da Vinci Code, How to Win Friends and Influence People, Jaws, Rich Dad, Poor Dad, Twilight, Lace* or *Dune* on the beach while the other kids are body surfing. They often come from that wonderful crop of college graduates who don't know what to do with their lives, so decide to find work that pays them to read. They don't care so much about line-by-line writing perfection, deep universal truths, or post-modern metafiction pyrotechnics, these editors are just addicted to narrative velocity—stories that grab you by the throat and won't let you go.

At the top of commercial pyramid is Women's fiction—big bestselling books like *The Help, The Guernsey Literary and Potato Peel Pie Society*, etc. Women's fiction doesn't mean that male writers are excluded from the category. But rather that the books written by men must have themes, characters, or plotlines that women enjoy. They scale and can reach the million-copy-sold mark if not with ease, at least with greater regularity than a war novel.

Estimates reach as high as 70% of the entire book buying market being women. So in order to really hit a book out of the park, a writer/publisher needs to bring women to the party. The male writers who do count women as devoted readers write stories that often include a love Story within their overarching plot. Nicholas Sparks is a terrific example of a male writer embraced by a female audience.

Male writers with female readers also feature strong female characters in their novels. Stieg Larsson's *Girl...* thrillers are an example. So too are works by James Patterson, John Grisham, Pat Conroy, David Baldacci, and Dan Brown. These guys are not seen as "boys' book" writers. They have BIG crossover appeal.

Talent and desire aren't enough to make the registers ring at retail. For that, you need to have identified your audience and have written your book in such a way as to give them the reason, or "hook," to buy it.

Ultimately, the question *Who's the target reader, and why?* must be answered by everyone in the publishing chain (writer, editor, marketer, publicist, publisher). Identifying the audience (the people who will buy your book) defines which of these two cultures "Literary" or "Commercial" you belong to.

I see commercial publishers and editors as the empiricists of the industry. Whether they consciously know it or not, they use data from previous successes to support their editorial selections. They think about markets and Genres and make as informed decisions as possible when choosing whether or not to publish a particular novel.

For example, years ago I was put in charge of acquiring the rights to mystery novels for Dell Publishing and later St. Martin's Paperbacks. I was given a limited budget and told to publish two, and later three, mysteries in mass market paperback every month. That's right...twenty-four and then thirty-six titles per year.

How did I do it?

First, I familiarized myself with all of the Subgenres of the mystery Genre. There are quite a few...Hardboiled Private Eye, Cozy, Amateur Sleuth, Domestic, Locked Room, Historical, and Police Procedural. (I've probably forgotten one or two.) Then I looked at the sales figures for previous mysteries the company had published in each of these Subgenres over as many years as I could get data for (back then, mid 1990s, about seven years). What I found was pretty interesting.

For the most part, each of these Subgenres was profitable, but inconsistent. One year private eye novels would be on top by a wide margin, and cozies were all red ink. A few years later, cozies were in the black, and private eyes took it on the chin. Armed with this information, I decided that the best course of action would be to publish a wide net of Subgenre mysteries. So I literally divided the number of Subgenres into the number of titles I had to publish each year and came up with a number—eight Subgenres, twenty-four titles needed per year. I'd publish three novels in each Subgenre each year.

Then I looked at the historical performance of the Subgenres. I wasn't the only editor publishing mysteries. I had competitors at every other major publishing house. What they published would influence the marketplace too. One year the market would be flooded with cat cozies (yes there is a Sub-subgenre of mystery that features a cat as a lead protagonist), and while the top brand-name writers in the Subgenre would still perform in big numbers (Lilian Jackson Braun, Rita Mae Brown, Carole Nelson Douglas…they all had three names for some reason), the unknowns found themselves scrambling. The cat cozy market was just about fixed. If there were too many books offered to that limited market, many would fail.

So I made the leap that each Genre of mystery had a fixed number of fans. If I knew that one Subgenre was being abandoned by my competitors (back then it was the hardboiled private eye on the ropes), I'd publish more of those kinds of books into the marketplace and fewer of ones that seemed to be "overpublished." The fan base would be starved for more hardboiled mysteries and I would be the only one offering them. I used this method to justify publishing some extremely talented writers who had just not found their audience yet—Harlan Coben and Ian Rankin among them.

So, that year, even if your cat cozy mystery was exceptional, better than even the best one on the market, your agent would have a tough sell to me. But if you had a compelling lead private eye mystery in a unique setting and a head-scratching plot, even if you weren't the best thing since sliced bread, you'd get yourself a contract. And perhaps vice versa the next year. Commercial editors listen to the market as best they can and then try and find the best books to fill a particular void.

While I can't attest that every commercial editor uses this sort of model to help them choose which books to get behind, I can say that each one of them has some sort of inner empirical strategy.

About two years after I moved out of mystery Genre publishing and into the big ticket lead commercial hardcover fiction arena, I read Steve Pressfield's *Gates of Fire* on submission. I loved the book. I thought it was extremely well written and the sense of time and place were remarkable. But what was the "hook?" Who was the audience? If I couldn't answer those questions when my publisher and the sales force asked me, there was no way in hell I'd be able to acquire the book.

I went back to my mystery model.

I looked at the arena. How many war novels were being published in 1996? *The Killer Angels* by Michael Shaara was a big bestselling book and his son Jeff's prequel *Gods and Generals* was climbing the charts too. W.E.B. Griffin's military novels continued to sell in big numbers year after year. And of course Tim O'Brien and James Webb's Vietnam novels were evergreen backlist bestsellers. But few other titles stood out.

After doing the research, I learned that the military fiction market was under-published at that time.

And as the Spartans were the epitome of warrior culture with Thermopylae holding the preeminent place in western military history, *Gates of Fire* could reach an audience starved for a brilliantly told historical war novel. The men who read Griffin, O'Brien, Webb, Shaara, even Conroy (his early novels *The Boo* and *The Lords of Discipline* are "boy book" military themed classics), and every military nonfiction book sold would love this book.

The argument worked.

But I was pitching to a commercial publisher and a commercial sales force. If I had been pitching *Gates of Fire* in a literary house back in 1996, and used these same arguments, I may have been granted approval to acquire the novel, but I don't think the literary house that published it would have targeted the wide swath of readers we did at Doubleday. That is, they would have "packaged it" (cover treatment, positioning to sales force and retailers, and eventually the message to the consumer) as something compelling for an intellectual crowd as opposed to a good old fashioned sword and sandal epic.

Back to the two cultures (Commercial and Literary) and why I think they are beginning to merge. Publishers can no longer afford to rely purely on the literary category. The audience for literary books has shrunk considerably over the twenty years I've been in the business. I think it's because there is no longer that select New York based media industry intelligentsia that can influence booksellers and book reviewers (both rapidly vanishing) to push a particular novel based on subjective aesthetic literary excellence.

There was a time when the book publishing industry was obsessed with finding the next great American novelist and while there certainly continues to be a longing for such a thing (Jonathan Franzen, Nicole Krauss, Jonathan Safran Foer, etc.), grooming one is expensive. Every publisher wants one of these tasteful literary figures to prop up as proof that their lists are fully rounded, but the fact is they just don't sell like they used to. As for scale, they will never approach a book like *The Da Vinci Code*.

That doesn't mean there is no place for the literary anymore. It just means that publishers have had to move the pendulum closer to the commercial. Knopf publishes the Stieg Larsson trilogy and has sold millions. And Knopf's paperback arm, Vintage, publishes the *Fifty Shades of Grey* trilogy. They publish certain kinds of commercial fiction because they can pay the bills while they search for the next Roberto Bolaño.

What this means is that there is a great demand for novels that can be positioned at the top of the commercial list—thrillers and/or dramas that women will want to read. All of the big publishers (with a contracting list of exceptions) are on the hunt for a female friendly literary/commercial commodity. They don't care about Genre so much as "will it scale?" A crime novel from a National Book Award nominee or a literary novelist taking a crack at a vampire trilogy is the result.

If you are a screenwriter, LITERARY AND COMMERCIAL translates to INDEPENDENT AND STUDIO. If you are a playwright, LITERARY AND COMMERCIAL translates to CHARACTER DRIVEN AND PLOT DRIVEN. If you are a nonfiction writer LITERARY AND COMMERCIAL translates to JOURNALISM AND NARRATIVE NONFICTION. No matter your intended Story career path, the divide remains...and always will.

More on all of this later when I write about INTERNAL AND EXTERNAL forces of Antagonism.

6

WHERE I TURNED TO LEARN HOW TO EDIT

Just about everywhere.

I asked seasoned book editors who told me that editing depended on what kind of Story was being told. You didn't edit a mystery the same way you edited a love story or a thriller or a coming of age novel. Each kind of Story has its own conventions and obligatory scenes.

There are also two kinds of editing—global and line-by-line. Copyediting is a separate discipline—a grammar, spelling, and punctuation checking stage that Story Editors left to the specialists. I breathed a sigh of relief. I didn't much care for that kind of stuff. I wanted to decipher what made me burn through books like *The Bourne Identity* and *Red Dragon* far more than knowing the best use for a semicolon.

Okay, so editing first depended on the kind of Story being told and what Genre it fit into. That made sense, but weren't there some hard and fast principles that all Stories had in common? Was there some sort of fundamental unit of Story that could be deconstructed? How would you do that?

Prior to entering book publishing, in one of my past enthusiasms after college, I studied acting. During that humbling experience, I'd learned how to break down a scene. How to figure out what the intention of the writer was and then extrapolate truthful actions that I could take to make the purpose of the scene clear to the audience. At its most basic, a scene starts one place and ends another. It starts with a positive (man meets woman of his dreams) and ends with a negative (woman rejects man's advances). Or it starts with a negative (rejected man calls his best friend for consolation) and ends with a positive (friend convinces rejected man to get a dog and try again). It can also begin negative and end double negative (someone falls…and then gets hit by a car) or positive and end double positive (man wins a hand of blackjack, puts it all on a number at roulette table and wins big)… That's about it.

Simple, but I can't tell you how many books I've read where the scenes just never shift valences. They never turn. And when a scene doesn't turn, it's not a scene.

I was attracted to a newish acting philosophy that came out of a bunch of classes that David Mamet and William H. Macy taught at New York University in the early 1980s. It was called the Practical Aesthetics Workshop. Mamet and Macy were (and still are) all about de-bullshitting stuff. Mamet's love of language and the crystal clear dramatic confrontations in his work always appealed to me. What he and Macy put forth just made sense. They offered a means to make the theory of acting (how to authentically give an audience a truth while living in a lie of fake circumstances) practical. They gave me a process to make choices and then a means to practice those choices. They gave me tangible things to do so that I could get better on stage. If you want to get stronger, you don't think about the proper way to lift weights. You learn the proper way and then you actually lift weights. Pretty simple.

We need this approach for editing too. Figure out the work and then do it.

PAW is a stoic, blue-collar, no-talent-required-if-you-work-your-ass-off kind of philosophy. And while I eventually abandoned my quest to become the next Daniel Day-Lewis, the training proved incredibly helpful when I did find my calling. I'll get more into what I learned at PAW and why it is such a crucial skill for an editor to have later on when I take a deep dive into the scene. But for now, suffice it to say that Mamet and Macy's method to deconstruct the fundamental unit of a novelist, a playwright or a screenwriter's Storytelling is a Godsend. Read *A Practical Handbook for the Actor*, the meat of what came out of Mamet and Macy's lectures and the foundation of The Atlantic Theater Company in New York. It's so simple, direct and easy to understand, it's mind blowing.

Now understanding how to throw a knuckleball is one thing. Doing it well is another. Same with acting. And writing of course. But understanding lends itself to repetition of action, which is the only way to get good at anything.

So with a skill I thought was a waste of time learning after I left the drudgery of living the starving New York actor life, I was able to apply a rigor to analyzing scenes in the novels that crossed my boss' desk.

I knew when a scene worked and when it didn't. And that has made all of the difference in my career.

7

WORKS, DOESN'T WORK

How many times have you read this snippet of a book review, either on Amazon.com or in a major newspaper or blog?

This book is badly in need of an editor.

It is not without irony that these sorts of reviews are most often attached to titles that have sold hundreds of thousands of copies. Rare is the *"where was the editor?"* decree for a work of meta-fiction from the writer with an MFA from the Iowa Writers' Workshop.

Why is that?

Beyond *The Emperor's New Clothes* factor many reviewers succumb to, an Alfred A. Knopf press release or advance praise from last year's bright young thing is often enough to move a snooze of a book to the top of the superlative review pile. "Literary" works are given a much wider critical berth than the commercially appealing salted peanuts kind of Storytelling. The reason is that there is no comprehensive formal education available for learning the essential fundamentals of Story. Let alone how to take those fundamentals and turn them into clear tasks capable of being objectively (or better still subjectively) evaluated. While reviewers, by the very nature of their critical point of view, profess to have such knowledge, most do not. They just don't get "works, doesn't work."

It's as if a person alien to the qualities of life were presented with a live mongoose and a perfectly preserved taxidermy of a mongoose and asked which one is "better." The stuffed carcass, while perfectly quaffed and "life-like" is impressive. But given a choice of having to look at a dead mongoose stuck to a plank of cedar and a live mongoose in its natural habitat for four hours, which choice would you make? I'll take the wild thing over the pretty thing every day of the week. Even if it has only one eye, its hair is matted, and it has an uncontrollable rabidity. Sometimes, especially because it has those immediately recognizable scars and afflictions.

Others say, quite volubly, that they would choose to contemplate the stuffed animal. (I think they're putting on airs no matter what they say…)

For me, as long as the thing is alive and I have no idea what it's going to do next, I'm in.

There are plenty of ways to praise or critique a writer's sentences, or a taxidermist's fur fluffing for that matter, but few critics are capable of explaining why some novels or histories or narrative nonfictions read like bats out of hell while others put you right to sleep.

It's easier to attack the bestsellers than it is to de-bullshit MFA fiction. And deep down, the "where was the editor" reviews are not really there to shame the bold name writers who know how to spin a wildly intoxicating tale but are not the best sentence to sentence. They are to show off how erudite the reviewer is, be it a *Wall Street Journal* review or the 1123rd amateur review at Amazon.com.

The subtext, of course, is that editors aren't doing their job at the very least and publishers are idiots at the worst. *Why don't they help the poor Story savants out and teach them how to write a proper sentence? If they did, the collective culture wouldn't be subjected to such pablum* is the ad nauseam refrain.

But, the reality is that editors **are** doing their jobs. Very well in fact.

You just need to remember one primary tenet of business to understand why this is so. People collect pay when they satisfy their employers. Editors at publishing houses don't work for writers. They work for for-profit corporations. So, you might reasonably ask, if these editors are doing their jobs, how in the world do such books escape the editorial process?

How do these cheesy, poorly drawn line-by-line writers escape without being re-written?

The answer is that a Story either works or doesn't work. It either engages the reader or it doesn't. It's alive or it's dead, like our mongooses. And the last thing an editor wants to do is kill a living Story, no matter how mangy.

And thus, the oath of the professional editor is like that of the physician, a Hippocratic one.

First, do no harm!

But there's a catch. And the catch is the hypocrisy of the business.

Working "literarily" and working "commercially" can be two very different things. A Story can take the reader through expertly crafted sentences with innovative metaphors that would be the envy of Proust. Technically, its sentence-by-sentence craftsmanship is beyond reproach. And perhaps many novels are honed to line-by-line perfection through a dynamic relationship between the writer and a word-by-word, sentence-by-sentence editor. But for all of the minutial skill of these novels, the Story may have absolutely no narrative drive.

This book may "work" literarily, but in no way does it work as a Story. These books are the equivalent of our perfectly preserved mongooses.

This is not to say that these well tended corpses can't sell a lot of copies and become bestsellers through the forces of the previously mentioned *The Emperor's New Clothes* phenomenon...*If everyone says it's great, it must be great even though I can't get past page nine.* And there are some editors who are experts at finding these properties that today's *Emperor's Court* will lavish praise upon and make the work that year's must read...or that is, must buy. But as there are fewer and fewer trusted arbiters of genius in the media these days (there are only a handful of newspapers that even review books anymore), it's getting more and more difficult to sell copies of a book based purely on its literary cachet.

Mind you, there are writers who take on a project knowing that they are more interested in fluffing fur than caretaking a wild beast. For them, a success is defined almost academically. That is, they know they are experimenting with technique and know that getting the attention of likeminded intellectuals is their preferred goal...not necessarily *The New York Times* bestseller list. They're pushing the boundaries of form intentionally and understand when they make that decision they will inherently limit their audience. They're pros though and thus, they're cool with it.

Knowing exactly what it is you are doing is the key.

And making a conscious decision about your project as best fits your goals for that project is crucial to managing your own private expectations. I think it doubtful that James Joyce thought he'd make a killing writing *Finnegans Wake* or that Samuel Beckett put down a deposit for a beach house while he was writing *Waiting for Godot.* They knew what they were doing—breaking Story form and taking the chance that the project would die in a desk drawer.

You better believe they knew the form, though, before they broke it. Just as Beethoven knew symphonic form before he smashed it with his *Ninth Symphony*.

Those form breaks were so well constructed that they pushed Story structure's edges out further.

On the other end of the spectrum, a writer's prose that wouldn't challenge an eight-year-old's vocabulary or ability to follow a sentence can be impossible to stop reading. And when one finishes that book, it's most often disingenuous for the reader to say that he wasn't satisfied. He may have quibbles, but he read the whole thing to the very last word. That's a Story that abides Story form but will not end up in the pantheon of Western civilization.

So what's the bottom line here?

Learn the form. Master the form. Then if you want to try and write the next *Gravity's Rainbow,* knock yourself out.

8

YOUR OWN WORST ENEMY

A few years ago, a very talented line-by-line writer came to me for help.

A publisher I respected had recommended her to me. The publisher believed (rightfully) that the woman had what it took to write bestselling thrillers. The publisher had passed on a number of her books…not because he didn't find them compelling, but because ultimately they "didn't work."

The writer asked me to work with her from first idea to final draft. That is, she wanted to start from scratch…seek my opinion about the right kind of character to feature, the particular Genre of thriller that I felt was the most underserved and to basically engineer a new novel from start to finish using *The Story Grid.*

She could not afford to pay my usual editorial fee, but I too believed in her, so we came to a profit sharing relationship. We would be business partners, just like a couple of scientists figuring out how to create a new kind of light bulb. I'd done this sort of thing before with narrative nonfiction as well as fiction, and while the work required a multiple year commitment, I've never regretted taking it on. I always learn something new.

We got to work.

I walked her through *The Story Grid*, how I work, etc. and she was over the moon. It turned out that she was as much of a Story nerd as I was. She had read and studied many of the same Story experts I had as I developed my editorial method, so we spoke the same language. She immediately understood my principles and jumped right into the process.

We began by both agreeing that she'd write a contemporary thriller that would introduce a brand new series character, a woman with a Jason Bourne-like ignorance of her past. While the External Genre was "spy thriller," the Internal Genre of the book would be a "disillusionment plot." (More on this later.) Coincidentally, she told me she had a draft of a book she'd written with a similar character in her closet.

She suggested that we begin with that draft to see if there was anything salvageable from it.

This is when I started to get nervous. But I relented. Maybe the manuscript could give us some direction…never say never, right? Why reinvent something that works?

I read the book and it had some really great moments. Innovative turns of phrase, some seriously frightening scenes. Overall, it gave me even more confidence in her abilities. But it most certainly did not work. It never paid off the promise of the hook in an inevitable, yet surprising way. She did not disagree.

I ran it through *The Story Grid* and then we sat down to go through the places where it went off the rails. Weeks later, I thought we had a very clear understanding that the new lead character for our reverse engineering project would not be based on the character from her previous, unsold novel. Rather we'd use a few of the scenes from the novel that really worked and perhaps adapt them to suit as major turning points for the new novel. I left her with a working map of about sixty scenes/chapters that included all of the conventions and obligatory scenes of the spy thriller form (more on this later). I thought the conventions and obligatory scenes that we'd sketched out were uniquely twisted and innovative to a degree that would delight a thriller fan.

I even cold pitched the Story, like Hollywood screenwriters do, to a few friends who held very high editorial positions at Big Five publishing houses. These friends had purchased millions of dollars' worth of stories from me before, so I knew they had zero interest in humoring me. They wanted me to give them the first crack at the book for their publishing houses, so they were happy to give me quick notes and/or tell me what worked and didn't work. This is what happens at agent/editor lunches sometimes and it's the only reason I still have them.

I finished my job as a sort of "co-creator/editor/agent" and now it was time for my business partner to do hers.

We shook hands and she walked away with the road map to complete the novel. Keep in mind that it took us a good nine months to get to this point. We debated scene after scene until we both felt it was the best solution we could come up with at the time. Were they turning correctly? Were we mixing up the positive and negative resolutions enough? Did we progressively complicate the Story effectively? Did we pay off the hook?

We both recognized there would be a very great chance that what we anticipated to work would need to be completely re-thought after we had a draft in hand. But as a reference guide to write a workable thriller, it was spot on.

She came back six months later with a book far closer to the original manuscript she pulled out of her closet than I thought possible. While scenes were changed, the very problems that made it unworkable a year and a quarter before riddled the narrative. And an obligatory scene—the hero at the mercy of the villain scene, crucial to nail in a thriller—was gone entirely.

I took a deep breath and went through her draft scene by scene again and confronted her about the lack of the crucial obligatory scene.

"Well, I wrote it, but then I didn't like it, so I cut it," she said.

I explained that it was fine to do the scene differently, but without it, the book wouldn't work.

"That's not true, I read THE LATEST THRILLER BESTSELLER BY A BESTSELLING AUTHOR and he didn't have that scene…why do I have to?"

So that was when I knew this project would never come to fruition. I now knew the reason why this very talented writer kept getting to the one-yard line and was never able to score a touchdown—a working thriller. Instead of dedicating herself to nailing the form of the thriller/Story, she decided she was above it. She wanted the fruits of the labor (bestsellerdom) more than the labor itself (writing a brilliant and innovative hero at the mercy of the villain scene no matter if the book was ever published or not). She wanted to be a bestselling thriller writer so badly, she decided doing what BESTSELLING THRILLER WRITERS did was more important than abiding by centuries-old Story form.

In her mind, conventions and obligatory scenes were all well and good, but because a BESTSELLING THRILLER WRITER was able to ignore one or two in his novel and still become a bestseller, she felt she must do that too. No matter how hard I tried to explain that she couldn't copy what a BESTSELLING THRILLER WRITER did and get the same result, she refused to change her mind. Over and over again, I told her there was no Formula, just Form.

Her argument of course was that if a BESTSELLING THRILLER WRITER was able to break the conventions of the form, she should be able to as well.

Here's a difficult concept to grasp and I'm sure I'll go to my grave trying to explain it. Just because a book becomes a bestseller doesn't make it something to emulate. There are a myriad of reasons why some books become bestsellers and still don't work as Stories (See *The Emperor's New Clothes* phenomenon). Sometimes, there's just a hunger for a particular kind of book (Vampires, Zombies, BDSM novels) based on some ephemeral need in humanity's collective subconscious that drives sales. Trying to write one of those books that get swept up in the tide or even, the ultimate for some, a book seen as the cause of the tide, is folly. It's like selling your house and putting all of your money on number seven at the roulette table because you have a feeling number seven is going to hit!

Chasing the vagaries of the bestseller list (believing in formula and not form) is the mark of the amateur. That's putting the by-product of the Story (money, fame, etc.) ahead of the Story itself. Your contempt for form and lust for formula may even give you what you want. You write the next huge thing that makes you hundreds of millions of dollars.

Now what? That kind of writing is equivalent to winning a lottery.

Why not just play the lottery?

The truth is I don't think my business partner really had contempt for Story form. I think it scared her. She had the stuff to write a terrific Story that played off of century-old themes, but to do so required adherence to fundamentals. Not formulaic rules. Despite all of their desire to live by their own lone wolf ways, ironically what amateur writers really want is a recipe. And certainty. And guarantees.

Form scares the big bestselling writers too. That's why they often write books that do not abide by the obligatory scenes and conventions of their Genres. But just because they have a wide audience that will buy whatever they write does not mean they wrote a Story that worked.

In their desire to be unique and powerful, creative people become their own worst enemies. To abide by "rules" seems antithetical to why we're artists in the first place. So when presented with things that look like rules (form) we subconsciously rebel. We resist it with everything we have. And even when we talk ourselves off of the "I'm not going to write that scene because it's stupid" cliff, it's really hard to actually see the form for what it really is—an opportunity. Form gives you the place to throw down your best stuff.

Take the Hero at the Mercy of the Villain scene. It's been done to death. Try not picturing Bruce Willis or Liam Neeson chained to a pipe and being tortured when you hear "hero at the mercy of the villain." How do you keep from writing that setup, but instead, innovate it and still deliver the form?

Thomas Harris did it in *The Silence of the Lambs*. He didn't run away from it. Instead, he probably wrote two hundred versions of it and none of them worked. He probably didn't really figure it out until his tenth draft. What's important to remember is that he didn't quit until his thriller WORKED. And working means abiding by conventions and obligatory scenes of Genres.

The writer/business partner and I never did get on the same page about her thriller and we parted ways. Unfortunately, it's five years later and she still hasn't been able to get a publisher to take her on. I think about her every day and have faith that she will one day set aside her Resistance to form and create something remarkable.

9

KNOWING THE RULES SO YOU CAN BREAK THEM

There is a reason why I first divided long form Story into business terms. A very good reason, and believe it or not, it has more to do with Art than Commerce.

Every writer wants to be read. And the best way to learn whether your Story is reaching people is to tally the number of them willing to part with their hard-earned cash to experience your work. Understanding exactly how and why certain kinds of Stories find an audience much faster than others allows an artist to make informed choices. Long form Story creation requires years of devotion. Knowing the general sense of how many people will want to read your Story before you set off to do the work will help manage your expectations.

That is, wouldn't it be better knowing up front that your novel about the conquest of an adolescent by a pedophile will in all likelihood fail to reach a wide readership no matter its packaging?

The Professional writer, whether consciously or subconsciously, knows exactly where his idea sits on the Literary and Commercial spectrum long before he starts to work.

Some even take on the challenge to prove a commercial "truth" wrong. They succeed or fail based on their Story Craft. Incredibly inventive line-by-line writing matched with superlative Story form charts new ground, while lackluster line-by-line matched with derivative Story execution fails to do much of anything.

There are innumerable reasons why the premise of *Lolita* (pedophile pursues adolescent and gets his conquest) should alienate an audience, but for the great majority of readers, it doesn't. Vladimir Nabokov probably didn't literally say to himself, "I know this book I'm writing will be impossible to actually sell, but I gotta be me. I'm gonna do it anyway."

But I'm confident he did set out to challenge himself in a way no one else would dare. He knew that writing about a taboo subject, not just writing about it, but writing about it from the point of view of the predator, was a ridiculous business decision. It was obvious in his day, and even today I don't see many who'd be willing to go down that road.

Nabokov wasn't a part of our postmodern, digital age either. There weren't three hundred thousand books coming out every year vying for the attentions of literary agents, editors and publishers. There was no way to effectively "self-publish." The marketplace was much smaller then and the business elements far more Draconian. And his chances of getting his novel published pre-e-book pale in comparison to today.

But he refused to allow the impossible odds of his book reaching a critical mass of readers to stop him from writing it. Instead he probably used the unlikelihood of *Lolita* making it to the front table of the equivalent of Barnes and Noble in his day to free his inner darkness. The result was that we got a game-changing novel that proved the irresistible nature of human longing as narrative.

To know the rules of the Story Business and of the Story Craft gives you the freedom to break them. Not knowing the rules is a recipe for disaster. Trust me, Nabokov knew the rules of Story and the rules of publishing. That is why he was able to break them so skillfully.

Lolita is a classic "quest/hero's journey" Story, the one that is so deeply ingrained within our cells that we can't help but root for even the most despicable protagonist like Humbert Humbert to get what he wants. Nabokov knew that the structure of the Quest Story is irresistible to readers. He knew that with a lot of hard work, he could use it to get people to not just sympathize with a monster like Humbert, he'd get them to even empathize with him. Talk about powerful. The book was so good it was banned.

The point is that you should know what you are getting yourself into before you dive in. Nabokov did. That's why he used the power of Story form to beat the odds.

10

THE REALPOLITIK OF BOOK PUBLISHING

When a Story "works," it makes you want to keep listening to it, or reading it or watching it. And what will happen next, while completely in keeping with its initial promise (a Western, a Bildungsroman, a ghost Story around a campfire, whatever), delights over and over again. But the kicker is that the climax will be utterly refreshing. By Story's end, the listener or reader or watcher has to be at the very least surprised and satisfied by the payoff of the Story's initial promise.

And sometimes, rarely unfortunately, the ending can bring an emotional catharsis large enough to change the way we see our world and even make us change our behavior because of it.

This from David Mamet's *Bambi vs. Godzilla* on what makes a Story work. "They start with a simple premise and proceed logically, and inevitably, toward a conclusion both surprising and inevitable."[1]

A Story has the exact same structure as a joke. When someone tells us a joke, the Genre ("knock-knock," "a horse walks into a bar," "take my wife") sets us up for an expectation. When the payoff is inevitable, but surprising, "orange you glad I didn't say banana," "Why the long face," "PLEASE"), we laugh.

Later on in the book, I will ask you to outline the major scenes in your long form Story (*The Foolscap Method*). Now, if you wish to know if your Story will "work" before you bang out a hundred-thousand-word manuscript, or revise a hundred-thousand-word manuscript, I suggest you take someone out to dinner (someone you trust who won't tell you what you want to hear, but won't undermine you either) and tell them the fifteen crucial movements from your Foolscap Page.

---

1 Mamet, David. Bambi vs. Godzilla: On the Nature, Purpose, and Practice of the Movie Business (Vintage) (Kindle Locations 1028-1029). Knopf Doubleday Publishing Group. Kindle Edition.

In Hollywood, this is called a "pitch."

You will know if your Story works if the person across the table actually pays attention. If your Beginning Hook doesn't grab him, you'll know it in a microsecond just by his expression. If your Middle Build doesn't raise the tension and make him desperate to know what they hell is going to happen, you'll know. And obviously, if your Ending Payoff is flat, he'll be trying to get the waiter's attention to get the check.

But if your Story works, he will beg you to write it for others. In Hollywood, that's called "buying it in the meeting" and it is nothing short of Nirvana. To speak for twenty minutes and to walk out of a meeting with the promise of tens of millions of dollars, if not hundreds of millions, committed to putting the stuff inside your head into the global marketplace must be both exhilarating and terrifying.

But the screenwriter knows that if he delivers what he pitched, he'll be fine. Even if the movie never gets made…

Is it possible to bring both great line-by-line and cathartic Story work to a project? Can there be an innovative literary novel that is also a barnburner of a read? Or a potboiler that is exquisitely written? Such is the Holy Grail of publishing.

And of course, the answer is a resounding "YES."

When line-by-line and global Story magic come together, our jaws drop. It's why we pick up any book, hoping that this one will join the short list of those that have changed our lives.

I will run you through *The Story Grid* of such a novel at the end of this book, Thomas Harris' *The Silence of the Lambs.* You'll see the sixty-four pieces of his puzzle and how he was able to put them together in perfect order, all the while staying truer than true to Story form. And he ended up innovating the conventions and obligatory scenes of his chosen Genres too.

And guess what? You can run any novel (or narrative nonfiction) through *The Story Grid* and see the same kinds of pieces and choices.

But back to the state of editing in today's book-publishing landscape.

Can you expect that the book you've written, which was good enough to attract an agent and also good enough to be acquired by a publishing house, will be raised to a higher level by your new editor? Remember, editors are paid by the publisher.

The primary job of the Big Five publishing editor and/or independent publisher hanging on by his financial fingernails is to concern himself with whether or not the book works commercially. That is, will the book excite and satisfy a critical mass of readers who will fork over their hard-earned cash to experience the Story? Will they come back for the author's next book too? Will the Story in its present form make money?

If the answer to that question is yes, the Big Five or independent publisher will invariably deem it ready to go. However, if the editor at the Big Five house or independent publisher suspects that the core audience for the book may reject it based upon the fact that the critical conventions and obligatory scenes in the book (more on this later) are not surprising enough, he'll put the writer through the editorial process. He'll make the writer re-write the clunkers and get them to a place where he believes the Story will satisfy its core audience.

The truth of the matter is that today there are so many Stories vying for the validation of major publishing that Big Five editors don't even acquire books that have clunker obligatory scenes or conventions anymore. The editor passes on them because there are enough books coming in to him that are ready to go. Why waste time fixing something when you've got plenty of things on offer that already work?

Remember that the Big Five or Independent publishing editor's first job is **not** to bring a Story to its creative epitome. It's to make the damn thing good enough to sell.

In my career I've seen the number of full-time editorial positions and full-functioning publishing companies cut in half, while the number of titles published and imprints started has at least doubled. Do the math on how much time an editor today can indulge his desire to understand Story. So give your editor some slack and remember that the first rule for him is DO NO HARM!

If he thinks your book can sell ten thousand copies as is (the usual place that will send a book into profitability, and they would not have offered you a contract if they didn't think it would sell ten thousand) he isn't going to ask you to re-write the act 2 climax. He may not even know what that is. If he did ask you to do that work, and you do, and your book sells 9,999 copies, it's going to be his fault.

And even if the book sells 12,500 after you've fixed the scene, who do you think will get the credit? The editor? Not so much. In fact, there will probably be a bunch of reviews about the book asking, *Where was the editor?* You'll forget about his contribution and think that the marketing team hit it out of the park.

So will everyone else. Even him. Trust me.

This is the realpolitik of book publishing and it's one you need to understand.

This is why you need to become your own editor.

11

FLASH FORWARD: *THE STORY GRID* IN ACTION

Just for fun, the next two-page spread is what *The Story Grid* infographic for the writer looks like for Thomas Harris' novel *The Silence of the Lambs.*

Don't panic. It's not nearly as complicated as it looks.

Like a human being, a Story has global systems from which extremely specific features develop.

The Story Grid, at its most fundamental, concerns just six questions that you will ask yourself over and over again. My business partner, Steven Pressfield, has an organizational technique he uses before he starts any novel or narrative nonfiction piece. He calls it *The Foolscap Method* because the whole thing fits on a single sheet of yellow foolscap paper.

The Foolscap Method is *The Story Grid* in miniature. It's a one-page version of *The Story Grid* and it is the first stop on the way to creating the big matrix that tracks all the pieces of a Story. We'll go through it in depth in part 3.

In *The Foolscap Method,* we ask ourselves just half a dozen questions of the Story we're about to write, or have already written…over and over again:

1. What's the Genre?
2. What are the conventions and obligatory scenes for that Genre?
3. What's the point of view?
4. What are the protagonist's objects of desire?
5. What's the controlling idea/theme?
6. What is the Beginning Hook, the Middle Build, and Ending Payoff?

Do you think of your Story in these terms? Do you ask yourself these questions? This is how an editor works to make a Story work. This is how they identify problems and how they discover the fixes for them.

In part 6, I will use *The Story Grid Spreadsheet* to break down, scene by scene, Thomas Harris' masterpiece *The Silence of the Lambs*. But before we get into such post-graduate detail, let's start with the absolute basics.

The Story Grid
The Silence of the Lambs by Thomas Harris

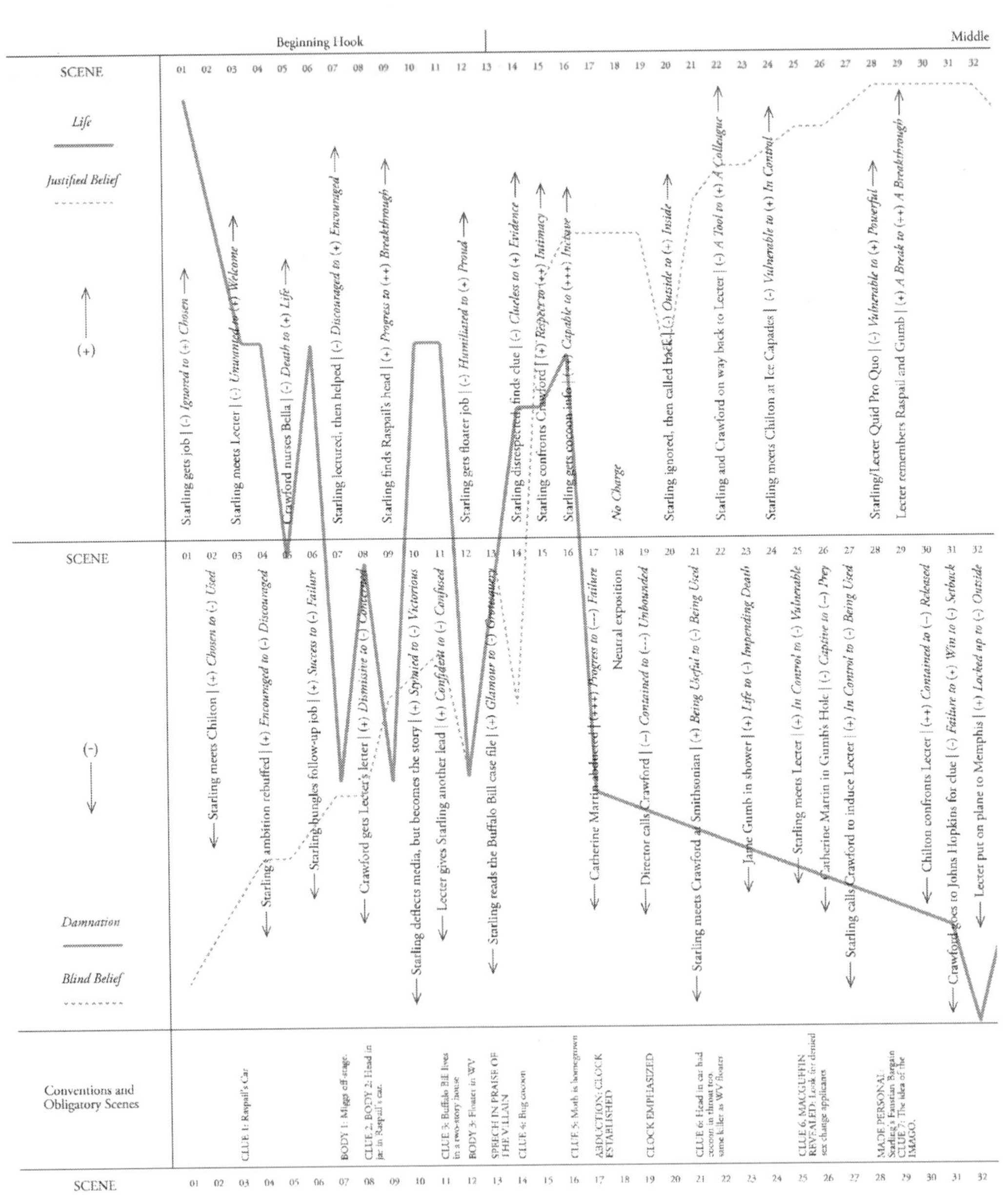

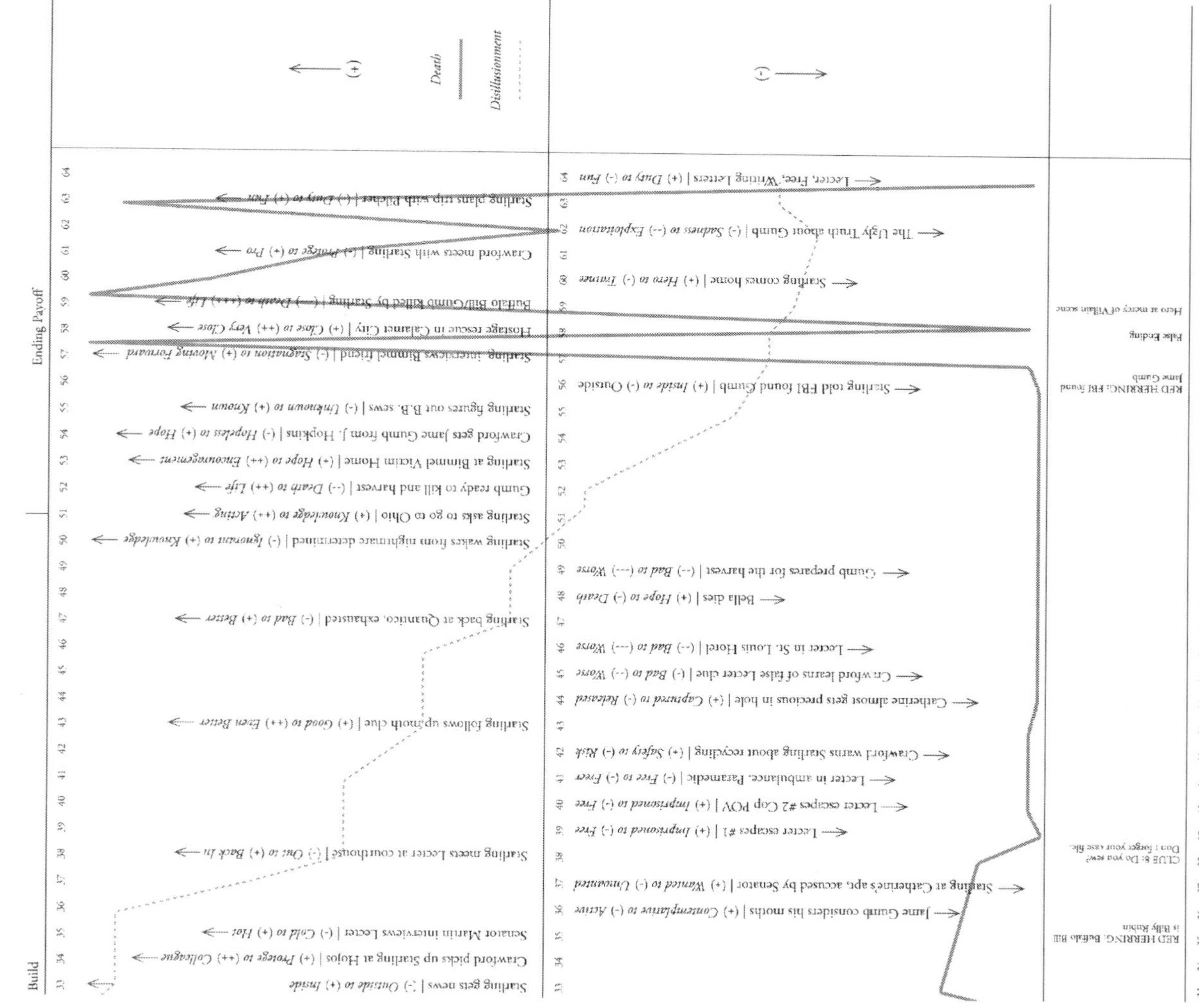
Build
Ending Payoff
33 34 35 36 37 38 39 40 41 42 43 44 45 46 47 48 49 50 51 52 53 54 55 56 57 58 59 60 61 62 63 64
Starling gets news | (-) Outside to (+) Inside
Crawford picks up Starling at Hojos | (+) Protege to (++) Colleague
Senator Martin interviews Lecter | (-) Cold to (+) Hot
Starling meets Lecter at courthouse | (-) Out to (+) Back In
Starling follows up moth clue | (+) Good to (++) Even Better
Starling back at Quantico, exhausted | (-) Bad to (+) Better
Starling wakes from nightmare determined | (-) Ignorant to (+) Knowledge
Starling asks to go to Ohio | (+) Knowledge to (++) Acting
Gumb ready to kill and harvest | (--) Death to (++) Life
Starling at Bimmel Victim Home | (+) Hope to (++) Encouragement
Crawford gets Jame Gumb from J. Hopkins | (-) Hopeless to (+) Hope
Starling figures out B.B. sews | (-) Unknown to (+) Known
Starling interviews Bimmel friend | (-) Stagnation to (+) Moving Forward
Hostage rescue in Calumet City | (+) Close to (++) Very Close
Buffalo Bill/Gumb killed by Starling | (---) Death to (+++) Life
Crawford meets with Starling | (-) Protege to (+) Pro
Starling plans trip with Pilcher | (-) Duty to (+) Fun
(+)
Death
Disillusionment
Jame Gumb considers his moths | (+) Contemplative to (-) Active
Starling at Catherine's apt, accused by Senator | (+) Wanted to (-) Unwanted
Lecter escapes #1 | (+) Imprisoned to (-) Free
Lecter escapes #2 Cop POV | (+) Imprisoned to (-) Free
Lecter in ambulance. Paramedic | (-) Free to (-) Freer
Crawford warns Starling about recycling | (+) Safety to (-) Risk
Catherine almost gets precious in hole | (+) Captured to (-) Released
Crawford learns of false Lecter clue | (-) Bad to (--) Worse
Lecter in St. Louis Hotel | (--) Bad to (---) Worse
Bella dies | (+) Hope to (-) Death
Gumb prepares for the harvest | (--) Bad to (---) Worse
Starling told FBI found Gumb | (+) Inside to (-) Outside
Starling comes home | (+) Hero to (-) Trainee
The Ugly Truth about Gumb | (-) Sadness to (--) Exploitation
Lecter, Free, Writing Letters | (+) Duty to (-) Fun
(-)
RED HERRING: Buffalo Bill is Billy Rubin
CLUE 8: Do you sew? Don't forget your case file.
RED HERRING: FBI found Jame Gumb
False Ending
Hero at mercy of Villain scene

PART TWO

GENRE

12

GENRE IS NOT A FOUR-LETTER WORD

When we hear a book or movie described as "Genre," the speaker is usually denigrating the Story. The designation connotes cheesy slasher films, lame mysteries, Ed Wood-esque science fiction, and bargain-bin romances.

When all of the above can be categorized as one of a particular kind of Genre, Genre is not limited to pulp fiction.

Genre's an incredibly broad way of cataloguing all Stories. Like the category Coffee includes all varieties from Sumatra to Folgers, Genre includes *War and Peace* as well as the pedestrian (to some people) entertainments described above.

Genre choices are the most important decisions you need to make.

Those choices will tell the reader what they are in for if they pick up your book. They will direct all efforts from your publisher from the front cover art to the publicity tour. If you are not writing in "Genre," you're lost. Every Story ever told has Genre classifications.

The Corrections is a Realistic, Long form, Mini-plot, Society, Domestic Drama.

Moby Dick is a Realistic, Long form, Arch-plot, Action, Adventure, Monster Drama.

The Iliad is a Fantastic, Long form, Arch-plot, War/Education, Literary Story.

Deciding what Genre(s) your Story will inhabit will also tell you exactly what you need to do to satisfy your potential audience's expectations. Genre will tell you the crucial conventions and obligatory scenes you must have in your novel. Knowing Genre is the single best way to avoid doing a helluva lot of work for naught. If you don't know you are writing a horror novel and you spend four months working on a character's past history for an epic flashback, you're wasting your time. Better to know up front what Genre best fits the idea or theme you want to convey to your audience before setting off on the work, no?

Most importantly, if you fail to abide by your Genre's requirements, you will not write a Story that works.

The only way to write a Story that works is to know exactly what Genre(s) you are exploring and deliver exactly what is required from those Genres. You must know what your reader is expecting before you can possibly satisfy her. And yes, if you are writing a Story, you must think of your audience. A Story means nothing if it is not experienced. If you do the work exceptionally well, you do that thing that we all dream of, you'll overdeliver on audience expectations. You won't just satisfy them, you'll shock and invigorate them. And the reader will have an experience that she will never forget.

The first questions we need to ask ourselves are, "What are the Genres of our Story?" and, "What will we have to do to meet those Genres' expectations?"

13

GENRES HAVE CONVENTIONS

If I hand you my novel and tell you it's a murder mystery, what would you expect from the book before you even turned the title page?

- You'd expect a dead body.
- You'd expect that an investigator—a police officer, an amateur sleuth, a PI, a cat—will set out to solve the crime.
- You'd expect certain stock characters to appear throughout the novel. The "Watson" to the novel's Sherlock Holmes or the "prime suspect" for example.
- You'd expect false clues in the plot otherwise known as "red herrings."

These are a few of the conventions of the mystery Genre. They are elements in the Story that must be there or the reader will be confused, unsettled or so bored out of their skull that no matter how beautiful the sentences, they'll quit reading.

Conventions are not obligatory scenes, which I'll cover in the next chapter. Rather they are specific requirements in terms of the Story's cast or methods in moving the plot forward (minor revelatory turning points that must be there but can be weaved into the Story at the writer's discretion). For example, the Gothic mystery would require the convention of being set in or around an ancient castle circa nineteenth or late eighteenth century. The mystery Genre evolves as new writers try out new kinds of conventions.

Agatha Christie took a tried and true convention (her brilliant sleuth like Hercule Poirot) and freshened it up when she created the amateur sleuth Miss Marple. But you'll notice that Christie did not eliminate the central clue-hunter from her Story. She just changed the personality and background of the investigator. She abided by the convention, but innovated its execution.

To go back to the joke analogy as emblematic of Story, a convention in a "knock-knock" joke would be having the punch line revealed as a play on words.

Knock-Knock

Who's There?

Banana

Banana Who?

Knock-Knock

Who's There?

Banana

Banana Who?

Knock-Knock

Who's There?

Orange

Orange Who?

Orange you glad I didn't say Banana?

The convention of the knock-knock joke is satisfied with punch line word play. It can change from Banana to Orange or from Boo to Boo Who? Doesn't matter as long as there is word play.

Knock-Knock

Who's There?

Boo

Boo Who?

Don't cry… it's just a Knock-Knock joke.

But the "Knock-Knock" and "Who's there?" elements of the joke are obligatory. They have to be there literally. In their exact form. These obligatory elements are so familiar and identifiable to the listener/reader that they immediately induce an expectation. Once we hear "Knock-Knock," we expect the convention of the joke form...a fun play on words payoff. If we don't get the play on words convention, the listener won't laugh. The joke will die. It doesn't work.

Similarly, to not give the listener the actual "Knock-Knock" and "Who's there?" obligatory elements for the joke is ridiculous right? The punch lines, *Orange you glad I didn't say Banana* or *Don't cry...it's just a Knock-Knock joke,* mean nothing without the obligatory setup of Knock-Knock and Who's there.

Whenever you start mulling whether or not to include a convention or obligatory scene in your Story, think of the "Knock-Knock" joke and what it would be like without a play on words punch line or "Who's there?"

14

GENRES HAVE OBLIGATORY SCENES

While conventions of particular Genres often concern a Story's cast of characters (the best friend sidekick in a love Story or the monster in a horror Story), setting (the labyrinthine castle setting in a Gothic romance) or method of turning plot (red herrings in a mystery/crime novel), obligatory scenes are the must-have elements to pay off the raised expectations of those conventions. They are the equivalent of the place markers, "knock-knock" and "who's there?" in a knock-knock joke.

Back to our mystery novel:

- You'd expect a "discovery of the body scene."
- You'd expect an eventual confrontation between the investigator and the murderer—what I call the "J'accuse" scene.
- You'd expect an ending scene that clearly results in justice (the murderer pays for his crime), injustice (the murderer gets away) or irony (the investigator gets his man, but loses someone or something in the process or the investigator does not get his man, but the loss results in a greater good).

So what happens if I fail to deliver even just one of these obligatory scenes from the above list?

I haven't written a mystery novel. I've written a book that doesn't work.

There is nothing more infuriating to blue-collar novelist pros than listening to amateurs who obviously haven't done the work necessary to know their art form. You can't help but lose respect for them. It's akin to your cousin Lou who makes "Pot-au-feu" without meat or vegetables calling himself a French chef.

In order to write a professional novel, you must know the conventions and obligatory scenes of your chosen Genre. (I'll detail those of the thriller Genre later on when I dive into *The Silence of the Lambs* in part 7.) If you don't know the conventions and obligatory scenes for your chosen Genre(s), learn them.

How do you do that?

Read the top novels in the Genre (yes, the most commercially successful ones) and write down what they all have in common. And "literary novels" are of a Genre too... If you are going to write a Testing Plot novel about endurance and tenacity, you better read *The Old Man and the Sea* and *Deliverance*.

Once you know them, how do you go about writing obligatory scenes?

Obligatory scenes are the most difficult ones for a writer to crack—*the discovery of the dead body scene, the hero at the mercy of the villain scene, the first kiss scene, the attack of the monster scene*, etc. The reason is that these scenes can easily devolve into cliché. They've been done to death. To come up with something fresh and surprising is an extremely difficult task.

A lot of writers have contempt for obligatory scenes for the very reasons I described above. They don't want to write them because they find them cheesy. A few even insist that their work is so intellectually challenging and above "Genre," that they are exempt from having to fulfill these expectations. They'll tell you that their work is more of homage to a Genre, not really part of the Genre, etc. Which is complete bullshit.

If the writer's global Inciting Incident is one associated with a particular Genre and she doesn't innovatively pay it off in the way that the Genre demands, the book won't work. People won't buy it.

Other writers (some call them hacks) love Genre because they think they can just recycle old scenes from the Genre's vault to fulfill these obligations. But if you rehash something you saw on a *Mannix* episode from the 1970s, you will sorely disappoint your reader. They may not have seen that particular episode, but they will easily be able to tell that what you've written is unoriginal. If you're re-using the setup and payoff of a particular obligatory scene from the past, chances are someone else has too.

Remember that the earliest readers in a particular Genre are experts.

When I ran mystery programs at the major publishing houses, you can be sure I was aware of the thousands of hardcore crime readers. I couldn't help but run into them at conventions and specialty bookstores. These readers are desperate for innovation. Their first question is always, "What's new?" These core two to four thousand readers will give new writers a shot. If the writer creates something unique, the aficionado will buy the next book too. And the book after that if the second one pays off too. This is how careers were made back in the day. Still are, even with the big publishing houses abandoning core Story categories for the big book. There's a reason why Amazon.com's most successful publishing programs all involve the core Genres.

But if the writer is rewarming old Rex Stout plotlines and somehow makes it into a big house without being found out, rest assured these first readers will know. They pride themselves on their expertise and if they find you lacking, they'll tell their fellow mystery junkies to skip the book. It's "meh," not worth their time. They won't brag about having a first edition of your first novel. They won't look forward to your next book. They won't give you another chance.

But what about those hugely successful novels that defy what I'm saying? What about those books that don't deliver fresh obligatory scenes and are still huge bestsellers?

Sometimes, an influential group of readers (usually critics) fall in the love with a book or just its prose and talk it up incessantly. The sophisticated and *The New York Times* reading metropolitan cocktail crowd (a dying tribe if there ever was one in the new connected age of "Weird") hear the chatter. Wanting to be "in the know," the swells repeat the hubbub and quite a number of books are bought and displayed on coffee tables across the country. But many if not most go unread.

Writing for that kind of attention is not going to fill the hole in your soul. It's certainly not a business plan. Again, it's like buying a lottery ticket.

Instead write for the Genre nerds desperate for new stories. They won't desert you when you push the envelope too far, either. Just knowing where the envelope ends will warm their hearts.

15

THE KEYS TO INNOVATION

Genre craft demands innovation. And that innovation is found in the way a writer handles audience expectations…the obligatory scenes and conventions of your chosen Genres.

This requirement is exactly the same thing that Steve Jobs and Apple faced when they decided to create a new cell phone. Jobs knew that the iPhone had to be compatible with cellular networks, at least one of them. He knew that it had to "ring." He knew that the connections between callers had to be clear. And tens of other obligations and conventions (a North/South hearing and speaking convention) had to be met. So the question Jobs asked himself was not, "How do I make something completely unique and change the way people speak to each other?" but, "How do I build on and reinvent those things that phone users demand while also giving them an intoxicating original experience?" Jobs worked inside the phone "Genre," and then moved the Genre forward.

As you'll remember, the first generation of iPhones had a tendency to disconnect in the middle of calls. The obligatory antenna required in the phone did not deliver. It wasn't until Apple fixed that problem that the iPhone moved from Apple baseline cult first generation adopters (its Genre experts) to middle managers abandoning their BlackBerrys. The core fanatics cut Apple some slack on the first iteration of the iPhone, but they didn't evangelize to non-cult members until all of the bugs were out of it.

It's the very same thing for books.

Win over the experts and keep banging away at the keyboard. When you've knocked out something extraordinary, the experts will beat down their neighbors' doors to get them to read your book.

I know one thing is for sure. Apple opened up every single cell phone they could find to see what they all did and how they did it before they started working on the prototype of the iPhone. Shouldn't writers do the same thing?

There's no shame in not knowing something. The only shame is when you willfully ignore and then blame the educated for your failures.

16

GENRE'S *FIVE-LEAF CLOVER*

Genre is the one of the most difficult foundations of Story to wrap your mind around. There are so many theories and categorizations of Genre, the editor/Story student can easily fall into an intellectual whirlpool. I've been sucked in so many times by so many different ways to look at Genres that my head spins thinking about it.

I'm so susceptible to Genre inside baseball that I even named my literary agency Genre Management Inc. to remind myself of its importance.

Not surprisingly, where I finally come out on Genre serves the purposes of my method of editing a Story. My goal is and always has been to take comprehensive theory and make it practical. So I started my deep dive into Genre with a few core goals.

- What combination of Genre theories can best serve the writer adrift at his desk?
- How can the conventions of a particular Genre be codified and written down as a list of must-have obligatory scenes or conventional characteristics?
- How can we use those conventions and obligatory scenes inherent in Genres to best effect?
- How can we make practical use (taking an idea and extrapolating a "doable" and "testable" task) of the deep thinking about Genre in order to best evaluate our work?

So my exploration of Genre is purely practical.

What follows is a combination plate of theories from many different sources from Aristotle and Plato, to Goethe, Georges Polti, Norman Friedman, Will Wright and others.

But the biggest influence on my thinking is Robert McKee, bestselling author of *Story: Style, Structure, Substance and the Principles of Screenwriting*, and his colleague Bassim El-Wakil. When McKee and El-Wakil release their own book on Genre, I will, without hesitation, recommend that you read and digest everything they have to say about it. But until we get their masterwork, here is a crash course from my experience to get you started.

The most ingenious ideas that McKee and El-Wakil put forth revolve around the interplay of their five distinct categories of Genre, which I will explain shortly. But before I do, just to keep us on track, here is a working definition of Genre so that we know exactly what we're breaking down:

A Genre is a label that tells the reader/audience what to expect. Genres simply manage audience expectations. It's really that simple. Don't let the French etymology and pronunciation scare you.

We all know what to expect from a mystery novel, a love Story, or an action movie. These categories tell us what we're in for when we pick up a book or go to the movies or the theater. But what are those buried specific expectations that must be satisfied before a Story lands with us? What do we expect to know about a Story before we'll even consider listening or reading or watching it? As per McKee and El-Wakil, there are five primary expectations of the audience.

1. We expect to know how long the Story will last.
2. We expect to know how far we'll need to suspend our disbelief.
3. We expect to know the style, the particular experience of the Story.
4. We expect to know how the Story will be structured.
5. We expect to know what the general content of the Story will be.

With these five questions in mind, McKee and El-Wakil sorted the myriad of familiar Genres we all know intuitively into five major categories.

I find it helpful to think visually and with most of the blood flowing through my veins being of Irish origin (the book publishing company I co-founded with Steven Pressfield is called Black Irish Books) I think of the five categories as leaves on a five-leaf clover. Each of the five leaves nourishes the central locus of the clover, the Global Story.

In order to manage the most primal of reader/audience expectations, writers must make at least five clear choices, at least one from each leaf. And more often than not, with secondary and tertiary subplots, they'll use more than one from a particular offshoot. But more on those choices later.

Here is how I define McKee and El-Wakil's five big categories, our leaves on the five-leaf clover that answer each of the questions above.

1. **TIME GENRES** answer how long the Story will be.
2. **REALITY GENRES** answer how far the audience will have to suspend their disbelief.

3. **STYLE GENRES** answer how we'll experience the Story.
4. **STRUCTURE GENRES** answer how broad or minimalist or nontraditional the global telling of the Story will be.

The last leaf, the **CONTENT GENRES**, are the ones everyone thinks of when they think of Genre. I further divide CONTENT into two sub categories, which I call the EXTERNAL and the INTERNAL. More on why I do this later on.

5. **CONTENT GENRES** answer the theme/controlling idea of the Story.
   a. EXTERNAL CONTENT GENRES determine the conscious object of desire for the protagonist(s). More on objects of desire later on.
   b. INTERNAL CONTENT GENRES determine the subconscious object of desire for the protagonist(s).

And here are specific choices a writer has at his disposal for each of the big categories. This list is by no means exhaustive, but it's comprehensive for our purposes.

1. **TIME GENRES**
   A. Short Form—short films, short stories, or individual scenes in a play.
   B. Medium Form—episodic television shows or documentaries, novellas, multi thousand-word journalism, one act plays.
   C. Long Form—feature length films/documentaries, novels, or three acts or more plays.
2. **REALITY GENRES**
   A. Factualism—stories that refer to facts of history or biography. They refer to part of the historical record implying "This Story Did Happen," like the movie *Argo* or *12 Years a Slave* or *Serpico.*
   B. Realism—stories that could happen in real life, but are imagined, *Law and Order*, the crime novels of Ian Rankin, etc.
   C. Absurdism—stories that are not remotely real, like Eugene Ionesco's play *The Bald Soprano* or *Looney Tunes*
   D. Fantasy—stories of wonder and imagination that require a comprehensive suspension of disbelief, the type of which is delineated by three Subgenres.
      1. Human—anthropomorphized reality like George Orwell's novel *Animal Farm* or fantastical experience like the movie *Groundhog Day* that can be set in one of two time periods.

a. Contemporary

b. Historical

2. Magical—stories about fantastical worlds with magical laws that can be mastered by certain beings, but not everyone, like *The Lord of the Rings*.

3. Science Fiction—stories about technology turning into magic with no special requirements of the user. That is, it is not necessary to be a wizard or an elf to employ the magic. Anyone with access to the technology can use the magic. Examples include the Sub-subgenres:

   a. Alternate History, *Watchmen* by Alan Moore

   b. Cyberpunk, *Neuromancer* by William Gibson

   c. Hard Science, *Solaris* by Stanislaw Lem

   d. Military, *Ender's Game* by Orson Scott Card

   e. Post-Apocalyptic/Dystopian, *The Road* by Cormac McCarthy

   f. Romantic, *Outlander* by Diana Gabaldon

   g. Soft Science, *Star Trek*

   h. Space Opera, *Star Wars*

3. **STYLE GENRES**—the various ways in which we experience a Story.

   A. Drama—a tone of solemnity, facing reality as it is. Emotions are truthful and fulfilling.

   B. Comedy—funny, making jokes at the worst possible time in order to avoid truthful emotion.

   C. Documentary—fact based tone like the film *The Battle of Algiers* or "mockumentary" styles like *This is Spinal Tap.*

   D. Musical—characters breaking into song,

   E. Dance—Martial arts films like *Crouching Tiger, Hidden Dragon*.

   F. Literary—a sensibility of "high art" as pronounced by a particular intelligentsia

      1. Poetry—*Pale Fire* by Vladimir Nabokov

      2. Minimalism—short fiction from writers like Raymond Carver, *Will You Please Be Quiet, Please?*

      3. Meta—self-referential works that present stories about stories, like *The Crying of Lot 49* by Thomas Pynchon or *Infinite Jest* by David Foster Wallace.

4. Postmodern—fragmented and subversive of formal Story Structure, *Naked Lunch* By William Burroughs.

G. Theatrical—qualities of the theater.

H. Cinematic—qualities of film.

I. Epistolary—qualities of letters.

J. Cartoons—anthropomorphized silliness.

4. **STRUCTURE GENRES**—more on these later.

A. Arch-plot

B. Mini-plot

C. Anti-plot

5. **CONTENT GENRES**—more on these later.

A. EXTERNAL CONTENT GENRES—stories driven by a global external value and its positive and negative charge as outlined for each below.

1. Action—Life/Death
2. Horror—Life/Fate Worse than Death (Damnation)
3. Crime—Justice/Injustice
4. Western—Individual/Society, Freedom/Civilization
5. War—Righteous/Corrupt
6. Thriller—Life/Death...possibility of damnation with a combination of Justice/Injustice (a merging of Action, Horror and Crime)
7. Society—the value at stake determines the Subgenre, for example the Domestic Story is about the Individual/Family dynamic.
8. Love—Love/Hate/Self-Hate/Hate masquerading as Love
9. Performance—Respect/Shame

B. INTERNAL CONTENT GENRES—stories driven by the nature of the protagonists' inner conflict.

1. Status—Success/Failure moving from one ladder of society to another.
2. Worldview—a change in life experience from one value charge to its opposite
3. Morality—a change/revolution of the protagonist's inner moral compass

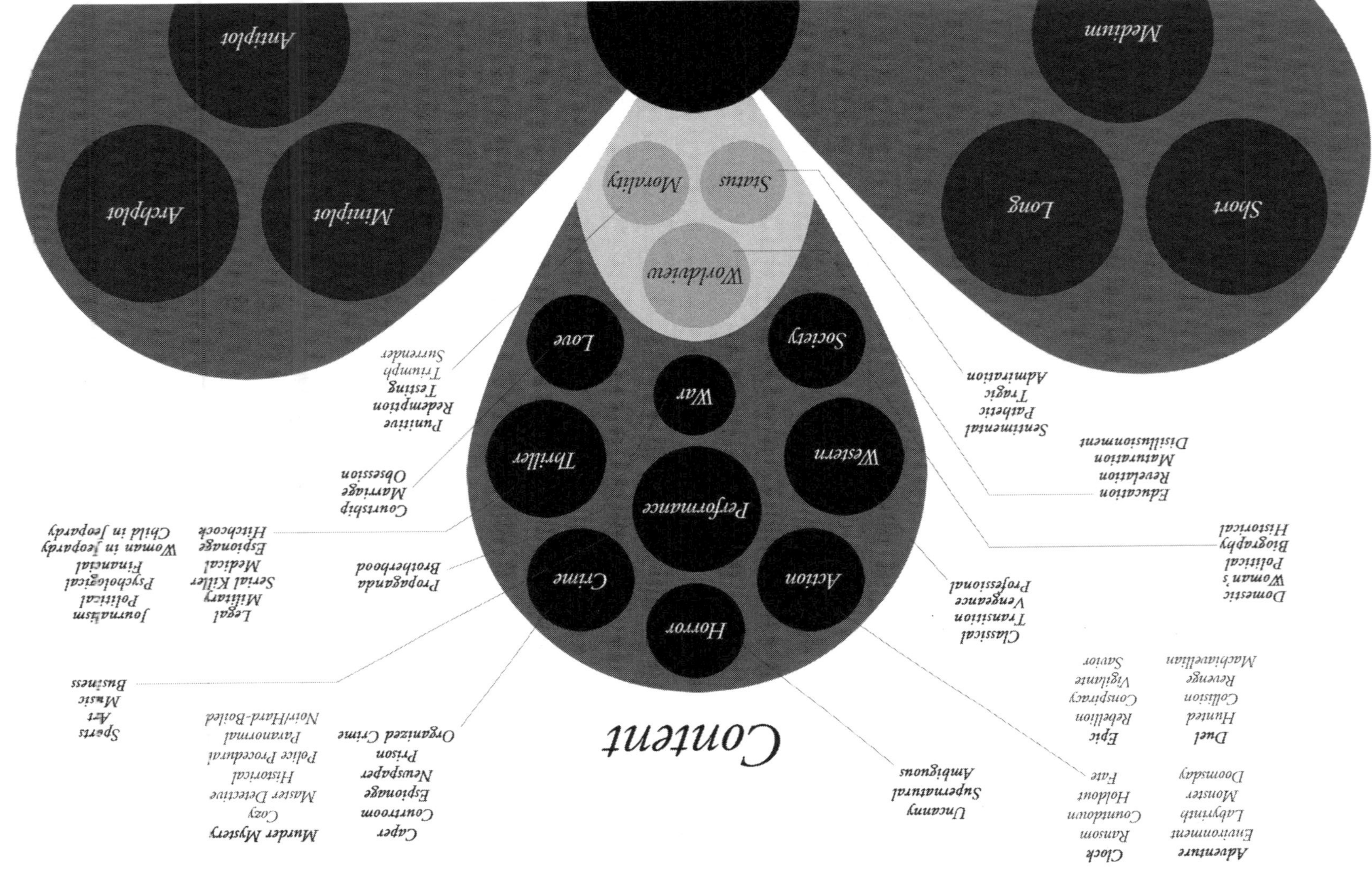
Content
Horror
Crime
Thriller
Love
Performance
War
Action
Western
Society
Worldview
Morality
Status
Archplot
Miniplot
Antiplot
Long
Medium
Short
Uncanny
Supernatural
Ambiguous
Caper
Courtroom
Espionage
Newspaper
Prison
Organized Crime
Murder Mystery
Cozy
Master Detective
Historical
Police Procedural
Paranormal
Noir/Hard-Boiled
Sports
Art
Music
Business
Propaganda
Brotherhood
Legal
Military
Serial Killer
Medical
Espionage
Hitchcock
Journalism
Political
Psychological
Financial
Woman in Jeopardy
Child in Jeopardy
Courtship
Marriage
Obsession
Punitive
Redemption
Testing
Triumph
Surrender
Adventure
Environment
Labyrinth
Monster
Doomsday
Clock
Ransom
Countdown
Holdout
Fate
Duel
Hunted
Collision
Revenge
Machiavellian
Epic
Rebellion
Conspiracy
Vigilante
Savior
Classical
Transition
Vengeance
Professional
Domestic
Woman's
Political
Biography
Historical
Education
Revelation
Maturation
Disillusionment
Sentimental
Pathetic
Tragic
Admiration

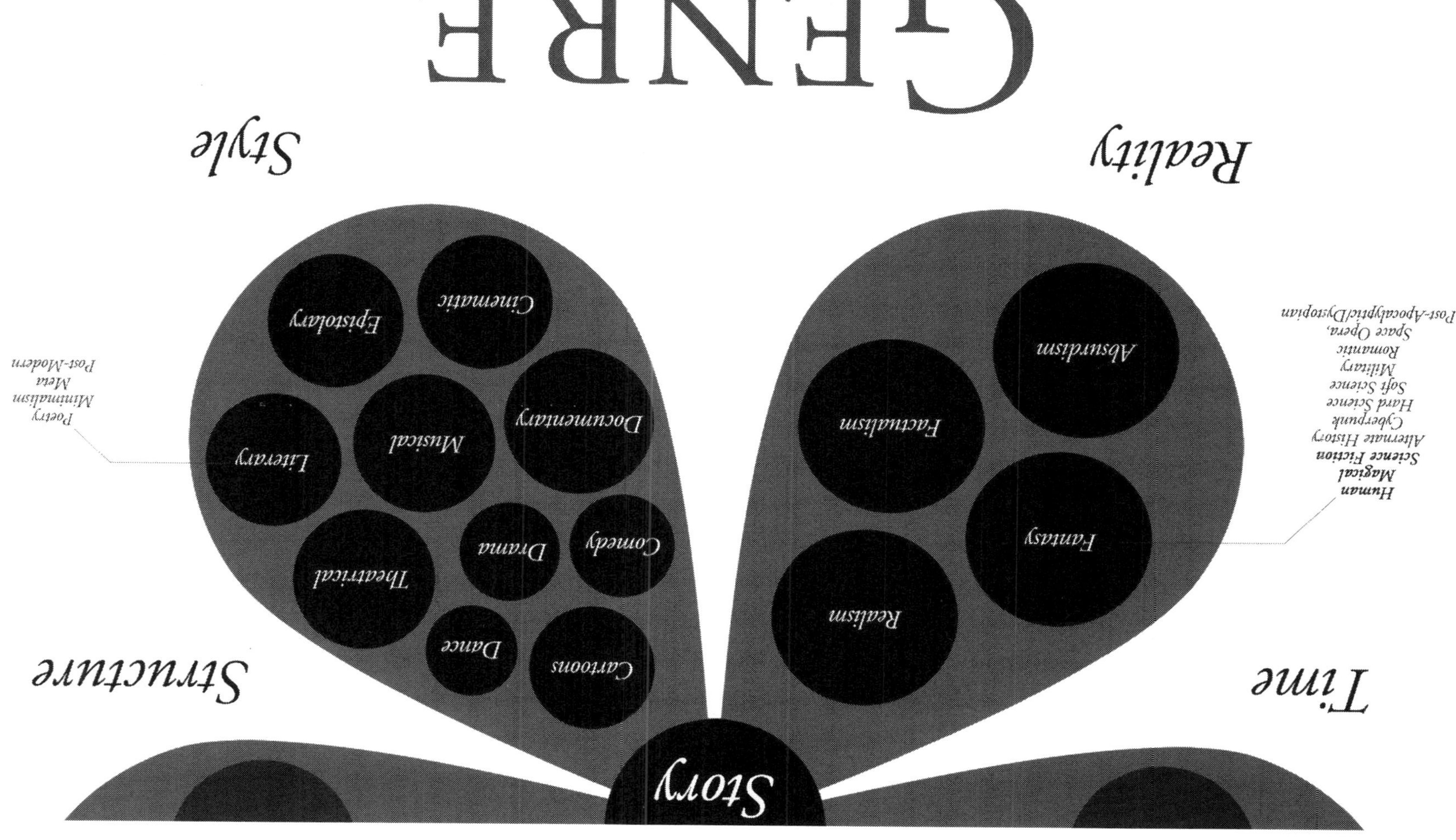
GENRE
Reality
Style
Time
Structure
Story
Realism
Fantasy
Factualism
Absurdism
Human
Magical
Science Fiction
Alternate History
Cyberpunk
Hard Science
Soft Science
Military
Romantic
Space Opera,
Post-Apocalyptic/Dystopian
Cartoons
Dance
Theatrical
Comedy
Drama
Documentary
Musical
Literary
Cinematic
Epistolary
Poetry
Minimalism
Meta
Post-Modern

17

CHOOSING YOUR GENRES

You probably have a general idea of the kind of Story you've already written or the one you want to write. You know it in generic terms. Now is the time to reconsider and clearly define your choices. Doing so will ground your work so that when you get stuck, you can always go back to these choices and evaluate whether you've abided their conventions and/or obligatory scenes.

On the first leaf of our Five-Leaf Genre Clover are the TIME GENRES, which are usually self-evident. You want to write a novel or a short Story or a screenplay for a short film. Any one of them is valid. Any one is easy to label. The same Story and *Story Grid* principles abide for all of the time Genres.

Chances are you've picked from the REALITY and STYLE leaves too without thinking too much about them. And that's fine. Micromanaging the choices you make in Time, Reality and Style can result in paralysis by analysis. Remember, *The Story Grid* and everything it entails is a tool. It is not an end in itself. So to obsess about whether your Story is a drama with comedic elements or a comedy with dramatic elements is time best spent elsewhere. *Terms of Endearment,* the novel and the film, use both comedy and drama in the telling. You can too with your Story. But when push comes to shove, I think we'd all agree that *Terms of Endearment* is globally a drama. It concerns itself with real emotional truth. Whereas, the global comedy, *There's Something about Mary* relentlessly avoids emotional truth.

It's important though to clearly write down exactly what choices you've made. Doing so will allow you to go back later on and make sure that you consistently abided by the conventions of those choices.

For the nature of the REALITY leaf, if your lead character is anthropomorphized, you're definitely working in the fantasy arena. If it's a novel based on a historical event, you're in the FACTUALISM arena.

Again, what's important is to write all of the choices down.

I'll suggest a one-page *Foolscap Global Story Grid,* a phrase I've borrowed from Steven Pressfield and his mentor Norm Stahl, later on that you'll use as a lifeline to track your global Story. It will be the thirty-thousand-foot view that will put you back up in the sky and settle your nerves when you inevitably panic and think you've crashed your Story. You'll use the *Foolscap Global Story Grid* along with *The Story Grid Spreadsheet* (which tracks the micro movements in your Story) to create your final *Story Grid* infographic.

Now with the first three leaves of our Five-Leaf Genre Clover considered (**TIME**, **REALITY** and **STYLE**), we're ready to detail the complementary relationship between the fourth leaf—**STRUCTURE**—and the fifth leaf—**CONTENT**.

18

THE STORY BELL CURVE

If you were to somehow plot all of the Stories that have ever been told, what would it look like?

It would look a lot like other natural phenomena such as the distribution of height of human beings, or blood type or women's shoe sizes. Which makes sense because Stories are as natural to human beings as air and water. The graph would look like a bell curve, in statistics what's called a normal distribution (or Gaussian distribution).

In order to map "Story" though, the first thing you'd need to do is figure out how to judge the stories, right? How about we evaluate the global popularity/commercial appeal of a particular Story along the vertical axis, or the y-axis, versus the three different Story Genre structures from the fourth leaf of our Five-Leaf Genre Clover on the x-axis?

So the further up the y-axis you move, the more appealing the Story will be to larger and larger audiences. That is, the y-axis is a reflection of the relative popularity of every kind of Story ever written…one where each Story perfectly aligns with its content Genre's conventions. Needless to say, no Story ever aligns perfectly with a single Genre, and like Heisenberg's uncertainty principle, the closer you analyze and pick at a particular Story to classify it, the more it moves away from your microscope. Also remember that those structures and their corresponding content Genres with the greatest potential for a large audience are also those that are the most difficult to innovate.

On our graph, let's make the East/West x-axis, the horizontal one, represent the three main structures—**Arch-plot, Mini-plot (often referred to as Minimalism) and Anti-plot.** (More on these three structures in the next three chapters.) Let's put the oldest structure, the Arch-plot, in the middle, the Mini-plot on the left hand corner and the Anti-plot on the right hand corner. So the East/West x-axis progression moves from the purest qualities of a Global Mini-plot to the purest qualities of a Global Arch-plot to the purest qualities of a Global Anti-plot. The further you move from left to right on the x-axis, the closer you move toward the qualities of the next Global Story Structure and the further away you move from the qualities of the previous structure.

Here's what it would look like:

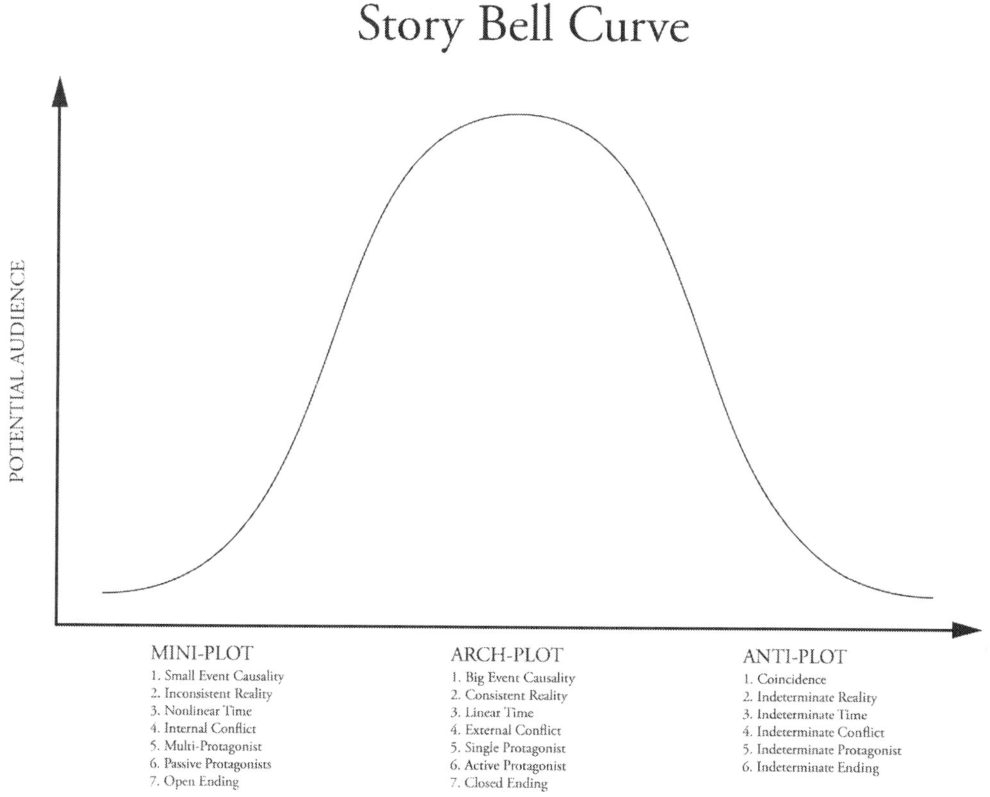

I recommend that you consider where your Story sits on this Story bell curve before you write it and after you have your first draft. Is it a pure Arch-plot? A pure Mini-plot? Can you shift the focus of your Story to find a sweet spot between your literary ambitions and a critical mass of audience who'd be interested?

It's important because the coordinates of your Story will be immeasurably helpful for you to home in or choose your global content Genre and any supporting content Subgenres. Knowing the relationship between the **CONTENT** Genres and the **STRUCTURE** Genres will save you from much pain later on. More on these relationships in the next chapters, but generally the External Content Genres (action, horror, crime, thriller, love, performance, society, war and western) live inside the meaty middle of the Story bell curve, while the Internal Content

Genres (worldview, morality and status) tend to move toward the outlying/thinner sections of the curve.

No matter how incredible an Anti-plot war Story may be, the potential audience for it is very small. Which is fine as long as you know what you're getting into before you sit down to write it. Charlie Kaufman doesn't write screenplays that he expects will do over a hundred million dollars in the box office their first weekend. So when they don't, he's not disappointed. If you're going after the idiosyncratic and you find that many readers of your work just don't "get it," don't fret. But don't expect to reach number one on *The New York Times* bestseller list either.

In addition to avoiding unnecessary work, understanding to whom your work will eventually be marketed and why will prepare you for the business of selling your Story to either a publisher or a select group of readers. But most importantly a comprehensive understanding of the Story bell curve will help you match what you want to say with the best way to say it.

For example, at the onset you may think the horror Genre best serves your controlling idea (we'll review controlling ideas later on) about the insidious nature of mass media. But after refreshing your knowledge of horror, you may find that it really would be much better served if you approached your work as a love Story/ political social drama instead. Perhaps Paddy Chayefsky had that debate before he began writing *Network*. Knowing the breadth of Story possibilities and the limitations of each Genre will focus your energy and pinpoint exactly where your Story will best live.

Let's now review the qualities of these three Story structures. I'm going to begin in the middle, the big meat of Story and then progress to the left tail and then the right tail.

19

ARCH-PLOT

The middle of the Story Bell Curve is Arch-plot, the classic Story form, sometimes referred to as the "quest" narrative.

In summary, it has the following qualities:

In a consistent and cause/effect reality like the one we all inhabit in our everyday lives, Arch-plots feature a single active protagonist. This lead character pursues an object of desire (a new job, the love of his life, a college education etc.) while confronting primarily external forces of antagonism (more qualified candidates, a better-looking suitor, a high school teacher out to get him). The Story ends "closed" with absolute and irreversible change in the life of the protagonist. There is no going back to the way things were at the beginning of the Story. Novels like *The Firm*, *Sense and Sensibility*, *Carrie*, *The Hobbit* and movies like *The Fugitive*, *Chinatown*, *Kramer vs. Kramer* and plays like *Death of a Salesman*, *A Raisin in the Sun*, and *The Importance of Being Ernest* are all Arch-plots.

Arch-plot is human life Story, the one we all use to evaluate and direct our own lives. This is why Arch-plot has the greatest potential for the largest possible audience. Every person on the planet is a potential reader/viewer.

The Arch-plot is the narrative form made famous and delineated so well by Joseph Campbell in his seminal work *The Hero with a Thousand Faces*.

Having evolved over thousands of years, it has the structure that every single human being on earth can relate to. We see our own lives within the frame of Arch-plot. We all strive to fulfill our desires, be they material, romantic, or professional and believe that there are forces aligned against us to keep us from what we really want and deserve. It is only through active confrontation and defeat of these antagonistic forces that we believe we achieve anything of value.

Once we achieve or fail to achieve our desires however, we find that we can't go back again. Once we've left our hometown and conquered the big city or fallen flat on our face, going back to the way things used to be is impossible. It is like Adam and Eve eating the fruit of knowledge. At the end of a particular quest—getting into college, finding the right mate—we can't reverse course and go back to the way we saw and felt before we successfully attained or unsuccessfully botched it.

Arch-plot is linear. This is the way we view our own lives.

We love Arch-plots because they mirror the way we choose to privately examine ourselves. There is nothing more powerful in a Story than having a lead character desperately pursuing something. The reader or viewer cannot help but attach himself to that character because he has objects of desire too. If the lead character in a Story gets what he wants, our brains are wired to believe that we can too. Stories fuel our courage and offer the cautions that we believe will help guide our own paths.

Whether you know it or not, your desire to write comes from the urge to not just be "creative," it's a need (one every human being on earth has) to help others. A well-told Story is a gift to the reader/listener/viewer because it teaches them how to confront their own discomforts.

In his wonderful book *The Examined Life: How We Lose and Find Ourselves*, psychoanalyst Stephen Grosz tells the Story of Marissa Panigrosso, who worked on the ninety-eighth floor of the South Tower of the World Trade Center. She recalled that when the first plane hit the North Tower on September 11, 2001, a wave of hot air came through her glass windows as intense as opening a pizza oven.

Panigrosso did not hesitate. She didn't even pick up her purse, make a phone call or turn off her computer. She walked quickly to the nearest emergency exit, pushed through the door and began the ninety-eight-floor stairway descent to the ground. What she found curious was that far more people chose to stay right where they were. They made outside calls and even an entire group of colleagues went into their previously scheduled meeting.

Why would they choose to stay in such a vulnerable place in such an extreme circumstance?

Because they were human beings and human beings find change to be extremely difficult, practically impossible. To leave without being instructed to leave was a risk. What were the chances of another plane hitting their tower, really? And if they did leave, wouldn't their colleagues think that they were over-reacting, running in fear? They should stay calm and wait for help, they must have thought to themselves, maintain an even keel. And that's what they did. I probably would have too.

Grosz suggests that the reason every single person in the South Tower didn't immediately leave the building is that they did not have a familiar Story in their minds to guide them. This from his book:

> *We are vehemently faithful to our own view of the world, our Story. We want to know what new Story we're stepping into before we exit the old one. We don't want an exit if we don't know exactly where it is going to take us, even – or perhaps especially – in an emergency. This is so, I hasten to add, whether we are patients or psychoanalysts.*[2]

Even among those people who chose to leave, there were some who went back to the floor to retrieve personal belongings they couldn't bear to part with. One woman was walking down alongside Panigrosso when she stopped herself and went back upstairs to get the baby pictures of her children left on her desk. To lose them was too much for her to accept.

That decision was fatal.

When human beings are faced with chaotic circumstances, our impulse is to stay safe by doing what we've always done before. To change our course of action seems far riskier than to keep on keeping on. To change anything about our lives, even our choice of toothpaste, causes great anxiety.

How we are convinced finally to change is by hearing stories of other people who risked and triumphed. Not some easy triumph, either. But a hard fought one that takes every ounce of the protagonist's inner fortitude. Because that's what it takes in real life to leave a dysfunctional relationship, move to a new city, or quit your job. It takes guts, moxie, inner fire, the stuff of heroes.

Change, no matter how small, requires loss. And the prospect of loss is far more powerful than potential gain. It's difficult to imagine what a change will do to us. This is why we need stories so desperately.

Stories give us scripts to follow. It's no different than young boys hearing the Story of how an orphan in Baltimore dedicated himself to the love of a game and ended up the greatest baseball player of all time. If George Herman Ruth could find his life's work and succeed from such humble origins, maybe they could become big league ball players too.

We need stories to temper our anxieties, either as supporting messages to stay as we are or inspiring road maps to get us to take a chance. Experiencing stories that tell the tale of protagonists for whom we can empathize gives us the courage to examine our own lives and change them.

---

2 Grosz, Stephen. *The Examined Life: How We Lose and Find Ourselves* (p.123) W. W. Norton & Company

So if your Story doesn't change your lead character irrevocably from beginning to end, no one will deeply care about it. It may entertain them, but it will have little effect on them. It will be forgotten. We want characters in stories that take on the myriad of challenges to change their lives and somehow make it through, with invaluable experience. Stories give us the courage to act when we face confusing circumstances that require decisiveness.

These circumstances are called CONFLICTS. What we do or don't do when we face conflict is the engine of Storytelling.

What I'm describing is the Arch-plot's inherent quest. It is the structural narrative of humanity and it's irresistible. Primal Arch-plot (from cave drawings to oral tradition) is all about external antagonism. There is little, if any internal struggle in the lead character. Which makes sense. When life's concerns are all about finding water, food and shelter, there is very little time to indulge one's inner development. The equivalent Arch-plots today live inside the External Action Genre.

Pure action Genre protagonists are not plagued by inner doubts or perversions or deeply seated anxieties. In these Stories, a heroic protagonist overcomes arch Villains and/or nature and ultimately sacrifices himself in order to save another human being or even the entire planet from annihilation. While often derided, the action/comic book Story is one of the most difficult to write/innovate and thus is rife with cliché. It's been with us since the first campfire Story, so it ain't easy to reinvent.

The commercial Story marketplace is Arch-plot central and is the stuff of two-hundred-million-dollar movie budgets from film studios and blockbuster novels from big publishing. Pure Arch-plot is all about external conflicts. And there is nothing wrong with a great fastball external-only Arch-plot Story. When done well, they're better than peanuts and popcorn.

But, Arch-plot can also be used to explore inner conflict. The way a writer can do so is to combine a big External Content Genre with a compelling Internal Content Genre. This is exactly what Thomas Harris chose to do in *The Silence of the Lambs*. The result is an Arch-plot structure for his global External and Internal Content Genres. The conventions and obligatory scenes of the serial killer thriller drive the external, while the internal hinges on the progression of the protagonist from blind belief to disillusionment. Much more on both the External and Internal Content Genres to come.

But next up is the second structural Genre, Mini-plot.

20

MINI-PLOT

While the Arch-plot is the stuff of tent-pole action movies and master detective murder mysteries, Mini-plot is most often associated with the literary Story culture. Moving to the left from the fat middle of Arch-plot on the Story Bell Curve, we come to Mini-plot, which is best thought of in terms of internal antagonism.

The content Genres most associated with Mini-plot are the Internal ones—Status, Worldview, and Morality. And as the Internal Content Genres concern the trials and tribulations of the individual, Mini-plot concerns the inner wars of internal antagonism.

Here are the qualities of Mini-plot:

Lead characters, and often multiple protagonists, face off with their inner demons. As opposed to the Arch-plot's action oriented lead character who battles people and the natural world around him on his quest for an external object of desire (and sometimes, as in the case of *The Silence of the Lambs,* an added internal one), Mini-plot characters passively move through the world avoiding external confrontation at all costs. These characters are passive, not active.

Inside, however, these characters are in a fight for their lives.

Their inner voices (those of their merciless inner parent, their pragmatic negotiator self, and their rebellious authentic self) are at odds. Oftentimes their inner confrontations are so violent that the character presents a practical catatonia to the physical world. Think of Anne Tyler's protagonist Macon Leary in her novel, *The Accidental Tourist.* To take on any external drama is to risk melting down entirely.

That is, until the Story forces them to overcome or succumb to the struggle within.

The Mini-plot also differs from the Arch-plot in that it has an "open" ending. There is no happily ever after or life sentence of misery at the end of a Mini-plot. Questions remain unanswered. It's open to interpretation by the reader/audience. And thus Mini-plot demands a deeper connection to the protagonist from the audience than just the dopamine rush of an action Arch-plot Story like Ian Fleming's *Goldfinger* or J.C. Chandor's film *All is Lost*. We don't really mind the fact that James Bond is a superficial human being or that we have no idea why Robert Redford's character in the film has no backstory beyond an unnecessary voiceover at the beginning of the movie. (I bet the producer made Chandor stick that in.) We're overjoyed just to find out what happens next.

While the Arch-plot produces an irreversible external change by Story's end that answers all of the questions raised throughout the Story concretely and satisfies all of the curiosities of its audience, the Mini-plot (while it does produce irreversible internal change in a character) leaves one or two questions unanswered by the Story's end. It leaves its audience with a level of uncertainty to debate and contemplate what could happen to the lives of the characters after the "ending." Something to talk about after the experience beyond the Chris Farley-esque declaration "That was Awesome!"

Time can also be played with in the Mini-plot Story.

The Story can move from the ending to the beginning like Harold Pinter's *Betrayal*. Playing with time is not a feature of the Arch-plot, which must be linear in design. But like the Arch-plot, the Mini-plot still must have the traditional beginning, middle and end. That is, the writer can put the end at the beginning, the beginning in the middle, and the middle at the end, but the Mini-plot cannot just stop the Story in medias res without satisfying the requirements of global Story form. It must abide by the logical (or illogical) rationale of the Reality Genre choice. A good example of Mini-plot virtuosity is the realistic, long form, but time playing Story *Pulp Fiction* by Quentin Tarantino.

Adherence to philosophical causality, crucial in Arch-plot, is not absolutely necessary in Mini-plot.

Causality is our innate belief that all Causes produce Effects in the world. Something happens and then something else results. An ill character coughs into his hand and then greets another character with a handshake. The cause of putting germs into one hand and transferring them to another creates the effect of the second character contracting the disease of the first.

One counter cause/effect philosophy often explored in Mini-plot stories is the idea that *Character is Destiny*; that our fates have been sealed at birth. The Greek classics like Sophocles' *Oedipus Rex* take that concept to unforgettable extremes.

Another notion is that the universe is indifferent to the actions of man…that one person's moral and/or ethical choices in the world amount to nothing. There is no damnation or salvation. We don't reap what we sow because in fact there is no farm. Deep stuff.

In order to effectively dramatize this kind of philosophical exploration, though, the Story often needs a wide net of characters to reinforce this underlying big controlling idea/theme. Here's why:

With just a single point of view, the reader intuitively expects Arch-plot. We just can't help it. The reader will attach himself to that POV and expect a palpable external object of desire for that protagonist, one closely associated with the External Content Genres. If no such object of desire reveals itself in like the first scene or two, many readers/viewers get turned off.

Mini-plot masters like Raymond Carver, John Cheever, George Sanders, and Alice Munro, who live at the top of the "short Story writer" pyramid, are capable of creating entire universes with multiple characters confronting the absurdity and/or sterility of existence. There is a reason why many short Story writers never write the single Big Novel that becomes their masterwork. It's because their entire body of work and the core themes they are exploring require precision and tight spaces. To expand a perfectly executed short Story into a novel just won't work.

So they don't try to do that.

But if you add up all of the short stories from these masters, you'll find a consistency of compelling and multifaceted philosophies about life and its contents and discontents within. Take a look at Robert Altman's movie *Short Cuts*, an adaptation of Raymond Carver's short stories spliced together as only Altman could do, to see what I mean.

So Arch-plot is all about Active Single Protagonists facing down External Antagonism and is the domain of the Commercial Book Culture, the Studio system in Hollywood, Narrative Nonfiction in journalism, and the Plot Driven Play.

Mini-plot is all about Passive Single (or Multiple) Protagonists contending with Internal Sturm and Drang and is the domain of the Literary Book Culture, the Independent Film world, Long Form Journalism in Nonfiction, and the "Character" Driven play.

Next up? Anti-plot.

21

ANTI-PLOT

If Arch-plot is the structural backbone of the External Content Genres and Mini-plot serves the Internal Content Genres (see Genre's Five-Leaf Clover), what's the deal with the third structural Genre, Anti-plot?

This is the kind of question a Story nerd like myself loves to noodle.

The Anti-plot came of age in the bloody twentieth century.

Faced with the realities of mass impersonal slaughter from two global wars and the very real prospect of complete annihilation of the human race, a coterie of artists stared down the prospect of the end of civilization. They dug deeply into the foundations of Story form to respond. Was there as much potential darkness as light in Storytelling? In fact, was Storytelling itself complicit in the systematized murder—not just of soldiers—but also of innocent civilians whose only "crime" was the content of their as yet quantified, let alone unqualified, genetic material?

There is no question that masterful propagandists can use Story form to ultimately horrific effect. In 388 BC, Plato urged Athenian leaders to exile poets and Storytellers. He understood how powerful a well-turned Story is. Plato would not have been shocked that convincing entire populations of their hegemony while arguing the necessity of eradicating defective human specimens who would degrade their omnipotent bloodlines would prove chillingly manageable with the use of a finely spun Arch-plot.

The rise of mass media (the printing press, film, radio and eventually television and now the Internet) to trumpet Stories visually and wirelessly moved the form from a linear to an exponential phenomenon as quickly as the technological adoption allowed. And how hard really is it to get people to adopt "entertainment" technology? Modern/civilized man no longer heard stories from just a small group of fellow tribe members. He heard them from third-party authority figures and beautiful new gods called "stars" from the screen and radio. Just as it did way back in Greece, the well-turned message from a charismatic presence proved irresistible.

They still do. Ask any child today who "Elsa" is or their adult parent what's going on with Angelina Jolie...

The Post WWI and WWII artists understood that Arch-plot—the dominant Story form and the communication device of Tyranny as well as Public Relations/ Advertising/Salesmanship—requires causality. Which means that one event causes another. I sneeze without covering my mouth. The germs reach the air. They travel to your nose and you get a cold. My sneeze causes your infection. They understood too that Mini-plot also (predominantly) requires causality, albeit at an internal level. For example, in stories of the time one's inability to control a sexual desire caused an effect...that wonderful go-to event used by nineteenth and early twentieth century Storytellers, hysterical fainting.

What baffled artists in the post-war years was that to attribute a single "cause" for mass-murder was ridiculous. That is, if the artist did not believe the rationale of the eugenists, the national socialists, the communists, the capitalists, the Vatican, or any other figure of authority or social movement, they'd find themselves at a loss when trying to conceive of a work of art to express their point of view.

The two Story structures available to them, (Arch-plot and Mini-plot) proved practically impossible to convey the absurdity.

To abide by the Arch-plot conventions, artists wishing to examine and/or comment on the state of the world were confronted with coming up with some sort of "explanation" for inexplicable human behavior. Unless one was writing pure propaganda [and a lot of people do write pure propaganda, yes even today] the notion of blaming the victims for their own extermination (they did x, therefore they got y) proved maddening.

As a response, Mini-plot first came to the forefront of Story, especially in intellectual circles.

But soon even the Mini-plot's fail safe big idea themes proved insufficient to describe just what sort of world we lived in. *Character as Destiny* drama relied on unseen higher powers to imbue humanity individual by individual with a certain outcome. Some were just flat-out "evil" and born that way. While the *Indifferent Universe* Story required multi-player casts and the specificity of bourgeois angst and navel gazing to realize—and nothing deadens a Story faster than authorial pontificating—try and read Clifford Odets today.

The big idea Mini-plots proved banal. Storytellers could choose from only two columns of Mini-plot's thematic Chinese Menu. There were Supernatural forces at play or there weren't. So if Stories intent on supporting the notion of a higher power or no higher power at play in the travails of human existence proved insufficient, perhaps Story structure itself required a new approach.

And it is such failures of traditional Story form that gave rise to **Anti-plot**, the rebellion against Story itself.

Anti-plot breaks all of the rules.

- There is no requirement that there be a consistent reality.
- There is no requirement of causality.
- There is no requirement to adhere to any time constraints.
- The protagonist(s) at the end of the Story are the same as they were at the beginning.
- The characters neither defeat nor surrender to external or internal antagonistic forces. They just remain as they ever were, like plants with voices.

Anti-plot gave birth to the Theater of the Absurd, Existentialism, The Beats, Meta-Fiction, and countless masterpieces on canvas. It changed the way the world saw itself. Man was no longer the rational progressively improving being he thought he was. All of his fundamental beliefs were called into question and scrutinized.

And the verdict was not so comforting. Masterwork Anti-plot Stories like *Waiting for Godot* and *No Exit* cut humanity to the quick.

Anti-plot sounds like fun, right?

You can break all of Story's rules and in the process become an avant-garde Artist with a capital "A" by doing whatever you wish. Just call yourself a serious writer and you don't have to deal with any of that "Genre" nonsense. Why learn Classic Story form when you're just going to throw away all of its rules?

The reason why is that you will never be able to achieve anything close to universality using the Anti-plot form if you do not know what it is rebelling against. Writing Anti-plot with no knowledge of Arch-plot or Mini-plot is the equivalent of trying to build a car with no understanding of the drivetrain.

As fair warning, *The Story Grid* derives from the principles of Story form for Arch-plot and Mini-plot. It will be of limited use to the Anti-plot Story beyond as an exercise to check that particular Story's consistency breaking the rules and/or achieving some sort of inspired randomness. That is, as a method to make sure that you have not accidentally built a cause/effect relationship into a particular moment or have changed any of the lives of the characters.

But once you have a comprehensive knowledge of the Arch-plot and Mini-plot forms, writing the next *The Trial* will be far easier. You'll know what "not" to do. If you never learn the "rules" of those forms, though, you'll never be able to break them.

22

CONFLICT AND OBJECTS OF DESIRE

If we boiled every Arch-plot and Mini-plot STRUCTURE GENRE down to its component parts we'd find that the chain of events in each is very much in keeping with what Joseph Campbell referred to as *The Hero's Journey*.

A protagonist or multi-protagonists go on a mission at the beginning and by Story's end, after overcoming or not overcoming forces of antagonism (inner, personal or extra-personal conflicts), he or they are irrevocably changed. That's it.

Well not quite it.

Something must happen at the very beginning of the Story—an event that throws the lead character's life out of balance. That something is the Inciting Incident (more on this down the road).

Either a good thing happens or a bad thing happens. The event can be a random coincidence [aliens attack] or a causal occurrence [your lead character's wife leaves him]. A positive change or a negative change in the life of the character unsettles his world and requires that the character do something to get back to "normal." Just like we do when our world gets weird.

This event gives rise to an object of desire in your lead character's conscious and often subconscious mind, a tangible object (a conscious want) and something intangible (a subconscious need). Perhaps he wants to stop the aliens from destroying earth (conscious) while he needs to prove to his family that he's worthy of their love (subconscious). Depending on your choice of Genre, the balance of these desires (which one dominates and which one is underneath the telling of the Story) varies. The key thing is that the lead character believes if he attains his conscious object of desire (his want), all will right itself in his world. Whether or not that is true is a whole other ball of wax.

For example, let's say that at the beginning of a Story, a lead character's father-in-law confesses to him that he only has enough money to take care of himself for six months. After that, the father-in-law will need the lead character's help to not just survive but keep up appearances as a respectable wealthy man. This Inciting Incident (family member desperately demanding help) throws the lead character's life out of whack.

He has to do something.

And doing nothing is doing something too.

Let's say the lead character chooses to blow off the father-in-law. He nods his head during the heart to heart talk but takes zero action afterward. So, the father-in-law turns up the heat. He tells his daughter about his predicament. The heat from her father (*I went to your husband for help and he's done nothing!*) puts her under a great deal of stress. She's now torn between her love and obligation to her father and the love and obligation she has to her husband.

Perhaps after the lead character is confronted by his wife's *Daddy says you won't help him!* duress, he chooses to do something. He decides to find a way to get the meddlesome father-in-law out of his life…for good. Let's say the conscious/tangible/external object of desire the protagonist chooses in this case is to get his hands on a lot of money. Once he has the money and gives it to his father-in-law, he'll get his life back.

Now, we could stop right here and map out an entire Arch-plot Story based on this Inciting Incident. We could come up with a crime Story or action Story or horror Story to drive the narrative velocity in such a way that the reader/viewer/listener will be held spellbound about what will happen next. The entire Story will ride on whether or not the lead character will succeed in getting the money. That's fine. (Check out the film *Sexy Beast* which has a similar setup, except it's an old "co-conspirator" who visits with some demands.) But you better be sure that you have wonderful turns of external plot to keep the reader/viewer/listener engaged. *Sexy Beast* certainly does.

If you want to explore the moral or internal conflicts inherent in a father-in-law using his son-in-law's love for his daughter as a means to maintain his country club lifestyle, though, you better add an internal element to the Storytelling. The way to do that is to build in a subconscious object of desire.

So what could be the subconscious/intangible object of desire for this lead character?

It could be a lot of things. And again, it will depend upon the Genre you've chosen to tell this Story, or alternatively you could choose the Genre that best fits the subconscious desire you wish to explore and make the Story less externally Arch-plot driven and more internally Mini-plot driven.

He could want his father-in-law to at long last give him the respect he deserves. Subconsciously the protagonist may believe that if he hands over a chunk of cash to the old man, he'll at long last gain his approval—for not only taking such good care of his daughter, but for now providing for him too. In this case, the subconscious desire could be *to place an authority figure in debt as proof of inner power.* This would be a choice to explore among the options in the Internal Status Genre—pathetic, admiration, tragic, or sentimental. (More on the Internal Status Genre to come.)

Or, the protagonist could want his wife to finally appreciate just how difficult it is for him to provide the lifestyle to which she has grown accustomed. Perhaps if she sees how he makes the sausage, she will no longer take for granted his hard work and sacrifice. In this case his subconscious desire could be *to gain unconditional love.* That would be an Internal Status Genre choice as well.

It is these two objects of desire, Money and Respect (or Unconditional Love) that will drive the two "plots" within the global Story. These two strands are what screenwriters refer to as **Storyline A** and **Storyline B**.

Storyline A is the external Story to achieve the conscious object of desire.

Storyline B is the internal Story to achieve the subconscious object of desire.

After an Inciting Incident that throws your character's life out of balance, he will go on a quest to achieve his objects of desire. He's got to make plans and execute the plans. But once he takes up the quest, forces of antagonism ally against him. His plans go wrong. He adjusts. His next plans go wrong. He adjusts. The stakes escalate until he's at the point of no return. His life will never be the same if he achieves or doesn't achieve his goals.

There are three levels of conflict that can thwart his plans to get his external and internal objects of desire.

1. **Inner conflict** is the Hamlet-esque inside-our-head dithering that we all do whenever faced with a difficult task. If we can't beat down the Resistance coming from the voices in our heads, we'll never get anything done.

2. **Personal conflict** is provided by an antagonist character or characters in the Story. And there must be a living and breathing character or characters intent on keeping our hero from reaching his goal. Without them, the Story gets more difficult to pull off than *Finnegans Wake*.
3. **Extra-personal conflict** is the threat of being ostracized by society at large or one's particular tribe of eccentrics. Or, it's a naturally occurring force like a hurricane or a frigid winter. Acts of God are extra-personal as are group and peer pressure in general.

You must take great pains to make the conflicts in your Story varied and surprising. How varied depends upon your choice of global content Genre. Again which of the three kinds of antagonism become the focal point of your Story is dependent upon your choice of Genre. A coming of age Story will hinge on Inner conflict, while a James Bond movie will be far more concerned with Personal conflict and a survival thriller on Extra-Personal conflict.

The quest for the external (conscious) and internal (subconscious) objects of desire is the heart and soul of Story. What the character wants (money) versus what the character needs (unconditional love). It's the foundation. And whenever you get stumped, you need to evaluate how surprising and interesting your character's quest to achieve his wants and needs are.

Here's the big takeaway:

Focusing on the struggle to get objects of desire will make up for almost every other kind of Story misstep.

But wishy-washy choices for the objects of desire will destroy the most stunning secondary subplots. Without fail.

The reader/viewer/listener has to attach and invest themselves in the Story's protagonist(s). And the way he attaches is through the fictional character's pursuit of objects of desire. There's no secret to the fact that we're all striving to get what we want. So it's only natural that we'll invest ourselves in characters pursuing someone or something that they think will raise their circumstances. Even if we don't like what they're going after.

Just about every one of Edith Wharton's novels features a lead character who is not a particularly appealing human being. Would any one of us want to step into Lily Bart's shoes in *The House of Mirth*? But, despite her shortcomings, her longing to be accepted in High Society is irresistible to us. We simply root for her even as she makes mistake after mistake after mistake.

No matter what Story you are writing—a sci-fi love Story, a master detective mystery, a fantastical allegory etc.—you must have compelling objects of desire for your lead protagonist. If the protagonist doesn't want anything or doesn't need anything, you don't have a Story. The book won't work.

So obviously, the first job you have as your own editor is to specify exactly what your lead character(s) want and what they need. What they will strive to attain and what it subconsciously represents to them in their deepest self must be clearly defined. If it isn't clear to you as the writer, there is no possibility that it will be clear to the reader.

The rough manuscript that you have in your drawer or the one you are preparing to write may be perfectly well crafted and may have compelling events, but without the foundation quests for an external and internal object of desire, it will not "feel" right to a reader or viewer. It will not compel people. It will seem sterile…too intellectual…too uninvolving. It just won't work.

Whenever you get stuck telling your Story…go back to the foundation…the quest for conscious external and subconscious internal objects of desire. Are you making those quests in your lead character clear? If you aren't, you must call up your inner demolition crew, break up that old cracked foundation and throw it away. And then go back to these two questions:

What does my character want?

What does my character need?

23

PLOT DRIVEN OR CHARACTER DRIVEN?

What comes first when you set out to tell a Story? The kind of plot you want to tell or the lead character you have in mind? This question is the equivalent of that old debate about whether something is plot driven or character driven. The distinction is meaningless, really, as a character's actions are what determine the plot and the plot is the sum total of a character's actions.

But what can be helpful when you are in the early stages of crafting a global Story or editing the one you have is to think about what excites your personal imagination. What kind of "What if?" do you like best? Some of us think in terms of external "What ifs?" while others of us think in terms of internal "What ifs?" Figure out which kind of person you are and this will help you immeasurably. Either way works. And finding the most exciting "What if?" will also be the key to creating your Story's Inciting Incident...the event that throws your protagonist's life out of balance.

If you are an external "What if?" thinker, you are probably a comic book fan, an action fan, a mystery fan, a horror fan or a thriller fan. You fantasize "What ifs?" like "what if a tidal wave hit New York in the middle of a U.N. assembly?"

If you are an internal "What if?" thinker, you are probably a coming of age novel, love Story, redemption Story, education Story or family saga kind of fan. You think of "What ifs?" like "what if a woman's husband leaves her on the same day she finds out she has Stage Four ovarian cancer?" "What if a mother didn't love her son but refused to acknowledge it?"

The first "What if?" is the thinking of someone who wants to write, for lack of a better expression, a plot driven Story. The second example is someone who wants to write, again for lack of a better expression, a character driven Story. One loves big Arch-plot while the other favors minimalism.

The truth though is that it just doesn't matter what kind of "What if?" you dream of exploring. The best "plot driven" Stories have compelling protagonists that chase subconscious internal objects of desire while they are also trying to get the President of the United States out of the U.N. before the tidal wave hits. And "character driven" Stories also require compelling quests for conscious external objects of desire, remission from cancer for example, while the lead character struggles with deep subconscious internal objects of desire like the need to attain some kind of meaningfulness before death.

STRUCTURE AND CONTENT are intimately related. No matter how you slice it, the Arch-plot and Mini-plot STRUCTURE GENRES require a foundational quest, which in turn requires an external conscious and internal subconscious object of desire. The ways in which the writer reveals those external and internal objects of desire is by making crucial choices.

These choices begin and end in the last Genre category, the CONTENT GENRES.

I've divided CONTENT GENRES into two distinct types.

1. EXTERNAL CONTENT GENRES define your protagonist(s) external objects of desire.

   What they want.

2. INTERNAL CONTENT GENRES define your protagonist(s) internal objects of desire.

   What they need.

24

EXTERNAL CONTENT GENRES

The External Content Genres are what we think of when we hear the word Genre—action, horror, crime, western, thriller, war, love etc. We know one from the other because each has its particular characteristics and because each has very straightforward forces of conflict at play.

The External Content Genres are driven primarily by extra-personal and/or personal conflict. These forces of antagonism are direct and easy to identify: the villains in crime and action stories, the potential mates in love stories, the monsters in horror stories, or the environment in action man against nature stories.

External conflict is the sizzle that gets bottoms in movie seats and books on bestseller lists.

As consumers, we have concrete expectations of these Genres as we've all been exposed to thousands of them since birth. Again, Genre conventions and obligatory scenes satisfy those expectations. While a reader/viewer may not be able to pinpoint what exactly it is they want from a Story, they know it when it's not there. Immediately.

Anyone who has ever been to a mind-numbingly bad play can tell you that. The writer needs to know and understand these Story requirements consciously and deliberately. If he doesn't know them, how can he possibly set them up and pay them off?

The External Content Genres are driven by Arch-plot quests to attain your lead character's conscious object of desire. The conscious object of desire is the tangible thing that the protagonist wants and actively pursues from the Inciting Incident of the Story forward. What's extremely helpful when considering whether to drive your entire Story by an External Content Genre is the fact that these objects of desire are conventions particular to each of the Genres.

That is, your protagonist's conscious object of desire is predetermined based upon your choice of External Content Genre.

The pursuit of the subconscious object of desire, however, drives the Internal Content Genres.

Perhaps you're working on an action Story or want to write an action Story. **The conscious external object of desire in an action Story is a convention.** The hero/protagonist (another convention in an action Story is that the protagonist must be a hero, someone who sacrifices himself to save others) wants to stop the Story's villain(s) and save the life of a victim or victims.

Perhaps you've written a love Story or want to write a love Story. **The conscious external object of desire in a love Story is a convention.** The protagonist pursues or runs away from an intimate bond with another human being—that's her object of desire, an intimate relationship.

Perhaps you've written a crime Story or want to write a crime Story. **The conscious external object of desire in a crime Story is a convention.** The protagonist wants to bring a criminal to justice.

Obviously the choice you make about your global External Content Genre is critical. It will drive the literal narrative of your Story.

Remember that readers don't have the capacity to read a man against time action thriller and then tell their friends not to bother with it because it didn't innovate "the hero at the mercy of the villain" scene. Instead, readers tell their friends that the book didn't work. It was missing something. It seemed thin. Don't buy it.

If you don't study the conventions and obligatory scenes of your chosen content Genre and don't know how writers before you satisfied them, how can you be sure that you've written anything remotely original? Just as to be a bodybuilder, you need to be a weightlifter first, to be a writer, you need to be a reader first.

If you want to write a particular kind of novel, you must dive deep into the history of the Genre itself…find the best books, read them, study them and understand intellectually how each of the conventions and obligatory scenes of the Genre were satisfied. *The Story Grid* is the perfect way to map out just how each writer did so. And having multiple Story Grids for your chosen Genre at hand will be an invaluable reference kit for your future work.

I'll show you how to create your own Story Grids later on when I put together *The Story Grid* for the thriller, *The Silence of the Lambs*. The thriller combines the conventions and obligatory scenes of three External Genres, action, horror and crime. So when I do analyze the conventions and obligatory scenes of the thriller, you'll also get a foundation in action, horror, and crime. I plan to offer analysis for the other Genres as well, but I just haven't written those works yet.

But with all of the above said, Genres are fluid.

They morph and combine and adapt to the tenor of time. That is, Genres shift and change to reflect the anxieties of the particular historical period. I'll make a case later on that the thriller is the dominant Story form today because it serves the largest segment of society, those overwhelmed by the threats of modern life.

I label the following External Content Genres because they concern primarily external forces of antagonism—other people or societal or natural forces—on a single protagonist. They primarily have closed endings, are causal, and happen in linear time in a consistent reality. Arch-plots. I write "primarily" because there are a number of works within these large Genres that move down the curve and approach Mini-plot.

These Arch-plot/Mini-plot stories still have an External Content Genre, but they have shifted the emphasis of the Global Storytelling to the subconscious object of desire. In these, the global Story is driven by the Internal Content Genre. The external one in these cases is usually used to grab the reader early on, only to shift later to deal with deeper internal issues within the lead character.

That is part and parcel of Genre fluidity.

Every once and a while, a writer like Thomas Harris comes along and abides by most of the conventions of a particular External Genre but tweaks them by morphing them with another Genre. In Harris' case, he melded the action Story with the crime Story and added horror to create the modern serial killer thriller with his second novel, *Red Dragon*.

Or, the writer places greater emphasis on an underlying Internal Genre beneath the external, like a crime novel laced with an overriding redemption plot, like one of my favorites, *Bait* by Kenneth Abel. Obviously, the more intimately you know more than one particular Genre, the better your chances of creating something fresh and unique by combining elements of both.

Here is an overview of the EXTERNAL CONTENT GENRES, along with a bit more description of each. These descriptions are by no means exhaustive. Each and every one of these could have an entire book devoted to its conventions and nuances.

EXTERNAL CONTENT GENRES are stories driven by a global external value (justice/injustice, life/death, love/hate) and its positive and negative charge.

The Action Genre

The core value at stake in an action Story is life/death. The core emotion is excitement and the most important event in the book is "the hero at the mercy of the villain" scene. Action is the primal Genre, the stuff of *Gilgamesh*, Homer's canon and *Beowulf*.

For more on this Genre, I highly recommend Robert McKee and Bassim El-Wakil's upcoming book *Action: The Art of Excitement* from which the Subgenres below are referenced. The key element to remember about action is that the villain is the driving force. He/she/it is the source of all conflict and antagonism in the Story and thus action can be broken down into the four Subgenres of extra-personal conflict.

Not to confuse you too much, but these four extra-personal varieties of conflict and their particular plot devices listed below can also be applied to the other External Genres. That is, you could create a horror Story that uses the Labyrinth Plot device, a crime Story that uses the Conspiracy Plot device, a thriller that uses the Savior Plot device etc. The action Genre is primal and its plot devices can easily be used to drive the other Genres.

1. **Action Adventure/Man Against Nature Stories**: These are stories that use the natural world or a specific setting as the villain/force of conflict. They can be further delineated by four kinds of plot devices:

    - *The Labyrinth Plot*: The object of desire is to save victim(s) and get out of a maze-like edifice. (*Die Hard*)

    - *The Monster Plot:* The villain is an animal. (*Jaws*)

    - *The Environment Plot:* The villain is the actual global setting. (*Gravity*)

    - *The Doomsday Plot:* The victim is the environment. The hero must save the environment from disaster. (*Independence Day*)

2. **Action Epic/Man Against the State Stories:** These are stories where the hero must confront societal institutions or tyrants.

    - *Rebellion Plot:* The hero is pitted against a visible tyrant like a Darth Vader from *Star Wars*.

- *Conspiracy Plot:* The hero is up against an invisible tyrant. (*Enemy of the State, The Bourne Identity*)
- *Vigilante Plot:* The hero is up against a criminal organization. (*Above the Law)*
- *Savior Plot:* The hero is up against someone who wants to destroy society. (*The Dark Knight*)

3. **Action Duel/Man Against Man Stories:**
   - *Revenge Plot:* Hero chases the villain.
   - *Hunted Plot:* Villain chases the hero.
   - *Machiavellian Plot:* Hero sets two villains against each other. (*A Fistful of Dollars)*
   - *Collision Plot:* Villain sets two heroes against each other. (*Troy)*
4. **Action Clock/Man Against Time**
   - *Ransom Plot:* A deadline imposed by the villain.
   - *Countdown Plot:* A deadline superimposed by circumstance. (*Andromeda Strain*)
   - *Holdout Plot:* Hero has to holdout until others can rally. (*The 300)*
   - *Fate Plot:* Time is the villain. (*Back to the Future)*

The Horror Genre

The core value in horror, like action, is also life/death, but here it is taken to the very end of the line…the fate worse than death. When dying would be a mercy. The core emotion is fear and the core event is "the victim at the mercy of the monster" scene. The element to remember about horror, like action, is that the forces of antagonism (the monsters) are key.

Generically, horror stories concern survival, those that go to the limits of human experience. They are by definition unrealistic and live inside the Fantasy Reality Genre leaf. An Inciting Incident featuring an attack by a monster of some kind throws a single non-heroic protagonist out of stasis in such a way that he must actively pursue a conscious object of desire, saving his own life.

One very important convention within the horror Genre is that the antagonist(s) are possessed by "evil." The antagonists cannot be reasoned with. They have no interest in anything other than annihilation. There are three Subgenres of horror and they divide along the lines of explaining the monster. Again, I must pay a debt to Robert McKee for these definitions. And remember that the action plot devices can be used for each of these Subgenres.

1. **Uncanny:** These are stories where the force of evil is explainable—a man-made monster, aliens, or a possessed maniac like Jason in the *Friday the 13th* movies. There is no way to convince these monsters to do anything but slaughter.

2. **Supernatural:** The monster in these stories isn't "real." That is, the force of antagonism is from the spirit realm and cannot be explained like a man-made monster, alien beings from outer space, or an axe-wielding freak. Rather they are of the zombies, vampires, Freddie Kruger variety. *The Amityville Horror* is a good example, as the father from the family becomes "possessed" by spirits in his home, which push him to slaughter his family.

3. **Ambiguous:** In these stories, the reader/viewer is kept in the dark about the source of evil. The sanity of the protagonist/victim comes into doubt. *The Shining* is a great example, one of my all-time favorite novels. Just a brilliant and beautifully written Story that mixes alcoholism, egotism, and despair into one hellish stew.

The Crime Genre

The core value in crime is justice/injustice, and the core event is the exposure of the criminal.

An unjust Inciting Incident (the compelling *"What if?"* event) throws a single protagonist out of stasis in such that he must actively pursue a conscious object of desire (a criminal) to restore justice. The type of protagonist and his point of view are what create the many Subgenres in crime.

1. **Murder Mystery:** The murder mystery is the most obvious Subgenre of crime. The Inciting Incident is the discovery of a dead body. For the most part, the end of the Story is the revelation of the murderer. Conventions of the Murder Mystery include false clues (red herrings), a crafty killer who has constructed the perfect crime, lots of interviews, lots of secrets, and an intrepid investigator, usually underestimated, who proves more

capable than the villain. There are numerous Sub-subgenres of the murder mystery and they divide along the point of view of the protagonist, as well as the category of investigator. Each Sub-subgenre has its own additional conventions and obligatory scenes.

- *Master Detective:* Sherlock Holmes, Hercule Poirot, Columbo... The core event is also the climax of the Story where the master detective lays out how the murder occurred and who perpetrated it. The murderer usually tries to escape but is thwarted by the intrepid investigator to resolution. Justice is restored by Story's end.

- *Cozy:* Miss Marple, Jessica Fletcher, Diane Mott Davidson's Goldy Schulz etc. These stories are told from the point of view of the amateur sleuth, who usually has some expertise that others lack that enables them to figure out the mystery. Readers love cozies because they learn quite a bit about an alien discipline while enjoying the standard investigation. Mysteries with recipes are quite popular. And of course there is that Sub-sub-subgenre that will never go away, the cat mystery where a cat is instrumental in solving the crime.

- *Historical:* These either feature historical figures as amateur sleuths, Eleanor Roosevelt, or they feature interesting professionals from earlier times like the monk investigator in *The Name of the Rose*. And like the cozy, the reader learns a whole lot about a particular time period while getting the honey of a perfectly crafted mystery.

- *Noir/Hard-Boiled:* These are a very specific mash up from a very specific time. The lead character is usually a good guy detective or lawyer or someone with skills that can be used for evil deeds. He gets seduced by a very specific character called a femme fatale, a woman who uses all of her feminine wiles to get the man to do as she pleases. She's a sort of modern day succubus. The innocent man decides to do the woman's bidding, commits a crime of some sort (most often murder) and then she sets him up to take the fall for it, escaping with some kind of treasure that only the innocent man can help her attain. The convention is that the Story is told from the schmuck's point of view, often in flashback. *Double Indemnity* by James M. Cain is a textbook example. The movie *Body Heat* is a nice update to it.

- *Paranormal:* These mysteries combine elements of the supernatural with the classic murder mystery plot. Charlaine Harris' Sookie Stackhouse mysteries/horror novels that began with *Dead until Dark* are a great example. HBO adapted the books into the series *True Blood.*

- *Police Procedural:* These are the classic cop point of view books. *Law and Order* kind of stuff, but just the first half of the show. There is a long list of these. Ed McBain/Evan Hunter's *87th Precinct* series of books epitomize the form. Another one of my personal favorites was a book I worked on years ago called *Eleven Days* by Donald Harstad. It was a terrific mash up of Police Procedural and Paranormal.

2. **Organized Crime:** is a crime (not necessarily murder) from the criminal point of view. The reader roots for the criminal to get away with it. *The Godfather* is an example of a crime novel combined with a political society drama. There is an amateur variety too where the good guy goes bad for good reason. *Breaking Bad* is the perfect example. The main thrust of the narrative is *Will he get caught*?

3. **Caper:** This is an offshoot of the organized crime Subgenre that has been done enough to earn its own distinction. This is a Story from the master criminal's point of view, movies like *Rififi* and *Sexy Beast* are two great examples.

4. **Courtroom:** These are crime stories from the point of view of a lawyer. One of my favorites is *The Verdict,* which meshes an internal redemption Story with the external crime Genre.

5. **Newsroom:** These feature reporters as protagonists. Ron Howard's movie *The Paper* and the nonfiction *All the President's Men* are prime examples.

6. **Espionage:** A spy is the lead character. These often walk the razor's edge between crime and thriller, depending on the presence of a hero at the mercy of the villain scene. *The Spy Who Came in From the Cold* and *Tinker Tailor Soldier Spy* come to mind.

7. **Prison:** These are from the point of view of a prisoner. Will they solve the riddle of how they were set up.

The Western Genre

The core values in the western concern the individual inside and outside of society, good/evil, strong/weak, and wilderness/civilization. The core event is the showdown between the hero and the villain. I recommend Will Wright's book *Sixguns and Society* if you really want the grand tour of this Genre, which had a very long run of popularity in the twentieth century.

1. **Classical:** A stranger comes into a small town, reveals that he has a special talent and is then tasked with saving the town from the influence of villains. By the end, the hero is welcomed into the fold. Even though he does not stay amongst the people at the end of the Story, *Shane* is the prototype. From the classical come three Subgenres.

2. **Vengeance:** The stranger is intent on righting a wrong. He's outside of society at the beginning, inside society at the end. Marlon Brando's *One-Eyed Jacks* is a perfect example.

3. **Transition:** The hero is inside society at the start, outside of society by the end. (*High Noon)*

4. **Professional:** The heroes are not out to save society. They're just doing a job, making a living outside of the law. (*Butch Cassidy and the Sundance Kid*)

The Thriller Genre

What would happen if you mashed up the action, horror and crime Genres? You'd get the modern thriller. Thrillers take the core values of action and horror (life and death) and adapt them to a very realistic human extreme. The life/death value escalates to what Robert McKee calls the Fate Worse than Death. Not just the external Fate Worse than Death that is present in horror, but all the way to include the internal Fate Worse than Death...Damnation. The core emotion escalates from the intrigue inherent in crime stories to the excitement level of action and then to horror's fear and ultimately terror. The force of conflict, the antagonist, is far worse than the single dimensional action villain, but just a shade less than the inexplicable horror monster.

The thriller explores the horrors of real life, real monsters who prey in our everyday world.

What distinguishes thrillers from action, crime and horror is that they require a supporting Internal Content Genre to drive the protagonist's "B" Story. The external threats and how the protagonist deals with them have a deep impact on his/her inner conflicts. James Bond doesn't think twice after he's killed a bad guy. The thriller protagonist, no matter his outward bravado, does. But more on that when we go over ***The Story Grid for The Silence of the Lambs***.

The thriller is very malleable. It can be used as a sort of honey to attract readers and then be circumvented by its underlying Internal Content Genre to become a much more symbolic treatise on contemporary life than one would expect on a first read. As such, it is embraced by both the commercial and literary publishing cultures. You'll often find books positioned and sold as "literary thrillers," promising such a deep experience. I'm going to examine the thriller at greater length later on when I go through *The Story Grid* column by column for *The Silence of the Lambs*. For now, let's examine the Genre broadly.

The thriller features a heroic protagonist (someone willing to sacrifice his own life for others) facing personal conflict just a hair's breadth short of the omnipotent horror antagonist. These are realistic threats of the highest order, crime antagonists at the peak of their strength. With outstanding action set pieces filled with derring-do to thwart the plans of the villain, the thriller must make the antagonism personal. That is, the protagonist of the Story must be revealed, usually by the middle of the novel or the end of the second act, as the victim. The victim in horror is the everyman protagonist. But in the thriller, he's a hero.

A sociopath has singled out the hero for the most extreme of the life/death values, the end of the line, what Robert McKee calls *the Negation of the Negation*, the fate worse than death...damnation. While horror stories also take the lead character to the fate worse than death, the thriller does so in a terrifyingly realistic way. Plus, the lead character has a deep inner life, filled with all three levels of individual conflict—inner, personal and extra-personal.

When done well, thrillers push all of our buttons. They entertain us in a way that action/adventure, horror and crime stories do, but in addition, they add on a deep layer of internal struggle that protagonists in literary Mini-plots contend with as their greatest challenge.

As you can use one or more of the sixteen plot devices in horror that you do in action, so can you use the same sixteen for the thriller. As most thrillers adhere to realism Genre within the REALITY leaf of our Five-Leaf Genre Clover, the variety of thriller is often determined by the setting. The setting is often referred to in

Hollywood as the "world." The point of view of the hero/victim protagonist is also a determining factor.

1. **Serial Killer**: *Red Dragon* by Thomas Harris, (police/FBI/PI as hero/victim)

2. **Legal**: *Presumed Innocent* by Scott Turow, (lawyer/judge as hero/victim)

3. **Medical**: *Coma* by Robin Cook, (doctor/nurse/researcher as hero/victim)

4. **Military**: *Seven Days In May by* Fletcher Knebel and Charles W. Bailey, (soldier as hero/victim)

5. **Political**: *Marathon Man* by William Goldman, (everyman/politician/gangster as hero/victim)

6. **Journalism**: *The Scarecrow* by Michael Connelly, (journalist as hero/victim)

7. **Psychological**: *Primal Fear* by William Diehl, (the core question "is he/she crazy?" drives the Story)

8. **Financial**: *Numbered Account* by Christopher Reich, (setting is financial world and how it works)

9. **Espionage**: *The Spy Who Came in From the Cold* by John Le Carre, *The Bourne Identity* by Robert Ludlum, (spy as hero/victim)

10. **Woman in Jeopardy**: *Sleeping with the Enemy* by Nancy Price, (woman as hero/victim)

11. **Child in Jeopardy**: *The Client* by John Grisham, (child as hero/victim)

12. **Hitchcock**: *A Coffin For Dimitrios* by Eric Ambler, (wrong man as hero/victim)

The War Genre

The core value of the war Story is victory/defeat for straightforward pro or anti-war propaganda Stories. These epics usually use Factualism as their REALITY Genre. *The Longest Day* and *The Battle of the Bulge* are prime examples. Another Subgenre of the war Story is what I call the brotherhood variation, which has a core value of honor/disgrace and would include *Gates of Fire* by Steven Pressfield and Oliver Stone's *Platoon*. The core emotion can be anything from excitement to fear to intrigue. And of course the core event is the big battle.

Love stories are often subplots within war stories, *Atonement* by Ian McEwan is a wonderful example of the use of love to ground the war Story.

The Society Genre

These are stories that are most driven by big ideas. That is they are often used to present a particular point of view/argument for political purposes. There are a number of varieties that hinge on the core values inherent in their choice of setting or character. They are often referred to as social dramas, but as we've defined drama as a particular category of the Style leaf of Genre, I prefer to reference these as just the society Genre. As society has many different strata, these stories usually have multiple protagonists. The core values at stake are dependent upon the Subgenre and the core events are also Subgenre specific.

1. **Domestic:** concerns the family dynamic and the core value is the health of the individual versus the bond of the family. The core event is what I call the "showdown" between the central force of control (father, mother, etc.) and the rebellious member(s) of the family. *Long Day's Journey into Night* is the masterwork of the form. All members of the family are both perpetrators of repression and victims of repression stuck in inescapable torment. But they are in it together.

2. **Woman's:** concerns the struggle of the independent woman versus an overbearing patriarch. The value is feminism/patriarchy and/or similar to the political, power/impotence. The core event is the rebellion and/or submission of the protagonist. *Anna Karenina* is a prime example.

3. **Political:** is the struggle for power. Its core value is power/impotence and the core event is the revolution where power is either lost or gained. *The Godfather,* while squarely in the crime Genre, is also a political drama too. We root for the gangster Michael Corleone to take down the five families and regain the power lost with the death of his father Vito.

4. **Biographical:** The value at stake in the biographical Story is dependent upon the figure as is the core event. Often biography takes on the dynamic of the performance Genre and/or one of the other External Content Genres to ground the narrative of a particular life Story.

5. **Historical:** The value at stake in the historical is also dependent upon the time period chosen as is the core event. What's important to remember is that when choosing the historical period to explore, it should be applicable to the present day dynamic. That is, the controlling idea of the Story should be applicable to contemporary life. Using historical details enables the writer to comment on a particular taboo or highly charged moment in contemporary life through the prism of the past. *Ragtime* by E.L. Doctorow has multiple protagonists as do the big epic novels of Edward Rutherfurd and Ken Follett.

The Love Genre

There are three Subgenres of the love Story: Stories of Courtship, Stories of Marriage, and Stories of Obsession. The core value of course is love/hate and the core event is the proof of love of one character for another.

1. **Courtship:** These stories concern the process of two people meeting and committing or not committing to each other. Beyond the core value of love/hate, they often concern dependence/independence, communication/misunderstanding, morality/immorality, social approval/disapproval, and togetherness/loneliness.

2. **Marriage**: These are stories about committed relationships going deeper into true intimacy or breaking apart. Beyond the global value of love/hate, they deal with notions of loyalty/betrayal, truth/lie, fidelity/infidelity, and self/other.

3. **Obsession**: These are stories about desire and passion, most often sexual. The core value beyond love/hate can often take a turn to survival/death. The core emotion can begin at romance/arousal and move to fear pretty quickly.

There are numerous popular Sub-sub-subgenres of love stories, including erotic, gothic, historical, paranormal, regency, romantic suspense, western and a very popular form in crime, thriller and horror...Buddy Salvation. Love stories are extremely effective as subplots in the other popular External Content Genres.

The Performance Genre

These stories are very popular because they concern the core value dynamic of respect versus shame. Will the big fight, performance, or presentation go well or will it result in dishonor? The core event, of course, is the big game or big performance.

1. **Sports:** *The Natural* by Bernard Malamud
2. **Music**: *The Commitments* by Roddy Doyle
3. **Business**: *Glengarry Glen Ross* by David Mamet
4. **Art**: *The Agony and the Ecstasy* by Irving Stone

25

INTERNAL CONTENT GENRES

Why do I make a distinction between External and Internal Content Genres?

The reason why is that today's Storytellers, especially long form television writers and series novelists, must have both components of Genre content to make their work compelling and sustainable over six or seven years of series television or ten to fifteen series novels. There are exceptions of course, but if you wish to create a Story that has the potential to play out over a long period of time, you need to think deeply about having both external and internal components in your work.

Years ago when I was at Doubleday Publishing, I worked with crime novelist Robert Crais. At the time, he'd written seven novels featuring a wise cracking and brilliant private investigator in Los Angeles named Elvis Cole and his dark compatriot Joe Pike. While the series was a commercial powerhouse, Bob wanted to go deeper. He wanted to stretch himself and I jumped at the opportunity to help him. I'll not get into the nitty-gritty of how Crais masterfully upped his game in his bestselling breakout novel *L.A. Requiem*, but it had everything to do with the internal wars within his two lead characters. Crais layered in multiple strands of Internal Genre to pitch perfect effect. So much so that today, most readers of Crais go to him for the internal battles he explores as much for his external plot machinations.

Remember that the External Genres concern outside forces aligned against the protagonist...nature, another person or society in general. These are represented by extra-personal and personal conflicts. They keep the protagonist from achieving his conscious desire...saving a victim, marrying his beloved, throwing down on the basketball court etc.

The Internal Genres concern forces inside the individual aligned against the protagonist's pursuit of a subconscious object of desire. The subconscious object of desire is the ultimate need within a protagonist whereas the conscious object of desire is the want, his immediate, on-the-surface identifiable goal. So in a thriller, a protagonist's external conscious object of desire will be to save a victim. But at a deeper level, he may need to sacrifice himself for another person in order to redeem himself from a past moral failing. Or he may need to finally learn the truth of who he is and why he does the things he does.

In the redemption plot, the lead character is conscious of wanting to save the victim. Beneath that consciousness, though, if the lead character were to sit down with a friend or a therapist and be asked why it was so important for him or her to save this victim beyond "doing their job," he'd eventually come to understand that his desire is a need to recover from a trauma/moral failing in his past. That buried-beneath-the surface need is the hero's internal object of desire. The redemption plot is just one of a number of possible internal content plot devices. More of those below.

So where did I come up with these classifications?

In 1955, Norman Friedman published the seminal Internal Genre differentiation "Forms of the Plot" in the *Journal of General Education.*[3] These Internal Genres are varieties of the hero's journey that reflect the quality of internal change at the beginning versus the end of the protagonist's mission.

Like choosing the global External Content Genre, choosing the Internal Content Genre is crucial to your Story. A poor combination of external and internal will result in an unsatisfying Story experience. A perfect combination will be a work of art. I'll take a hard look at one of the masterworks of the last fifty years, *The Silence of the Lambs*, and show you a pitch perfect combination of external and Internal Content Genres down the road.

From Friedman's work, I've adapted three internal Subgenres:

1. **Worldview:** connotes a change of seeing the world one way and by Story's end, seeing it differently.
2. **Morality:** connotes a change in the moral or ethical character of the protagonist.
3. **Status:** connotes a change in social position of the protagonist.

---

3 (Volume 8, pages 241-253)

The choice of global Internal Genre is driven by your lead character's subconscious object of desire, your character's unknown (to them at the beginning) inner quest. Remember that the quest is most often a two front journey. There is the external quest for a conscious object of desire like justice or survival or companionship or a prize of some sort like the rave review or victory. Then there is the internal quest, the one the lead character doesn't know he is in need of until a critical moment in the telling. The interplay of these two quests for objects of desire is what provides narrative drive on the one hand (the external) and insight into the human condition on the other (the internal).

Each of the three can be broken down further into recognizable Subgenres.

1. **Worldview: A Change in Perception of Life Experience**
    - Education: a shift in view of life from meaninglessness to meaning (*Tender Mercies*)
    - Maturation: a shift from naiveté to worldliness (*Saturday Night Fever*)
    - Revelation: ignorance to knowing (*Oedipus Rex*)
    - Disillusionment: belief to disillusionment (*The Great Gatsby*)
2. **Morality: A Change in a Character's Inner Moral Compass**
    - Punitive: good guy goes bad and is punished (*Wall Street*)
    - Redemption: bad guy reforms (*Drugstore Cowboy*)
    - Testing: willpower versus temptation (*Cool Hand Luke*)
3. **Status: A Change in Social Position**
    - Pathetic: weak protagonist tries to rise and fails (*Little Miss Sunshine*)
    - Sentimental: weak succeeds against all odds (*Rocky*)
    - Tragic: striver makes mistake that dooms him to failure (*American Tragedy*)
    - Admiration: principled person rises without compromise (*Gladiator*)

The Internal Content Genres are crucial to execute for novels or stories in the "Literary" Style, often referred to as those of "character." Literary novels most often use the Mini-plot structure and, for the most part, Mini-plot requires that the Internal Genre drive the global Story. That is, it is the change in the inner world of the character that compels interest in the reader/viewer much more so than the

External Genre's global value at stake. We read *Crime and Punishment* not for the external crime but for the internal punishment.

These Mini-plot stories are the stuff of the "literary" culture.

So a novel like *To Kill a Mockingbird,* while it has a wonderful external crime Genre within (the courtroom drama with Atticus Finch leading the defense of Tom Robinson), is a maturation plot first and foremost...the preeminent coming of age novel of the twentieth century.

Stories driven by the big set piece extra-personal antagonisms of horror and action, however, are far less dependent on the Internal Content Genres to work. In fact if you add too much internal hemming and hawing and "character development" in the pure action Story or horror Story, you may completely alienate your audience.

The master Stephen King is that rare novelist who can do both. But it's interesting to note how he pulls off this trick in his novels like *The Shining* and *Misery*. He does it by creating horror elements that can serve as symbols for inner turmoil. In *The Shining,* alcoholism's inner abuser takes form as supernatural spirits egging on the protagonist to kill his family. And in *Misery,* King has recently revealed that he created Annie Wilkes as a stand-in of sorts for his personal struggles with cocaine. Cocaine was his #1 fan...pushing and egging him on to furiously complete his pages.

Stephen King knows better than anyone how unchecked internal wars can morph into external horrors.

26

THE "A" STORY AND THE "B" STORY

Screenwriters often speak of these choices as Storyline A and Storyline B.

This is just another way of looking at their External and Internal Genre choices. If the Storyteller is telling a conventional murder mystery, the "A" Story would be the actual investigation…finding the killer and bringing him to justice. The External Genre, the crime Story, dictates the global object of desire. And the quest for justice that the lead character undertakes drives the global telling. The protagonist wants justice. He'll get it or he won't.

The "B" Story in a crime Story is usually determined by the choice of Internal Genre that the Storyteller makes. The "B" Story drives the theme or controlling idea. It's what the whole thing is really about. Under the surface of the external crime Genre, there is often another subconscious quest that the lead character/investigator/criminal undergoes. Keep in mind that this second quest is a deliberate choice by the writer. There are plenty of fun crime novels or films that do not have deep Internal Genres. Agatha Christie's master detectives aren't going on any internal quest in her stories. They are simply there to solve the crime.

In Robert Towne's screenplay *Chinatown*, though, the lead character does have an internal quest, a "B" Story. Jake Gittes is out to "find the girl," but underneath it all, he is out to prove to himself that he is capable of righting the wrongs of his past. He is out to beat the myriad of forces in the world that are out to keep him from living a righteous life protecting the people he loves.

Gittes wins the "find the girl" external object of desire, but he does not win the internal "redemption" Story. The bad guys win that one in the end. In fact, they've used Gittes to do their dirty work without his knowing and there's not a thing he can do about it in the end. Not only have they killed the woman he loves, they will take the innocence of a child.

Because *Chinatown* is a crime Story, the investigation drives the Story on the surface. Only with multiple viewings of the film do you discover that Gittes is haunted by a case in his past…back when he was on the LAPD and covered the eponymous Chinatown. He's asked at some point in the film about why he left the force and his reply is that he tried to protect someone and he failed. Back when he was a cop in Chinatown, his job was to do "as little as possible" but he refused. His meddling caused someone he cared about a great deal of pain if not her life. Towne wisely leaves the circumstances of that past trauma to the imagination of the viewer.

Jake Gittes doesn't know why he's decided to put his life on the line to help Evelyn Mulwray and her sister escape the clutches of Noah Cross, but he does it anyway. What's remarkable is that we, as the viewers of the movie, never question why he makes that choice. Because Robert Towne did such a masterful job revealing Gittes' deep character while he toils away toward his conscious object of desire—his wanting to find the girl—the audience is able to intuit his need. It's a need we all have.

Subconsciously, Gittes wants to redeem himself. To prove that his choice to help people is not in vain, that his deeds result in "truth" coming into the world. He exposes infidelities for a fee, what he calls "an honest living." This is why he gets so deeply invested in the Evelyn Mulwray case. He wants to prove to himself that he has the power to bring truth to the world and punish those who trade in deception, to redeem himself from his past failure in Chinatown.

Gittes may not know why he put his life on the line, but we do. Gittes needs to uncover the truth so that he can bring justice to the world. Like the Cerberus hellhounds who guard the Underworld, the authentic Jake Gittes (the self-actualized Jake Gittes) is a sentry for justice. He does what we know our better selves would do in the same circumstances. He fights for what's right. Even when Gittes fails, we never question his decision to try. He didn't get what he wanted (to save the world), but he got what he needed (a better understanding of the world).

That "B" Story is so deeply embedded inside of the "A" Story that it is almost invisible, as subconscious to the viewer as it is to Gittes. A first viewing of the movie leaves the viewer with a sense of deep sorrow for Gittes and the corrupt world he lives in. That feeling of empathy is the result of Towne not hitting the viewer over the head with the "B" Story. Instead he expertly drops hints in dialogue and description that make the catharsis palpable at the end. He never comments on the internal quest. But after multiple viewings, you can see and hear exactly where the screenwriter, Robert Towne, placed the critical mechanics of the "B" Story.

The perfect modulation of the "A" and "B" Stories reveals the ultimate theme/controlling idea of the global Story. *Chinatown*'s controlling idea is very much in keeping with the director of the movie, Roman Polanski's view of the world. *Evil reigns, to fight it is folly.*

PART THREE

THE FOOLSCAP GLOBAL STORY GRID

27

THE FOOLSCAP METHOD

It took my friend and business partner Steven Pressfield thirty years before he published his first novel. If he had to boil down the thick slurry of reasons why it took so long, he'd tell you that it took that long to figure out how to write a single foolscap page.

Years ago Steve was a struggling writer in New York, with a slew of unfinished manuscripts in his closet. He had no clue about why, but he knew deep in his heart that all of his efforts just didn't have "it" to convince a publishing house to give him a shot. He just knew there was something wrong with his novels but didn't know what.

One morning Steve was, yet again, whining to his friend Norm Stahl about this dark feeling when Stahl had finally had enough. He told Steve to meet him for lunch at Joe Allen's on West 46th Street in the Theater District of Manhattan that very day. His treat. [Joe Allen's is famous for its "Flop Wall," featuring posters of failed Broadway plays.]

So after Steve ordered his cheeseburger and fries and got his tall glass of ice tea, Stahl laid it on him. He reached into his briefcase and pulled out a legal sized yellow pad, known in the paper trade as foolscap.

"Steve, the good Lord wisely made one sheet of foolscap paper just long enough to outline an entire novel. The reason why your work is letting you down is that you may have a clear destination in mind when you start, but you have no map. How will you know if you made the best choices for getting to 'THE END' if you don't have a game plan before you set out? THIS IS YOUR MAP!" he pointed to the yellow lined paper.

Steve's friend wasn't just some civilian with no experience creating narrative Story. Norm Stahl is a highly respected and incredibly nimble and productive filmmaker with over three hundred feature-length documentaries to his credit.

And if you have no sense of Story when making a documentary, you are in deep trouble. Over the years, Stahl had learned not to be so precious with his material, but to be brutal and decisive about what he wanted to say and how he wanted to say it.

Stahl then pulled out a thick-felted Sharpie and drew two lines across the page, cutting the one sheet into thirds.

"The top third of the page is your first act, Steve. The second third is your second act and the third is your third act... You can only use the space allotted."

Steve sat transfixed.

"In the simplest way possible, write down your 'What if?' Inciting incident at the top of act 1. Say it's a murder mystery. Your Inciting Incident will be the discovery of a body. If it's a romance, it's the lovers meet scene. If it's a horror novel, it's the scene where the monster attacks. Now at the very bottom of the page, write down the climax of the entire novel. If it's a murder mystery, it could be the core event identifying the murderer…bringing him to justice or him getting away. If it's a romance, it could be the lovers reunite after falling out in the second act scene. If it's a horror novel, it could be the vulnerable victim overcoming the monster. Whatever. After you have the global Inciting Incident and the global climax of your Story, then all you have to do is fill in the rest!"

Steve was speechless.

The concept was so easy to get and understand that he had a hard time believing it was that simple. Like anyone else would, Steve resisted the notion.

"That's nice, Norm, but I'm trying to write something with real gravitas. My stuff can't be broken down like that."

Stahl smiled and said, "Oh yeah? Is your stuff better than *Moby Dick*? How about *The Great Gatsby*?" Steve shook his head. "Well both of those break down perfectly using the Foolscap Method. Try it!"

Eventually, in one of those *all is lost* moments we all reach when we're forced to change, Steve did try it. He decided to map out a novel that had been scratching inside his head for years. He just had no idea how to execute it. He only had a notion.

Steve put Norm Stahl's Foolscap Method to the test when he wrote his first published novel, which not only put his work into bookstores, but also onto big screens. *The Legend of Bagger Vance* adaptation was directed by Robert Redford and starred Matt Damon, Will Smith and Charlize Theron. Steve writes about the entire experience in *The Authentic Swing*, which lays out just how he practically applied Norm Stahl's advice. (Full disclosure: Steve and I published *The Authentic Swing* together under the same publishing house that this book is being released, **Black Irish Books**.)

Norm Stahl's Foolscap Method is remarkably similar to what took me a good twenty years to figure out myself as a struggling book editor. I have a similar, but a bit more obsessive method that involves an extra black line that divides the foolscap into four sections instead of three. It evolved as an editor's diagnostic tool rather than a "create from whole cloth" Story creator's point of view. But it's absolutely a similar concept.

In honor of my friend Steven Pressfield and his mentor Norm Stahl, I call it *The Foolscap Global Story Grid*.

28

AN EDITOR'S SIX CORE QUESTIONS

An editor handed a pile of manuscript pages must answer a whole bunch of questions before he can even begin to diagnose the effectiveness of the Storytelling. While he'll know after one read whether the book "works," in order to take the book to the next level, he'll have to figure out exactly how it is working. He has to put the whole book onto one page.

To refresh your memory, here are the six questions he must answer:

1. What's the Genre?
2. What are the conventions and obligatory scenes for that Genre?
3. What's the Point of View?
4. What are the objects of desire?
5. What's the controlling idea/theme?
6. What is the Beginning Hook, the Middle Build, and Ending Payoff?

The Foolscap Global Story Grid is that one page document. Once he's read the book [just one time] if the book is well conceived he should be able to fill in the blanks of *The Foolscap Global Story Grid* without having any serious head scratches.

When you boil down an entire Story to one page, there is no place for a writer or an editor to bullshit himself. It's an indispensable tool to check your work.

But don't forget that it is a diagnostic tool and not a recipe. You could have a brilliantly laid out *Foolscap Global Story Grid* before you begin writing and the Story itself could fizzle completely. Or you may have what seems to be a rather generic *Foolscap Global Story Grid* that results in a timeless work of art. Execution is everything.

If you cannot execute the plan, *The Foolscap Global Story Grid* will not result in a great Story. You could have the best architectural plans, but if you are a lousy carpenter or plumber or electrician, the house is going to have flaws. But those kinds of flaws are fixable through perseverance and hard work and dedication to craft. But an ill-conceived *Foolscap Global Story Grid* is fatal. The Story won't work.

But again, *The Foolscap Global Story Grid* is not an end to itself. It's not even something to show anyone else unless he is your editor or a fellow scribe in need of a helping hand. To go back to our metaphor, it's an architectural layout for a building, not a building.

Don't torture yourself over it unless you really have to.

What *The Foolscap Global Story Grid* can do for you if your Story isn't working is immeasurably helpful. It will show you where you went wrong. Where you jumped off track, got lazy, fell in love with a scene instead of making sure the scene served your Story, etc. It will show you where your problems are, where there's a leak in your plumbing, a short in your wiring etc. and thus it will take away quite a bit of that inner self-loathing and destructive behavior we all face when we have a very, very rough first draft. You as the writer are not the problem, the problem is the problem. *The Foolscap Global Story Grid* will tell you where your problems are.

It will take away a lot of emotional sturm and drang and keep you working. You'll use it to make discernible progress. It will keep you from desperately seeking "notes" from friends or acquaintances who know nothing about Story structure. It will make you a much better Storyteller and as you use it more and more, you'll become a far better writer.

Eventually you'll do the work of *The Foolscap Global Story Grid* intuitively. But you'll always be able to fill it in at the first sign of trouble.

Now, let's move down *The Foolscap Global Story Grid* from top to bottom and explain exactly what we need to fill in.

		FOOLSCAP GLOBAL STORY GRID		
		External Genre:		
G	S	External Value at Stake:		
L	T	Internal Genre:		
O	O	Internal Value at Stake:		
B	R	Obligatory Scenes and Conventions:		
A	Y			
L		Point of View:		
		Objects of Desire:		
		Controlling Idea/Theme:		
B			External	Internal
E			Charge	Charge
G	H	1. Inciting Incident:		
I	O	2. Complication:		
N	O	3. Crisis:		
N	K	4. Climax:		
I		5. Resolution:		
N				
G				
			External	Internal
M	B		Charge	Charge
I	U	1. Inciting Incident:		
D	I	2. Complication:		
D	L	3. Crisis:		
L	D	4. Climax:		
E		5. Resolution:		
			External	Internal
E	P		Charge	Charge
N	A	1. Inciting Incident:		
D	Y	2. Complication:		
I	O	3. Crisis:		
N	F	4. Climax:		
G	F	5. Resolution:		

The first line we need to fill out is the External Genre, which is one of the nine External Content Genres I detailed earlier along with its Sub and/or Sub-subgenre classification. So for *The Silence of the Lambs*, the External Content Genre would be THRILLER, along with its Subgenre classification SERIAL KILLER.

External Genre: Serial Killer Thriller

The External Value at Stake in a thriller is a convention. It is Life. To remind myself of the progression of the value, I'll move it from its positive value to its most negative. Again, I'll go into more depth regarding the external value in part 7.

External Value at Stake: Life to Unconsciousness to Death to Fate Worse than Death (Damnation)

One of the Internal Genres that I discussed earlier is also a very major component of *The Silence of the Lambs*. I'll do a much more in-depth analysis of why I've designated it the way that I have later on when I walk you through the entire *Story Grid* for *The Silence of the Lambs*.

Internal Genre: Worldview Disillusionment

The Internal Value at Stake in a Worldview Internal Story is what you'd expect—the way in which the protagonist views the world. It will arc from negative to positive or positive to negative depending upon your Subgenre. In the case of *The Silence of the Lambs*, it arcs from what I see as a "false positive view" to a proven negative and it does so through the prism of Clarice Starling's professional ambition.

Internal Value at Stake: Blind Belief to Justified Belief to Doubt to Disillusionment

I'll lay out the obligatory scenes and conventions of the thriller and we can fill in the next line on our *Foolscap Global Story Grid*, but before we do that it's worth the time to look at where the thriller Genre came from.

29

THE UNIVERSAL APPEAL OF THE THRILLER

Al Zuckerman, a very experienced and successful literary agent who founded and runs the esteemed literary agency Writers House, wrote a book some years ago (1994) that is still vital, *Writing the Blockbuster Novel.* In it, Zuckerman recommends that if a potential novelist wants to succeed commercially, he should write a novel with multiple points of view. This is sage advice from someone who represents the extremely successful writer Ken Follett. In his book, Zuckerman actually walks the reader through Follett's multiple outlines for *The Man from St. Petersburg.* I highly recommend reading it, as you'll get a very clear understanding of one writer's analytical process before he even contemplates writing his first draft.

Follett is a big believer in outlining. I worked for one of his editors years ago at Delacorte Press, the wonderful Jackie Farber, and had the pleasure of reading a number of his outlines before he wrote word one. While innovations in his Story came to him during the drafting that he hadn't anticipated before he dove in, his outline was comprehensive. That is, he tackled the very difficult work of creating a Beginning, Middle and End to his book before he began writing. He didn't depend upon the guiding light of the Muse alone to steer him to shore, he mapped out his journey before he set sail. And wouldn't you know it, while he worked fresh ideas that took his outline from a "B" Story to an "A" Story emerged.

He made sure he knew where he was going before he set out on the journey. Through his example (and many other extremely gifted and hardworking writers including the master Elmore Leonard), I began my quest to conceive and develop *The Story Grid.* Twenty plus years later...here it finally is!

Follett's kind of sweeping novel that is as much about a historical time and place as it is about its characters requires a very unique set of skills. Al Zuckerman is certainly right that when a novel of great scope hits the marketplace and touches a nerve, it can become a blockbuster success.

However, it is my contention that while the broad, often multi-Genre historical saga (*Dr. Zhivago, Pillars of the Earth,* the entire James Michener backlist etc.) can result in very compelling Story, it does not have the commercial potential today that it did only a few decades ago. That is, beyond Ken Follett, there are few writers making hay with this approach today. Just take a look at today's bestseller lists and you'll see that this kind of work is not as represented as it once was.

As time passes, things change. Like everything else, Story changes too. What was once a dominant Genre just a few decades ago often recedes in popularity. Why aren't there novels like *Rich Man, Poor Man* or *The Carpetbaggers* or even *Less than Zero* on bestseller lists anymore? Audiences grew weary of them and moved elsewhere.

But then again if I were to give advice to a young writer looking for an angle… I'd suggest writing a saga. When there is a hole in the marketplace, it doesn't necessarily mean that there is no market for that kind of book. It usually indicates an opportunity. Donna Tartt's *The Goldfinch* being a major bestseller and critical sensation stands as direct proof. In fact, I can anticipate that within the next few years, we'll have more of these epic realistic sagas with deep Story reaching larger and larger audiences. The good old-fashioned epic social drama is on the ascent.

What determine the degree of popularity of any one particular Genre are the vagaries of the time period in which it has been written. What were once the popcorn Stories of a time, decades later prove to be dusty and unpopular. Westerns were once the bread and butter of book publishing. Paperback houses survived on churning out westerns, sometimes five of them a month. Now the western is all but forgotten. Other than a few classics from the arena, *Lonesome Dove* and the Louis L'Amour oeuvre perhaps, or post-modern takes that splice the western into other Genres, you can't give away westerns today. There was once a Genre called the *Pennydreadful* that was hugely popular in the Victorian era. Not so anymore. Although there is a television series just out working hard to revive it.

So what is the Story Genre of our time?

THE THRILLER.

The thriller is the Story form of our time because it concerns the individual coping with omnipresent and often difficult to even comprehend antagonism. Thrillers boil down our modern experience to a psychological core that every literate person and even illiterate person on the planet can understand, sympathize and empathize.

Contemporary civilization is a dizzying mix of sensory input designed to elicit individual compliance and subconscious behavioral action. We are inundated with psychically damaging messages—*we're too fat, we're ugly, we're low class, we're not cool, we're lazy, we're never going to make it*. On top of those assaults are prescriptive solutions to overcoming our inadequacies—*go on a diet, join a health club, go to college, wear hip-hop clothes, take this seminar*. They are targeted to us every single day, hour, minute, and even second of our lives.

And these are no longer static images from the Mad Men era. They are loaded in full High Definition motion on billboards, in cabs, on buses, on the Internet and every single cable channel. While the commercial messaging is impossible to ignore or avoid, it is modern life's "control" messaging that really knocks us on our asses. I'll not get into the work of Sigmund Freud's nephew Edward Bernays here, but he's the ghost in all of these machines.

The granddaddy of all messages we receive is this: WE'RE NOT SAFE.

We are told that there are boogeymen at every corner. Al Qaeda, and now ISIS and a slew of other terrorist organizations that we know little of, want to destroy us. Pedophiles are stalking our children. Our government is failing us. The world is getting so hot, it will soon melt down. Floods, tornadoes, hurricanes, tsunamis, are imminent. Storm watches, breaking news, lone gunmen, sociopaths, psychopaths, liars, cheaters, swindlers, gangs, feral youth, pirates, unstable veterans, racists, sexists, drones, the NSA, the CIA, the FBI, the Police, MI5, MI6, the Stasi, KGB, DEA, IRS, drunk drivers, texting drivers, homeless people… The fear factory is churning out product like no other time in history.

To make matters worse? We all live alone. We belong to no protective tribe. The nuclear family is a couple or just one parent with a kid or two or three. Perhaps all from different partners. Single parents pulled in a million directions. It's just mano a mano.

This is why the thriller is the form that holds the blockbuster baton these days. [Let's not forget that Ken Follett has written one of the best thrillers of all time, *Eye of the Needle* as well as his epic sagas.]

I also think we are attracted to the thriller because of the chaotic and yet intricately connected character of our age. Modern man is assaulted with data from the moment he wakes to the moment he falls asleep. While we are all connected now by the World Wide Web, we don't see any real grand humanitarian design coming to bear as a result. There are millions of people starving, being slaughtered, used as slaves, and our economies are in complete flux. Everything that modern man once held dear and believed (technology will solve all of our problems) is now in doubt. There just doesn't seem to be any way to navigate the world without feeling in one way or another victimized by forces beyond our control.

In order to find our way in this chaos, we seek stories that give us hope and faith that we can persevere.

While over the top action fantasy stories are certainly still viable and commercially irresistible (hence the Batman, Superman, Avenger, comic book movie franchises), long form stories in novel form that do not sugarcoat reality or simplify success help satisfy our need for order. As we often feel like we have no impact on the world whatsoever and are treated by the powerful as consumption machines to be programmed by the latest algorithms, we deeply identify with thriller protagonists.

The thriller is all about one individual negotiating a complex world, living it to the limits of human existence, and usually triumphing over seemingly overwhelming forces of antagonism. Isn't this a description of what we often feel we are up against every day of our lives? We love thrillers because they reassure us that there is an order to the world and one person can make a difference, have an impact. When we leave a great movie thriller or finish a great thriller novel, we have a catharsis. The experience purges our gloom and gives us reinforcement to stay the course.

If Clarice Starling can survive having Hannibal Lecter in her head, all the while chasing a schizophrenic serial killer flaying women to make himself a woman suit, we can certainly make it through another day at work.

30

THE POWER OF NEGATIVE THINKING

So just how do you take your Story to the end of the line… to the limits of human experience?

The Storyteller needs a tool to not only understand this concept, but to evaluate whether or not they have successfully done so. And if you're writing a big Story, you **have to go to the end of the line**.

The trick to figuring out how to do that is discovering what Robert McKee calls the negation of the negation of your global Story value. Once you understand the negation of the negation of a global Story value, you will discover whether your draft or your murky foolscap sketch for a Story has legs. And in the process, if you do this work early and often, you'll be able to clearly understand the obligatory scenes and promises that you are making to the reader by your choice of Genre and/or mix of Genres.

Let's take a step back and look at Story values.

What the hell am I talking about when I use the phrase "Story value"?

A Story value has nothing to do with "family values" or financial currency. A Story value is simply a human experience (a judgment of reality) that can change from positive to negative or negative to positive. It's best to just list a whole slew of them so that you'll get the gist. Alive/dead, truth/lie, love/hate, justice/injustice, hope/despair, good/evil, right/wrong, happy/sad, naïve/experienced, young/old, smart/dumb, rich/poor, freedom/slavery, honor/shame, chosen/ignored, etc.

Where one goes off track is in forgetting that these Story values aren't just black and white polarities.

There are progressive degrees of positivity or negativity for each.

For example, the opposite of love may be hate, but there is something in between love and hate that is worse than love but less than hate. That in between is called indifference. And there is also something worse than hate. That something is what Robert McKee coined as the "negation of the negation." And for the love/hate spectrum, the negation of the negation is "hate masquerading as love" or "self-hatred."

Let's look at a very popular External Content Genre, crime fiction, and examine the core value at stake in four different ways.

The Story value at stake for crime fiction is JUSTICE.

A crime has been committed.

Will the crime be solved?

Will the perpetrator be brought to justice? That's basically it.

By choosing the crime Genre, the first promise you are making to a reader is an answer to these two fundamental questions.

But we'd all agree that there are varying degrees of crime, right?

Stealing a piece of candy from a drugstore is far less of a crime than the wholesale slaughter of an entire village. There is a wide spectrum of mendacity. Because there is such a wide band, the writer has a choice of how far to take his Story. As every Story must progressively complicate, a crime Story needs to begin one place, get more and more difficult to solve, and then end in a surprising but inevitable final solution or conundrum. Just how far you take the crime (how globally threatening it is) requires you to figure out exactly where the line ends in terms of the JUSTICE value.

To do that, we need to look at the negative progression (or degradation) of the value at stake.

So let's begin with the POSITIVE end of the spectrum, which is JUSTICE, and place that at the very left of our degradation line. And we know that the opposite of JUSTICE is INJUSTICE, so let's put that down the line on the right hand side, further away from the epitome of positive.

JUSTICE INJUSTICE

But we also all know there's more to the negative world than injustice. There's crime with extenuating circumstances…like the thief who steals a loaf of bread to feed his starving children. Did the man steal the bread and did the owner of the store lose a valuable asset? Yes.

But is this an offense that threatens society?

No.

So somewhere between JUSTICE and INJUSTICE lies a nether region of unfairness. It's unfair to the owner of the store not to be compensated for his bread. But the fact that the bread was used to feed starving children—a good outcome from a bad act—lessens the act's venality. So between justice and injustice, let's put UNFAIRNESS, which is something in between black and white.

JUSTICE UNFAIRNESS INJUSTICE

Now the question arises, is there something worse than an Injustice?

The bad mojo that off the charts sociopathic narcissists bring into the world is something more than just unjust, isn't it? The serial killer or warlord or fascist genocidal perpetrator is emblematic of a world that is always unjust. In this kind of world, there is no justice. By definition, it is run with complete unpredictability. The rules are changed whenever it suits the whims or desires of a central body or figure.

That kind of more negative than the opposite JUSTICE is the world of Tyranny.

So on a straight line spectrum from positive to negative, let's put Tyranny even further to the right of injustice.

JUSTICE UNFAIRNESS INJUSTICE TYRANNY

To recap, while there is a direct opposite of Justice (Injustice), the value has far more nuance than purely positive or purely negative. There is the degree of negativity less than the direct opposite, Unfairness, and the degree of negativity far more abhorrent than the direct opposite, Tyranny.

It is the darkest of the dark that McKee has termed the *Negation of the Negation*.

Here's the way I would chart the spectrum of positive to negative

JUSTICE (+)   UNFAIRNESS (+/-)   INJUSTICE (-)   TYRANNY (- -)

If we were asked to assign a power of ten number for each of these (the number one being the most positive and number ten being the most negative), it would look like this:

JUSTICE (1)   UNFAIRNESS (3)   INJUSTICE (7)   TYRANNY (11)

If you've ever seen the movie *Spinal Tap,* I think you know where we should try and reach by the end of our crime Story.

Using the power of ten system by assigning a numeric value to the degree of negativity can help you track the progression of your Story.

The beginning section of your Story should progress from say a 1 to a 4, the middle from 4 to an 8 and the end from an 8 to an 11. The resolution of the Story would then bring the Story full circle, back to 1, or end on a more somber note, ending on 8 or even 11.

If your crime Story is a straight action James Bond kind of thing like *Thunderball* or *Live and Let Die,* your resolution will circle back to Justice, 1...all's well again in the world. James Bond has fixed it. Major positive ending.

But if your Story is *Apocalypse Now* or *Chinatown*, you're going to end on an 11 on the negativity scale. The world is a mess and we've gone completely to the dark side. It's every man for himself.

What about those stories that have a positive ending for the global Story but have an ironic twist?

Is there a way for a crime Story to somehow return the global Story value back to Justice (or life back to life in the case of the thriller, action Story or horror Story) but do it ironically? That is, bring a criminal to technical justice but lose something in the process?

If your Story is *Dirty Harry*, you can accomplish this irony through your choice of theme/controlling idea.

Dirty Harry ends on a positive/negative combo plate of irony. Our cop gets the guy and justice is served, but he breaks the law doing it and leaves his job in disgust (remember he throws away his badge at the very end). The world no longer has a vicious killer in it, but the kind of man who can take him out has been lost too. The only way to stop the killers is to empower fascists/"good" killers is one interpretation of the theme/controlling idea of *Dirty Harry*.

Another way to add irony to Story is to add an Internal Genre along with its inherent value progression underneath the global External Genre. That is, the protagonist undergoes an internal quest as well as an external quest in the Story. The External Genre ends on the positive, while the Internal Genre ends on the negative, thus producing irony.

An example of that scenario would be the movie *The Social Network*... The lead character wins the business performance External Genre (Facebook is a huge hit) but fails his internal morality test plot (he succumbs to the temptations of wealth and power at the expense of real connection to fellow human beings).

Bottom line, should you wish to reach the pinnacle of your chosen Genre(s) (don't we all?) you must think deeply and clearly about the negation of the negation and how best to express its arrival in your Story.

31

THE OBLIGATORY SCENES AND CONVENTIONS OF THE THRILLER

We've been working our way down *The Foolscap Global Story Grid.*

Let's look at the spaces we'll need to fill in for the conventions and obligatory scenes of your chosen Genres. As our big payoff down the road will be a complete creation and analysis of ***The Story Grid for The Silence of the Lambs***, here is the breakdown of conventions and obligatory scenes for the External Content Genre, the thriller.

The thriller is its own Genre, but it came to be through a mashing up of three primal Genres that came before it: action, horror and crime.

Many place the thriller inside the action or crime Genres because a large number of the obligatory scenes and conventions of the thriller share elements with both action and crime stories. Few (Robert McKee being the very large exception) would associate thriller with horror, but the horror element is what puts the cherry on top of the thriller's three-Genre mash up sundae.

Here are the other necessities (beyond a supporting value of Justice at stake) in a thriller that derive from action and crime and stories.

1. The first convention of a thriller is that there must be a crime. And with a crime, you must have perpetrator(s) and victim(s), either corpse(s), the assaulted or hostage(s).
2. The crime must occur early on in the telling.
3. The crime must reveal a clue about the villain's MacGuffin.

   A MacGuffin is the object of desire for the villain. If the villain gets the MacGuffin, he will "win." Some familiar MacGuffins are a) the codes to the nuclear warhead, b) one thousand kilos of heroin, c) microfilm, d) and in the case of *The Silence of the Lambs*, the final pieces of skin to make a woman-suit. The MacGuffin must make sense to the reader. It doesn't necessarily have to be realistic, just believable. I think Alfred Hitchcock coined the term when asked about the device in *North by Northwest*. MacGuffins are essentially the antagonist's literal objects of desire.

4. There must be a brilliant and/or incredibly powerful master criminal and an equally brilliant and/or powerful investigator/detective/sleuth. But the balance of power between the two is heavily in favor of the villain.

5. The villain must "make it personal" with regard to the protagonist. The criminal may from the very beginning want to kill/humiliate/destroy/damn the investigator; or he may come to this attitude during the telling. But the crime must escalate and become personal. The protagonist must become a victim.

6. There must be clues and red herrings in the Storytelling. The protagonist investigates and follows leads in order to find and/or trap the criminal. Some of these leads are dead ends and misdirect the protagonist and the reader.

7. The value at stake in a crime Story can progress from justice to unfairness to injustice to tyranny. Most crime stories end at Injustice...will the detective get his man? He usually does. But in a thriller, the value is often driven to the limit. If the detective/investigator/protagonist does not bring the villain to justice, tyranny will be the result. The protagonist's failure to get the criminal takes on a universal quality. If our best investigators can't stop the worst villains, the villains have won. There is no justice. We live in tyranny.

So what does the thriller get from the horror Genre?

1. In the horror Genre, like the action Genre, the value at stake is life. But the value is taken to the end of the line…the fate worse than death, damnation. So while the thriller gets procedural elements from the crime Story, its global value comes from horror.

2. The villain in horror is far more powerful/intelligent/ supernatural than the protagonist. The balance of power is huge, so large that it's unrealistic. In the thriller, the balance of power is not as large as horror but far more than in a crime Story. And the thriller is realistic...that is believable, possible to occur in real life. The villain in a thriller is a human monster.

3. In the horror Genre, there is a speech in praise of the villain and/or awesomeness of the supernatural power. So too in the thriller. There is a speech in praise of the villain that clearly states how awesome the forces of antagonism are.

4. Also like the horror Genre, there is the hero at the mercy of the villain scene. The protagonist must be put into a position where they are seemingly incapable of overpowering the villain. That is, there is no way the protagonist can free himself. But somehow, the protagonist either outsmarts or overpowers the villain and escapes. This is the real nail biter scene of a thriller, the big moment, and as such it is the most difficult to innovate.

5. There is a false ending. Like those cheesy but wonderful *Friday the 13th* movies, the end of a thriller isn't really the end. Somehow the villain reasserts himself one final time. Just when you think it's safe to enjoy the resolution of the Story, BAM!

Let's put it all together. Here are the conventions and obligatory scenes for the thriller.

1. An Inciting crime
2. A MacGuffin
3. Red herrings
4. A Speech in Praise of the Villain
5. The stakes must become personal for the hero. If he fails to stop the villain, he will suffer severe consequences. The hero must become the victim.
6. There must be a hero at the mercy of the villain scene.
7. False ending. There must be two endings.

Lastly, many thrillers also have an additional convention that derives from the action Genre, a clock. At a critical point in the Story, a time limit is placed on the protagonist to get the villain. If the protagonist does not do so, the villain will get what he wants by default. The clock is one way for the writer to clearly define the end of the limit for the Story, the ultimate fate worse than death, damnation. If the hero dilly-dallies like Shakespeare's Hamlet, his indecisiveness will damn him.

It's his fault that the villain won because he refused to accept his calling. Clocks are not required, but they sure help escalate the stakes. You'll see how brilliantly Harris uses a clock in the Middle Build of *The Silence of the Lambs* later on. The Middle Build is the most challenging section of a Story, when a Story is most likely to lose its grip on the reader.

If you've decided to write a thriller and you know that you have to deliver these conventions and scenes, wouldn't it be a good place to start your work by mapping out some strategies to do so? That is, if you know you have to write the hero at the mercy of the villain scene, wouldn't it be a good idea to try to crack it before you dive into fleshing out the rest of the novel? The hero at the mercy scene is the big promise you're making to a reader when you tell her that you have written a thriller. Nailing it early on will help you immeasurably.

Obligatory scenes are a great way to give you a clear mission. You'll be surprised at how straightforward it can be to write the rest of the Story if you've created innovative obligatory scenes.

So this is why it's a good idea to remind yourself on your *Foolscap Global Story Grid* about the conventions and obligatory scenes you'll need to drop into your Story. Put them at the very top and you'll have them ever present in your mind. From first through final draft.

32

POINT OF VIEW

Next up on our *Foolscap Global Story Grid* is the space to fill in point of view.

Point of view is the vantage point the writer chooses to tell the reader a Story. Your point of view choices will dictate the tenor of each beat, each scene, each sequence, each act and the entire work. They are crucial choices. (I'll do a follow up chapter to this on Free Indirect Style next for more on how best to approach the literal telling.)

Let's say that you have two characters in a scene. Two brothers. The younger brother is the prodigal son. He's left town years ago and now has decided to come home to the family farm. He's coming back—not because he's broke and destitute and in need of help—rather because he's wealthy beyond whatever he expected out of life. But his material possessions have brought him no happiness. He's coming home to rekindle his love for his dear brother who stayed behind to take care of the family while he went out to make his fortune.

The older brother is the workhorse farmer who has sacrificed his own individual ambitions in order to care for the extended family. The farm survives only by his efforts.

How will these two greet each other? What will they want from one another? Will one get what he wants while the other doesn't? One of the best places to begin to answer these questions (if you haven't already) is by approaching them through point of view.

You'll have four point of view choices to describe this "coming home" scene. Your choice of global Genre will dictate which choice to make, hence why I've spent so much time laying out the Genres. Knowing what point of view will best serve your Genre is the key.

You could:

- Place the center of the narrative "inside the mind" of the rich younger brother coming home, and share his thoughts as if there were a magical parrot sitting on his shoulder capable of hearing and repeating the character's inner world to the reader. (See the Free Indirect Style chapter coming up next.)
- You could put the parrot on the farmer brother's shoulder.
- You could alternate between the two brothers' points of view and their respective magical parrots.
- You could place the narrative center above the world and describe the scene as if you are the child at play with two dolls and a farm set. This reportorial/neutral point of view is the strict third person omniscient voice that does not tell the reader what is going on inside the heads of the characters. Or if it does, it does so from a God-like perspective. (Again, read the upcoming chapter Free Indirect Style for more on this.)

How do you decide?

If the younger brother is the protagonist of your Story—your novel could be a modern society/redemption Story about the corrupting powers of ambition—I'd suggest you follow everything that happens from his point of view.

If your Story is a western/testing Story about the difficult choice someone might make to safeguard the lives of others at the expense of his own "self-actualization," I'd suggest you follow everything that happens from the farmer brother's point of view.

If your Story is a domestic drama/sentimental Story about the pressures of shifting from one kind of family dynamic and back again, then perhaps using both points of view would serve your purposes well. In this case, both brothers would serve as protagonists and antagonists, depending upon the particular circumstances of the global family saga Story's arc. See *Giant* by Edna Ferber.

If your Story is not about either of these brothers, but is a historical drama/punitive Story about a plague and the effects it has on regular people, you'll probably want to write it as strict third person omniscient with perhaps a smattering of indirect speech to invest the reader emotionally with one or more characters.

Here's my advice to get you started. If you are writing a traditional Arch-plot structured novel, write the first draft from the point of view of your protagonist. Either in the first person or by using third person omniscient (all knowing/Godlike) Free Indirect Style.

Quick reminder:

> **First Person** means the Story is told by the narrator...*I saw my brother in the field.*
>
> **Second Person** means that the Story is told with the narrator referring to the reader as you...*You saw him in the field.* Rarely do novelists use the Second Person. Jay McInerney did a remarkable job with it in *Bright Lights, Big City*.
>
> **Third Person** means the Story is told from a narrative distance—*Jim Smith saw his brother Luke in the field.*

If you can sustain interest in the trials and tribulations of that one character and use the inner life of that lead character to best effect, you'll get the most out of the Arch-plot form. But after you've finished the first draft, you may find places in the Story that would benefit from a shift in point of view. That is, you may need to get Story events onto the page that the protagonist is not privy to. Or you'll want to layer in another character's thoughts to counterbalance those of your protagonist.

For example, in *The Silence of the Lambs* Thomas Harris makes use of nine points of view. Primarily Clarice Starling (the protagonist), but he also gives at least two chapters/scenes to Buffalo Bill/Jame Gumb (the antagonist), Jack Crawford (the mentor) and Hannibal Lecter (the anti-mentor).

Starling is the dominant force of the novel. But if Harris did not stretch out and use the POVs of the other three characters, the reader would have a very generic sense of the forces aligned with her and those against her. Without seeing Buffalo Bill/Jame Gumb prepare to harvest his victim, the novel would lose a great deal of tension. Starling would not be privy to that preparation, so if Harris strictly maintained her POV, we'd lose a very chilling scene.

You'll notice though that Harris does not give us the antagonist's POV until the Middle Build portion of his novel, nor does he give us Hannibal Lecter's until even later on in the book. He does give us Jack Crawford's POV in chapter five. That choice allows the reader to attach to Crawford emotionally. Harris understood that Crawford's actions up to that point are very stoic and dictatorial, if not Machiavellian. By giving us his world early, the reader can't help but see that his behavior is a mask. A mask to cover up the horrors of his personal life experience. And thus, the reader allows him his misanthropy. Empathizes with him.

You'll also notice Harris using minor characters' points of view with Free Indirect Style to ratchet tension in critical moments. He does this so seamlessly that the reader does not mind the POV shifts.

Big caution: Too many POV shifts are irritating.

Especially in the Beginning Hook of a Story. You need the reader to get attached to your protagonist before you can branch out. Finding the perfect mix is the challenge. The simple rule to follow is...if the POV shift takes the reader out of the global world and confuses them for even a millisecond...don't do it.

33

FREE INDIRECT STYLE

How can you best tell a Story? Through the vantage point of one character? Or multiple characters?

If you decide to write in first person, *I went across the street to buy an ice cream cone,* then you have taken on the central limitation/strength of the novelist. Choosing to write a novel gives you the best opportunity to explore the deep inner conflicts of one or more characters. The intrapersonal world (what is going inside someone's head) is the novelist's domain. You must master it. No other Story medium (stage or screen) allows for such exploration into the inner life of a character like a novel. And the first person Storytelling method is a Godsend to do that very thing. *The Great Gatsby, To Kill a Mockingbird, Moby Dick, The Adventures of Huckleberry Finn*...these are among the great American novels and they all use first person narration.

But what of the many (if not majority of) novels that are not written in the first person? They are written in what is called third person omniscient point of view, meaning from a God-like stature above the action, *He went across the street to buy an ice cream cone.* The advantages of third person omniscient writing is that you can have a broad cast of characters doing a whole slew of actions in multiple places, even all at the same time. If you take that Godlike approach, you are not limited to what one-character experiences, but rather you can report on the actions of many. Of such scope are epics made. *War and Peace* anyone?

Most commercial fiction in the primal External Genres (novels written to be bought and enjoyed by strangers, not just your extended family and the Ivory Tower) is in the third person. So if the advantage of the novel is in being able to get inside a character's head, but first person narration only allows you to write from the point of view of one character, how do the third person omniscient stories work? In other words, is there a way to get inside multiple characters' heads while also maintaining the proverbial Godlike/reportorial narrative of third person omniscient?

The answer is YES!

We have the Stephen Kings, Nora Roberts, and John Irvings of their time…Johann Wolfgang von Goethe, Jane Austen, Gustave Flaubert (and many of his fellow French nineteenth-century realist novelists), to thank for the innovation. *Madame Bovary* (Flaubert 1857) is generally recognized as the model for the technique. These literary lions wrote in what is now called the "Free Indirect Style."

Essentially, Free Indirect Style is a combo plate of first person and third person. Meaning there are two distinct narrative beings present in Free Indirect Style. There is the third person narrator (you, the writer) and there is a character or multiple characters in the novel that also "narrate" through their thoughts.

For example, as I'll be analyzing *The Silence of the Lambs* in part 7, let's take a look at how Thomas Harris makes brilliant use of Free Indirect Style. What's more, he transitions into it seamlessly, allowing the reader to attach to his lead character as a virtual observer of her behavior before he lets us "hear" directly from her. Harris begins the novel by reporting her thoughts as if he (the Godlike narrator) were capable of tapping her consciousness. Later on, he'll drop the reporting element altogether and just give the reader her thoughts.

In chapter 1, Clarice Starling has been called into the big boss' office, Jack Crawford head of the FBI's Behavioral Science Unit.

> "Starling, Clarice M., good morning," he said.
> "Hello." Her smile was only polite.
> "Nothing's wrong. I hope the call didn't spook you."
> "No." *Not totally true*, Starling thought.[4]

The last two sentences in this dialogue "No." *Not totally true,* Starling thought. are written with direct ("No.") and indirect (*Not totally true,* Starling thought.) speech. Direct speech (quoted) and indirect speech (reported) abide by the traditional third person omniscient rules. The narrator quotes the action. Starling says "No." Indirect speech is the narrator retelling the character's thoughts. "*Not totally true*, Starling thought." So technically, the first chapter is written in third person omniscient.

What's interesting is that Harris chose to *italicize* "Not totally true," even though he's using the indirect approach and the phrase does not require it. I suspect

4 Harris, Thomas. The Silence of the Lambs (P. 2). Macmillan.

Harris made this choice to signal to the reader, subconsciously, that he was going to eventually use Free Indirect Style and get rid of the necessity of having to write "she thought... she said to herself... she wondered" etc.

In the very next chapter of *The Silence of the Lambs*, when Starling meets with Dr. Frederick Chilton, the head of the Baltimore State Hospital for the Criminally Insane, Harris makes the complete shift into Free Indirect Style. He's already let the reader get a global sense of who Starling is through his quoting and reporting her speech and thoughts. Now he's giving them the intimacy of being able to hear her thoughts without his authorial reporting attached.

After Chilton tells Starling that he suspects Crawford is just using her to "turn-on" the killer Hannibal Lecter, thus her being given the job to interview him, Harris makes the transition to Free Indirect Style.

> *Well fuck off, Chilton.* "I graduated from the University of Virginia with honors, Doctor. It's not a charm school."[5]

This may all be a bit inside baseball for our purposes. The bottom line, though, is that Free Indirect Style is a wonderful tool for the novelist. It gives you the best of first person and third person narration. Going inside a character's head and giving the reader her thoughts without third person reportage emotionally bonds the reader to a character. Jane Austen was one of its masters. She was so skilled that a novel without some free indirect speech in it today feels sterile, devoid of heart.

Remember, though, that you must limit the number of brains that you open up to the reader in a novel. The use of Free Indirect Style signals to the reader that this character is our protagonist...this is the main person we will view this fictional world through. Especially at the beginning. If you use the technique with more than one character, you better have a very good reason. And you better think hard about where in the novel to insert these kinds of shifts.

Thriller writers often use Free Indirect Style with their protagonists and with their antagonists. Thomas Harris uses the Free Indirect Style for nine different characters in *The Silence of the Lambs*. Every single time he did so was a critical and productive choice. Make sure your choices are too.

---

5 Harris, Thomas. The Silence of the Lambs (P. 11). Macmillan.

34

CONTROLLING IDEA/THEME

The most challenging line to fill in on our *Foolscap Global Story Grid* is Controlling Idea/Theme.

The controlling idea is the takeaway message the writer wants the reader/viewer to discover from reading or watching his Story. It's the whole reason many of us want to be writers in the first place. We have something to say about the way the world is and we want others to come to see it in the same way we do.

Wanting to say something and understanding exactly what it is that you are trying to say is the most difficult thing to crack. The truth of the matter is that there is a wide chasm between our rational and deliberately reasoned and specific inner philosophies and our creative energies. Oftentimes, our subconscious creative comes up with a strikingly good idea for a scene or description and we have no real understanding of where it came from. The more you write, the more you discover that those inspirations are clues to figuring out the controlling idea/theme of your global Story.

Many writers don't have a clue of what their theme is until far into the writing process. Some even refuse to acknowledge that they have any particular agenda or message to impart beyond keeping the reader guessing what's going to happen next... One of my clients is David Mamet and he'll pledge on a stack of bibles that he does not have any agenda in his work beyond keeping the audience transfixed. I absolutely believe him, but to think that there are no controlling ideas in Oleanna or Glengarry Glen Ross or Sexual Perversity in Chicago is to ignore the very truths that emerge when a writer is busting his hump to keep us guessing. I could devote entire books to these three plays and pull out very clear controlling ideas concerning tyranny, self-deception, humiliation, and the nature of intimacy, which all three of these plays explore. Mamet would deny that he had any intention of loading these works with any of my takeaways.

He would not be lying either. But his work is so damn specific and biting that to deny the truths that lie within the drama (put there intentionally or not) is ludicrous.

So it's fine if you don't want to overly concern yourself with the controlling idea/theme. If you can write scenes and structure progressive complications, crises, climaxes and resolutions like David Mamet, you certainly don't need me to tell you that your work isn't vital because you won't spell it out for me. But if you haven't been sitting at a desk for forty years like he has with a clear intention to keep people guessing no matter what, then you may find that codifying your controlling idea/theme can help direct your work.

This is the beauty of writing, the big payoff that keeps people staring at blank screens for hours on end banging out scenes and chapters that they believe are accomplishing one thing, while underneath the onstage action they are doing something completely different. The creative energy and hard work necessary to bring these bits to life truthfully will eventually coalesce and an "aha, that's what this is about!" moment will come. Perhaps not even to the writer, but to the reader.

One of the most difficult skills to develop as a writer is patience. And figuring out the controlling idea/theme requires it in abundance.

But once the controlling idea of the Story becomes concrete for the writer, and this may take far longer than you can possibly imagine, the Story will come to life. Problems will resolve themselves. Decisions will become much easier to make and the work becomes far more pleasurable.

What exactly is a controlling idea?

I like the approach that Robert McKee takes because it is extremely clear and specific.

1. A controlling idea must be boiled down to the fewest possible words and cannot be longer than a one-sentence statement.
2. It must describe the climactic value charge of the entire Story, either positively or negatively.
3. And it must be as specific as possible about the cause of the change in value charge.

For example, the controlling idea of the popular crime novel and film adaptation, *The Firm,* would be **justice prevails when an everyman victim is more clever than the criminals.**

That's a solid controlling idea. Is it incredibly innovative or deep? No. But it is perfect in keeping with the core value at stake in a crime Story—justice.

John Grisham told a wildly compelling Story using his deep understanding of the life of a young lawyer. While the controlling idea of his book isn't internally driven or existentially spectacular, the execution of the important cultural value that "Justice prevails" is very important. Justice is a value that we all want to deeply believe in.

Reading a Story like *The Firm*, gives us an initial anxiety about how justice can prevail if the stewards of the law are corrupt. But at climax when it does prevail surprisingly but inevitably, we find relief. The fact that a single individual can outsmart and defend an important societal value is a message we all need to hear. That's what the controlling idea/theme is all about. Taking a value that we all rely on to live peacefully day to day, challenging its stolidity and then paying it off with its confirmation or its vulnerability. So even though you may think the crime, horror, action stories that have no underlying internal messages within are purely entertainments...they serve society as certifiers of our values. When the bad guy is caught, we're relieved. Justice prevails, life is precious, love is sublime...we need to get these messages from our stories or we despair.

Did John Grisham sit down and write out his controlling idea before he wrote *The Firm*?

My guess is no. Instead, Grisham's life experience and grasp of compelling characters and scenes all flowed from an internal value that he perhaps never consciously spelled out for himself. When a writer chooses to have his Story driven by a broad External Genre, the controlling idea is often inherent in the choice. This is perfectly acceptable and even laudable when well executed. There is no requirement to pound your head on a table to come up with a brand new controlling idea for your particular Story. Knowing what the controlling idea is concretely, though, will help you stay on course.

Especially if you get stuck in the weeds on a particular draft.

But isn't there a way to have a deep controlling idea within a broad External Content Genre?

The answer of course is yes. The way to pull this off is to drive the Internal Content Genre as hard as you do your External. An example of a very deep controlling idea that is also a straightforward horror Story is *The Shining* by Stephen King.

I took away the following controlling idea from his book: **Narcissistic self-abuse annihilates all forms of human love.** The novel is one of King's masterpieces, written in the midst of his coming to terms with his own alcoholism and cocaine addiction. This Story fired on all cylinders because it was deeply horrifying while also being so intensely personal. It didn't just nail the ambiguous horror Story. It was a deeply moving punitive/cautionary tale for the overly ambitious/self-loathing striver in all of us...the one who insists that if he were just given the right circumstances to paint his masterpiece, he'd deliver...

Both Grisham and King wrote extraordinarily successful novels. And both men had something very important to say. While Grisham's was more of a deep dive into the dangers of powerful legal partnerships in the United States and its dominant global Genre was the crime thriller, King's novel was ultimately driven by its Internal Genre, the Punitive Plot. But he brilliantly wrapped it in the candy of an external ambiguous horror Story.

King somehow wrote a literary Mini-plot novel masquerading as a horror Story. That's extraordinary.

You may have imagined the most charismatic protagonist, the most detailed and inviting setting and the perfect foil, but without a clear understanding of what it is you are trying to get across to the reader, you'll never hear the magic words... "your book changed my life." And trust me. Every writer I've ever worked with would die happy to hear someone tell him that. Even just once.

There is a reason why writing a novel, a screenplay, a play, a television pilot or even launching a company is difficult. Practically impossible. You have to make a lot of choices. You have to make value judgments. You have to ask yourself: If I had to boil down all of the events in my Story to one sentence what would that sentence be? That sentence is the controlling idea. Once you figure it out, and again it will not come easily to you, you will gain immeasurable confidence.

35

BEGINNING HOOK, MIDDLE BUILD AND ENDING PAYOFF

After we've laid out the global elements of our Story at the top of our *Foolscap Global Story Grid,* we need to nail down the actual major movements. So you'll see that the final three quarters of our *Foolscap* is dedicated to mapping out the Beginning, Middle and End of our Story.

Boiling your pile of four hundred pages down to BEGINNING, MIDDLE and END and setting aside all of the other pieces in your Story is the single best advice I could give anyone. Remember, Stories are conceptually simple things...

A Storyteller hooks us: ***Once upon a time, there were three bad children...on their morning walk one day a wolf captures them and takes them to his lair...***

And then we get a Middle Build that raises the stakes: ***the three children are tasked to help the wolf slaughter their kingdom's only source of food**...**while they "help" the wolf, they make a dastardly plan that only wicked children could devise.***

Lastly, we get an Ending Payoff that is both surprising and inevitable: ***after the children trick the wolf and lead him to his death, his fur fades away, his snout shortens and he is revealed as their long lost father the King. The King awakens and tells them of the spell he'd been put under by an evil housemaid and of how that spell could only be broken by his children. With the return of their father, the children are no longer bad and the family is restored.***

It's very useful to remember that the BEGINNING is all about HOOKING your reader...getting them so deeply curious and involved in the Story that there is no way they'll abandon it until they know how it turns out. The MIDDLE is about BUILDING progressive complications that bring the stress and pressure down so hard on your lead character(s) that they are forced to take huge risks so that they can return to "normal." The ENDING is the big PAYOFF, when the promises you've made from your HOOK get satisfied in completely unique and unexpected ways.

STORY distilled is...HOOK, BUILD, PAYOFF. That's it.

The Beginning Hook of our little Story above would be the introduction of three bad children (why are they bad?) who get approached by a wolf on their morning walk. The appearance of the wolf is the Inciting Incident that leads to a crisis... to refuse the wolf could end in death for the three children, to abide the wolf's request could result in worse for the whole community.

The Middle Build would be the wolf and children's preparations for the slaughter of the kingdom's animals all the while having the children set up the betrayal of the wolf.

The ending paying is the revelation that the wolf was their father under a terrible spell. Once his evil persona has been destroyed through the efforts of his "bad/disobedient" children, he is restored to his normal self. He's now capable of providing for his brood, knowing that his children are resourceful. The Ending provides the answer to the Beginning Hook, *Why are the children bad?* They've lost their father and without one, they do not fit in with polite society, which is a very good thing when they meet up with a wolf. And it resolves their true selves. They are not "bad" or they would have abided the wolf's request, slaughtered the kingdom's food sources and then lived with the evil wolf. Once their father has returned to his normal self at the end of the Story, the world is restored to order.

The more time you invest in your global hook, build and payoff, the better your Story will be. You'll see that I've listed five scenes in each section of our *Foolscap Global Story Grid.* Now let's take a look at those crucial constituent parts of the Beginning Hook, Middle Build and Ending Payoff.

36

THE MATH

Creating a *Foolscap Global Story Grid* for a complete work is all well and good, but then what?

How do you begin to actually map out the rest? How long will it take you to write the first draft? Is there a way to take the "Beginning Hook, Middle Build, and Ending Payoff" concepts even further to break down the work into more "doable" parts?

This is where a little rudimentary math will help.

But before we dive into it, remember that you are not the problem. The problem is the problem. And the problem we're facing now is figuring out how to map out a course to get from idea to first draft or how to evaluate the first draft we have in hand. At the beginning of the long form Story process, the problems we face are innumerable. To demystify exactly how a lump sum of words can be broken down into component parts is extraordinarily helpful. If we can cut our problems into bite size pieces that we can contend with one by one, one day, one session at a time, then we can beat Resistance into submission and finish our first draft or edit our first draft.

I know. You hate math. That is why you became a writer/Storyteller. But, math is a Godsend. And a very cursory look at the math of a novel is definitely worth the time.

Why?

Math helps you break problems into little bits. It's much easier to figure out where to cut a piece of lumber than it is framing a house. Your mind can't really wrap itself around framing a house. But if you break the work down into its component parts, you'll reach a very doable level of skill…a skill that is relatively easy to master. Measuring the length of a board, marking where to cut it, and then taking a saw and ripping it at that mark is the primal skill for a carpenter.

If you can do that one skill well (and you can screw it up very easily too) you are well on your way to learning how to frame a house.

Same goes with writing or editing a long form Story.

So let's look a novel in mathematical terms.

Here are some facts.

The average length of a commercial novel today is between eighty thousand and one hundred thousand words. Are there exceptions? Sure, but this ballpark range is where the novel has settled over the last twenty years or so. It's the length the average reader is expecting—not too much and not too little. So, it's a safe assumption to make that if you want to begin a path that will satisfy a particular readership, your goal is to put together eighty thousand to one hundred thousand words in a unique and compelling way.

Let's break it down further using the Foolscap method.

To keep it simple, you'll need a beginning, middle, and an end to your Story. No matter how many acts you have (three to five to seven), you need a beginning to your Story, a middle section to your Story and an ending to your Story. As an editor, I don't worry so much about figuring out exactly how many acts are in a book. For me, the Beginning, Middle and End are all that matter. The beginning may comprise two acts, the middle three acts and the end two acts, but I don't really care. Instead I concentrate on the five building materials for each of the three sections. I think about the Inciting Incident scenes, Progressive Complications scenes, the Crisis scenes, the Climax scenes and the Resolution scenes for the beginning, middle and end of a book. (Don't worry; I'll go over these crucial elements of Story form in much greater detail in part 4.)

As you'll recall, the key building block for a long form narrative is the scene. Beats are the actor's domain. Scenes are the writer's. (I'll review the building blocks of Story in part 5.)

So the first breakdown of the eighty-thousand to one-hundred-thousand-word book are the scenes necessary to create the five building materials for your beginning, middle and end of your Global Story. So there will be at least fifteen scenes in your book:

1. You'll need a scene that is the Inciting Incident of the beginning of your Story.
2. You'll need a scene that is the Inciting Incident of the middle of your Story.

3. You'll need a scene that is the Inciting Incident of the end of your Story.
4. You'll need a scene that progressively complicates the beginning of your Story.
5. You'll need a scene that progressively complicates the middle of your Story.
6. You'll need a scene that progressively complicates the end of your Story.
7. You'll need a scene that creates a crisis question at the beginning of your Story.
8. You'll need a scene that creates a crisis question in the middle of your Story.
9. You'll need a scene that creates a crisis question at the end of your Story.
10. You'll need a scene that climaxes the beginning of your Story.
11. You'll need a scene that climaxes the middle of your Story.
12. You'll need a scene that climaxes the end of your Story.
13 You'll need a scene that resolves the beginning of your Story.
14. You'll need a scene that resolves the middle of your Story.
15. You'll need a scene that resolves the end of your Story.

But how long should they be? How many words should each scene be? And then how many words should be in the beginning? How many words should be in the middle? How many words should be in the end?

Here is a piece of information that professional writers spend ten thousand hours of their lives figuring out. After thousands of years of Storytelling, the beginning, the middle and the end for a long form Arch-plot or Mini-plot Story breaks down as follows:

> The Beginning is about one quarter of the Story.
>
> The Middle is about one half of the Story.
>
> The End is the last quarter of the Story.

Are there stories that do not break down 25/50/25? Absolutely. But if you were to average every Story ever told, 25/50/25 would be the result. I have a theory about why Stories break down like this. That's up next.

So, if you are writing a one-hundred-thousand-word novel, the beginning will generally be twenty-five thousand words, the middle will generally be fifty thousand words and the end will be the last twenty-five thousand words. We've already determined that we need at least fifteen scenes in the book, five in the beginning, five in the middle, and five in the end.

What about the rest?

Nerds like me have noticed that typically, in contemporary commercial fiction, scenes run between one thousand and five thousand words. Remember that a scene creates a clear value change in the life of a character through conflict. When I break down ***The Story Grid for The Silence of the Lambs***, you'll see where Thomas Harris fell on the scene word count spectrum. My personal recommendation is to take a page from the master and keep your scenes, like Harris', around two thousand words. I also recommend that you treat your scenes like chapters. That is, each scene should be a chapter in your novel.

Why?

Two-thousand-word scenes/chapters are potato chip length.

That is, if you are about to go to bed and you're reading a terrific novel and the scenes/chapters come in around two-thousand-word bites, you'll tell yourself that you'll read just one more chapter. But if the narrative is really moving after you finish one of these bites, you won't be able to help yourself reading another. If the Story is extremely well told, you'll just keep eating the potato chip scenes all through the night.

Whereas, if you cram five scenes into a chapter that ends up being forty pages, the bedside reader will have a much easier time just setting the book down before beginning the long slog through seventy-five hundred words.

People like to stop reading when they've finished a chapter, not in the middle of a chapter. This is probably the last thing they'll tell you at the Iowa Writer's Workshop, but it's a reality worth considering.

You can accomplish quite a bit in two thousand words, and if you successfully leave out the stuff that the reader does not need explained to them, two thousand words can often be way too much.

Anyway, let's assume that all of the scenes/chapters in our novel are two thousand words long. So if we're writing a one-hundred-thousand-word novel, we'll have about fifty scenes/chapters in our novel. From our earlier beginning, middle and end discussion, we know that fifteen of those fifty scenes are already spoken for. So we'll need to write thirty-five more.

I know. You are an artist and this mathematical manipulation is probably rubbing you the wrong way. I get it. But remember, the math is just a way to break down an extremely intimidating task into doable units.

So we have thirty-five scenes left. Let's set aside 25% of these for the BEGINNING, 50% of them for the MIDDLE and the other 25% for the END.

So we'll need seven to eight scenes in addition to our five obligatory scenes for our beginning (twelve to thirteen total).

We'll have twenty additional scenes to play with in addition to our five obligatory scenes in the middle (twenty-five total).

And we'll have seven to eight scenes in addition to our five obligatory scenes for our end (twelve to thirteen total).

Take a look at *The Story Grid* now based on this information. You can now see the entire form of your novel without having written a single word. You've got doable pieces of work that can be attacked one day, one session at a time.

But let me emphasize again that you may end up with six scenes for the beginning, thirty for the middle and fourteen for the end or the other way around. There is no "rule" about 12/25/13. We are merely trying to map out a course of work for us to bang out a first draft. After we have a first draft, we can go back and analyze exactly which scenes work and which scenes don't work. But if we never write a first draft because we get stuck after writing three scenes, we're never going to finish the novel. Better to have a map of the targets we need to hit in order to make it to the end. Once we get there, then we can fix our blunders.

37

THE KUBLER-ROSS CHANGE CURVE FOR STORY AND THE MATH

Elizabeth Kubler-Ross wrote the seminal book *On Death and Dying* (1969) in which she laid out a psychological model for the stages of extreme change...coping with the death of a loved one. In the years after publication, psychologists, sociologists and economists have applied Kubler-Ross' work to the process of dealing with many varieties of life change. Most notably, her stages of grief were applied to organizational change in an article entitled "Applying Grief Stages to Organizational Change" by P. Scire in Mark R. Brent's book *An Attributional Analysis of Kubler-Ross' Model of Dying*[6], an article that inspired me to think of Story as "coping with change" narrative.

The bottom line with change (and change is the substance of Story) is that it requires loss. Even when change is positive, we lose something of ourselves coping with its effects. Lottery winners are a great example of the monumental effect of positive change.

I promised to explain why I think Stories break down to 25% Beginning Hook, 50% Middle Build, and 25% Ending Payoff. So for our purposes, I've created a change curve that best aligns with the Storyteller process.

---

6 Harvard University, 1981

Here it is:

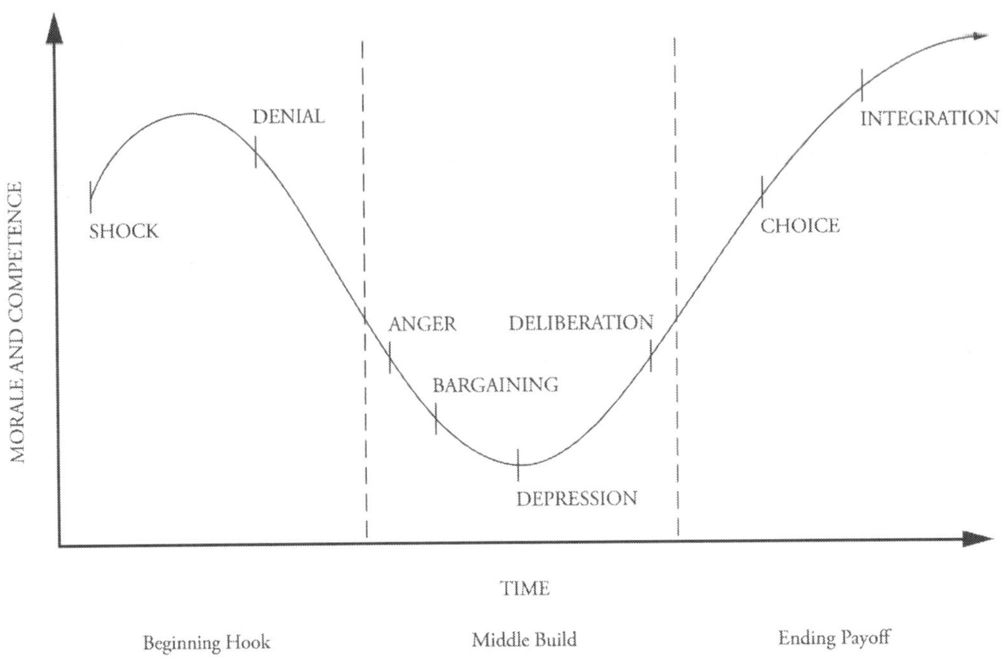

You'll see that the vertical axis reflects the effects of change on the protagonist(s) of your Story. The higher the position on the y-axis, the more comfortable and competent the character is. The lower the position, the less comfortable and competent. The horizontal axis represents Time. I've broken the Time into our three parts—Beginning Hook, Middle Build and Ending Payoff.

Let's begin at the beginning SHOCK.

Remember that when life throws us out of kilter, it takes us a certain amount of time to even realize that we're out of kilter. There is an initial shock about an event in our life and then shortly thereafter, a denial that the event even occurred. We just pretend that everything is as it ever was until we're forced to face the facts.

I think these two stages, SHOCK and DENIAL, comprise the BEGINNING HOOK of a Story.

The Beginning Hook of a Story ends when the protagonist or multiple cast of the Story can no longer deny the truth. The climax and resolution of the BEGINNING HOOK pushes us into the MIDDLE BUILD of our Story and also the middle of the change curve.

The middle forces us to react to the truth of the life event.

Once we can no longer bullshit ourselves about our circumstances, we get ANGRY. We blame others or the gods for what has stricken us, lash out, usually making our circumstances even worse. After we burn off our anger, we search for the easiest way out of our situation. We work to BARGAIN our way out of the problem. Perhaps we push the problem to someone else, who is sure to fail solving it.

Or we decide that if we change our environment, we will be able to slough off the problem. We move to another city. We change jobs. We find a new spouse. We buy a better lifestyle. Of course, the bargaining proves fruitless. The monkey on our back (coping with the shock necessitating a change in ourselves) gets even heavier.

When we discover that there is no easy solution to our predicament and all of our bargaining has left us broken and battered in worse circumstances than if we had faced the problem head on at the beginning, we finally come to the understanding that there is no way we can turn back.

Our lives will never be the same. We've lost. We bottom out in DEPRESSION.

This depression is dramatized in what screenwriters call the ALL IS LOST MOMENT scene. We despair. There is no way in hell that we're going to come out of this event anywhere near how we were before it happened. It's finally clear to us that life will never be the same.

Once we can no longer live with our sad sack, life-is-no-fair selves, we take a deep breath and get to work. We dig deep and confront our demon(s), stare down our problems and resolve to beat them into submission. We come to THE DELIBERATION stage. This is the moment we weigh the pros and cons about what we can do to cope with the big change in our lives.

We finally see the crisis for what it really is—a single question that has no easy answer. Whatever we do will require loss.

We must choose the best bad choice or an irreconcilable good, knowing that we have to lose something in order to gain forward progress and reach a new level of stability. We understand that we'll never get back to "normal," so we stop trying.

I think these four stages, ANGER, BARGAINING, DEPRESSION and DELIBERATION, thematically comprise the MIDDLE BUILD of a Story.

Now the beginning of the ENDING PAYOFF of a Story is how we choose to answer our crisis dilemma. CHOICE is the climactic moment when we actively do something that will finally metabolize the Inciting Incident event and change our lives forever.

Once we choose, we barrel forward, damn the torpedoes and act.

Lastly, there is INTEGRATION, which I would call the very end of a Story. INTEGRATION dramatizes resolution. We've found a new stability, one that is vastly different than where we began. We've got a whole new outlook on life and we're not the same person we once were. At INTEGRATION, we have come full circle and have recovered from the SHOCK of a big Inciting Incident in our life. No matter what, by the end of the Story we will never go back to where or who we were before.

This entire change process is eight stages.

In terms of telling a Story (a change process) the BEGINNING HOOK is two parts, the MIDDLE BUILD is four parts and the ENDING PAYOFF is two parts.

What do you know?

In terms of percentage of the change cycle, 25% of the cycle comprises the beginning, 50% for the middle, and 25% for the end. So the 25/50/25 rule mirrors the process that psychologists have hypothesized is required for a global personal point of view change. I don't think this is a coincidence.

Elisabeth Kubler-Ross' theories can be helpful in other ways too. Especially if you get stuck trying to understand how your protagonist will psychologically proceed through your Story. Here's how the building materials of Story break down psychologically.

The Inciting Incident SHOCKS our protagonist...throws them off balance to the point of DENIAL...hooking the reader's curiosity about how the denial will come back to haunt the protagonist.

This beginning to the Story transitions into the progressive complications in the middle, when the protagonist can no longer deny his predicament. He rages about his plight, bargains ineffectively to make it go away, realizes his life will never be the same and despairs during his ALL IS LOST MOMENT, until he regroups and deliberates about his crisis.

He makes a choice, often called THE POINT OF NO RETURN, and the Story moves toward the Ending Payoff. He makes that CHOICE active during the climax, which results in the INTEGRATION of a new point of view, which is the Story's Resolution.

So, if you get stuck and you're not sure where to take your character in any one place during your Story, think about these eight stages. Are you dramatizing the psychological turmoil of your lead character(s)?

38

FLASH FORWARD: *THE FOOLSCAP GLOBAL STORY GRID* IN ACTION

Later on, I'll go through it line by line, but it's worth looking at a complete page right now. Here's *The Foolscap Global Story Grid* for *The Silence of the Lambs*...The entire outline of the novel on one page.

		FOOLSCAP GLOBAL STORY GRID		
		FOR *THE SILENCE OF THE LAMBS*		
		External Genre: **Serial Killer Thriller**		
G	S	External Value at Stake: **Life to Unconsciousness to Death to Damnation**		
L	T	Internal Genre: **Worldview Disillusionment**		
O	O	Internal Value at Stake: **Blind Belief to Justified Belief to Doubt to Disillusionment**		
B	R	Obligatory Scenes and Conventions: **1. Crime/MacGuffin 2. Villain makes it personal 3. Red Herrings**		
A	Y	**4. Clock 5. Speech in praise of villain 6. Hero at mercy of villain scene 7. False Ending**		
L		Point of View: **Protagonist (FIS)+ Eight Others**		
		Objects of Desire: **Wants to rise in the FBI, Needs to "silence" the torment of abandonment**		
		Controlling Idea/Theme: **Justice prevails when the hero identifies with the vulnerability of the**		
		victims as deeply as she deduces the core pathology of the villain.		
B			External	Internal
E		**Move from Life to Unconsciousness**	Charge	Charge
G	H	1. Inciting Incident: **Starling accepts "errand" to interview Lecter**	+	-
I	O	2. Complication: **Lecter's valentine lead turns into a dead end**	-	+
N	O	3. Crisis: **Does Starling re-engage Lecter after discovering head?**	?	?
N	K	4. Climax: **Starling re-engages**	+	-
I		5. Resolution: **Lecter gives up Buffalo Bill clue.**	+	-
N		**Move from Blind Belief to Justified Belief**		
G				
			External	Internal
M	B	**Move from Unconsciousness to Death**	Charge	Charge
I	U	1. Inciting Incident: **Dead body found in West Virginia**	-	-
D	I	2. Complication: **Starling taken off of the case**	-	-
D	L	3. Crisis: **Should Starling rebel and investigate by herself?**	?	?
L	D	4. Climax: **Starling goes alone to Ohio**	+	+
E		5. Resolution: **Has Crawford's blessing but not the FBI's**	+/-	+
		Move from Justified Belief to Doubt		
			External	Internal
E	P	**Move from Death to Damnation**	Charge	Charge
N	A	1. Inciting Incident: **Clues found in Bimmel's House**	+	+
D	Y	2. Complication: **FBI says it has found Buffalo Bill in Illinois/False Ending**	+	-
I	O	3. Crisis: **Does Starling quit her investigation?**	?	?
N	F	4. Climax: **Starling stays the course**	+	+
G	F	5. Resolution: **Starling slays Buffalo Bill**	+	+
		Move from Doubt to Disillusion		

PART FOUR

STORY FORM

39

THE FIVE COMMANDMENTS OF STORYTELLING

It's now time to review the timeless principles that we rely upon to create and evaluate the building blocks of a long form Story—scenes. Scenes build into sequences, which build into acts, which create our Beginning Hooks, Middle Builds and Ending Payoffs.

The five elements that build Story are the Inciting Incident (either causal or coincidental), progressive complications expressed through active or revelatory turning points, a crisis question that requires a choice between at least two negative alternatives or at least two irreconcilable goods, the climax choice and the resolution.

Here they are in outline form:

1. Inciting Incident
   a. Causal
   b. Coincidence
2. Progressive Complication
   a. Active Turning Point
   b. Revelatory Turning Point
3. Crisis
   a. The Best Bad choice
   b. Irreconcilable goods
4. Climax
5. Resolution

These five elements must be clearly defined and executed for each unit of Story. I'll go into further detail about all of the units of Story later on, but for now it's important to note:

1. Every **beat** has an Inciting Incident, progressive complication(s), a crisis, a climax and a resolution.
2. A well-designed series of beats builds to the next unit of Story, the **scene**, which also has an Inciting Incident, progressive complications, a crisis, a climax and a resolution.
3. Scenes build into **sequences**, which also have Inciting Incidents, progressive complications, crises, climaxes and resolutions.
4. In turn sequences build into **acts**, which have their own Inciting Incidents, progressive complications, crises, climaxes and resolutions.
5. **Subplots** also have Inciting Incidents, progressive complications, crises, climaxes and resolutions, and can be tracked in exactly the same way as the global Story. They act more like add-on extensions or outbuildings to the property that make the global Story a deeper and more satisfying experience.
6. And lastly, **the global Story** itself has its own Inciting Incident, progressive complications, crisis, climax and resolution.

Like an organic structure, a Story has a base set of internal materials that integrally combine to form self-contained units of mini-Story, which in turn combine to form even more complex systems. Ultimately, all of the systems combine to create a work of intellectual property.

Just as cells form tissues, which interact to form organs that work with other organs to form systems (skeletal, nervous, circulatory etc.) with ultimately fourteen systems making up the anatomy of a human being, so do beats combine to form scenes which combine to form sequences which combine to form acts and subplots and ultimately the Beginning Hook, Middle Build and Ending Payoff of a global Story.

But without the engines of creation (the Inciting Incident, progressive complications, crisis, climax and resolution) beats, scenes, sequences, acts, subplots and the global Story will have no life. It is never a bad idea to revisit these crucial Story elements before we begin a new project or just after we've banged out our first draft of a project...just before we put on the editor's hat.

Knowing them and trusting their efficacy are mandatory. A writer who does not pound these concepts into her head will never come close to reaching her artistic potential. There is no escaping them. And anyone who tells you differently is either ignorant or a charlatan. Seriously.

So my advice is to surrender to them. Bow down to them. Hold them closely to your heart. They will save you from yourself. They will outwit and out duel any bullshit you or anyone else will come up with to get you to ignore them so that you can write "freely." Sure go nuts on your first draft and riff all you want. But when you dive into your edit, you've got to make sure that these five elements are present in every beat, scene, sequence, act, subplot and global Story.

When Moses' cousin, Morrie the writer, went up the mountain seeking a cure for his writer's block, God didn't have time to give him all of the answers. And wouldn't you know it, Morrie climbed up unprepared. He only had a crumpled coffee shop napkin and a leaky pen in his shirt pocket. So God did Morrie a solid and boiled Story down to just five commandments.

40

COMMANDMENT NUMBER ONE

Thou must have an Inciting Incident.

The Inciting Incident is the big event scene that kicks off your Story.

It is also an equal or somewhat lesser event scene that opens your Middle Build or Ending Payoff.

It is an even smaller event scene that kicks off a sequence.

It is also a minor event that destabilizes a supporting scene within a sequence.

And lastly, the smallest Inciting Incident is an action in a beat that unsettles the relationship between two characters.

No matter the unit of Story (beat, scene, sequence, act, or global Story) what the Inciting Incident must do is upset the life balance of your lead protagonist(s). It must make them uncomfortably out of sync…for good or for ill.

An Inciting Incident can occur in one of two ways:

1. **Cause**
2. **Coincidence**

A causal Inciting Incident is the result of an active choice—a wife leaves her husband, a man enlists in the Marines, a dentist molests a patient he's put under anesthesia.

A coincidental Inciting Incident is when something unexpected or random or accidental happens—a simple man wins the lottery, a woman takes the wrong suitcase at an airport, a piano falls out of a window and kills a man's dog.

What your choice of Inciting Incidents in every unit of Story (beat, scene, sequence, act, and global Story) must do is arouse a reaction by your protagonist. For the examples above: perhaps, the man resolves to get his wife back, the recruit decides to fight against his Parris Island instructor, the patient hires a detective to investigate the dentist, the lottery winner decides to give away all the money, the woman with the wrong suitcase decides to keep it, the man who barely escapes the piano quits his job.

Obviously, the most crucial Inciting Incident you must choose is the event for the Beginning Hook. If you have a weak hook, no matter the Genre (even the most mini of mini-plots requires a compelling hook), there is little that can be done editorially to make your Story work. Unless you start over.

Remember also that how your character acts—and refusing to do anything is an action too, especially in mini-plot stories…it's actively hiding—must be in tune with your choice of External and Internal Genres.

That is, the Inciting Incident of a global Story must make a promise to the reader… the ending. The ending must be a perfectly reasonable and inevitable result of the Inciting Incident. But it must also be surprising. If it is not surprising, it will not drive anyone to recommend it to his friend to read. Don't promise something and then not deliver it. That is the telltale mark of a writer writing a book that will not work, no matter how great bits and pieces are within.

Many Genres have conventional Inciting Incidents that set up obligatory climaxes. If you're writing a murder mystery, the Inciting Incident must be the discovery of a dead body. The climax of the mystery will be the solving of the crime. If you're writing a love Story, the Inciting Incident will be when the lovers meet. The climax of the love Story will be the answer to whether the couple stays together. If you're writing a horror novel, the Inciting Incident will be an attack by the monster, which sets up the obligatory climax, which is the ultimate confrontation between your lead character victim and the seemingly indestructible monster from your Inciting Incident.

Without Inciting Incidents, a writer has nothing…just a collection of riffs that don't add up in any coherent way…character sketches or meticulous Proustian descriptions of inanimate objects that have zero emotional payoff. That kind of writing is what most people think of when they think of what a writer with a capital "W" is and does. But being able to put words together in unique and poetic ways without anything happening that requires an action or reaction on the part of your cast of characters is not Storytelling. It is showing off your way with words, gold plating inertia. As Truman Capote said so well, "That's not writing, that's typing."

Without an Inciting Incident, nothing meaningful can happen. And when nothing meaningful happens, it's not a Story.

To put it in Hollywood terms, the Inciting Incident is the High Concept for every unit of your Story, the golden "What if?" It's the intriguing lure to get people to care not only about what you are going to tell them right now, but also what you are going to tell them later. If you are writing a novel and your Inciting Incidents are ho-hum, you're setting yourself up for a lot of pain. You'll twist and turn inside trying to use language as a crutch to inflate the importance of trivial events.

Instead why not take the time before you write anything—be it a beat, a scene, a sequence, an act, a subplot or the global Story—and make sure your Inciting Incident is compelling and appropriate for the unit of Story you are about to tell. Remember that every unit of Story has an Inciting Incident. So every scene you put in your Story has to have one, no matter its position on the work's progressively complicated hierarchy.

Years ago I had the surreal experience of working with Bill Murray on a book project. One day we were having a cup of coffee. I'd just returned from doing a lot of talking at a sales conference and my voice was shot. Bill laughed and told me I sounded like Mike Ovitz back when he worked with him.

"He spoke very softly so you'd really have to concentrate to make out what he was saying."

I asked what happened to that relationship. Bill no longer works with an agent, he just sort of lets people find him and offer him stuff to work on. If he likes the idea of it, the "What if?" he'll do it. If he doesn't, he won't.

Bill explained to me that Ovitz called him one day and told him that he'd met with a studio and pitched an idea to them that they loved. They were willing to write Bill a big check if he signed on to the project. Bill asked Ovitz what the idea was and he simply said, "Bill Murray and an elephant."

While not even close to half-baked, that five-word phrase inspired an Inciting Incident that Bill found attractive. All they needed now was for someone to bang on a word processor for a few months and they'd be ready to go. Roy Blount Jr., a wonderful writer and author of my favorite sports nonfiction *About Three Bricks Shy of a Load* was given that impossible task.

Blount took that single phrase and spun it into the far more fleshed out conceit "a down-on-his-luck motivational speaker finds out that his father has left him a huge inheritance...the twist is that his father was a circus promoter and the son's inheritance is an elephant..."

They did make that movie. It was called *Larger than Life* and unfortunately, it bombed.

Soon after that experience, Bill decided he could make those kinds of mistakes himself. He didn't need an agent to do it for him. From that point forward, Bill decided to only talk to the creators of material directly. If he gets a good feeling about the writer/director and their commitment to the Story (and of course what they've put down on actual paper), not just the Inciting Incident but the whole Story, he'll do it. If he doesn't, he won't.

But getting Bill to talk to you is a whole other Story. I left a message for him about five years ago and I'm still waiting for him to return the call. So Bill, if you're reading this, could you mail me back that laptop I lent you before you left for Tokyo?

Again, global Inciting Incidents are most often determined by the Genre the writer chooses. But what about the great American novels? What were their Inciting Incidents?

The Great Gatsby—the cousin of a man's long lost love moves next door to him.

Moby Dick—a young man gets a job on a monomaniac's whale ship.

Catch-22—fighter pilot can't get grounded for being crazy because he says he's crazy and crazy people don't know they're crazy.

These are examples of global Inciting Incidents. Like the peanut butter that lures a mouse into a mousetrap, the global Inciting Incident must be irresistible to the writer's intended audience. And yes, even the big literary writers have an intended audience.

But alas, a fantastic global Inciting Incident does not make for a slam-dunk commercial success. You must load every beat, scene, sequence, and act with tantalizing Inciting Incidents to keep the reader turning pages or to keep the viewer in their seat. Creating these kinds of Inciting Incidents is all about zigging when the reader expects a zag. They require singular imagination. Ideally, the writer fulfills the conventions of a particular Genre's obligatory Inciting Incidents in a completely unique way. A way that the reader never sees coming.

Here's some advice…

Mix up your Inciting Incidents. Don't make them all causal or all coincidental. When the reader is expecting a causal event, swap in a coincidence and vice versa.

41

COMMANDMENT NUMBER TWO

How does one know when a Story isn't working?

After more than ten thousand hours of publishing books, reading submissions and being pitched both fiction and nonfiction, here is just one of the criteria I use to separate the wheat from the chaff.

I simply track the Story's progressive complications…the escalating degrees of conflict that face the protagonist.

How do you do that?

Take this pitch as an example:

An ambitious actor/lawyer/chef/programmer graduates from Julliard/Harvard/Culinary Institute of America/MIT and looks for meaningful work. After months of rejections, the actor/lawyer/chef/programmer decides to take a side job while continuing to look for what will ultimately make him happy.

The Inciting Incident of the Story arrives (at long last) when he gets a part time job as assistant to a casting director/judge/Michelin star *restaurateur*/editor in chief of *Wired* magazine. As he works for the casting director/judge/Michelin star *restaurateur*/editor in chief of *Wired* magazine, he is exposed to all of the best new projects in Hollywood/Washington/New York/Silicon Valley and even gets to help out by being a reader during auditions/doing paralegal work/sous cheffing/writing code. The casting director/judge/Michelin star *restaurateur*/editor in chief of *Wired* magazine notices his talent and decides to promote him.

By dint of hard work the actor/lawyer/chef/programmer gets the big job and the rewards that come with it—status and money. But after a while, the actor/lawyer/chef/programmer grows weary of the big Hollywood grind/legal profession/food work/writing code and decides to go back to his first love, the theater/pro bono work/artisanal cheese making/new app innovation. He then auditions/takes up a cause/

makes cheese/devises a new app that no one takes seriously let alone buys into. Until, at last, he gets a small time director/not for profit/cheese monger/software company to take on his life's work. The performance/cause/cheese debut/app launches, but to little acclaim. The actor/lawyer/chef/programmer loses his shirt on the project, but learns a lot about himself. He decides that his happiness is dependent on his relationships and not the fantasies of finding meaning through work. The End.

And yes, the above is indicative of the kind of material that floods literary agencies and publishing houses. A very talented prose stylist could actually make the above rather entertaining too. And he'd also be able to hide behind a pseudo-Genre like "literary slice of life" to boot. But no matter the writerly artifice, this Story doesn't work. It may prove commercially viable depending upon the tenor of the times, but it will never last as a work of art. Let's assume the writer is not a celebrity or the hottest young thing to come out of the Iowa Writer's Workshop. So extenuating commercial potentialities are not in play here. That is, the literary agent can't sell the Story based on just the identity of the writer. She has to sell it on its Story.

Beyond the fact that there is no clear antagonist in the above, other than some vague hinted sense that the lead character is having "inner turmoil." Not to mention the fact that the execution of the Inciting Incident—getting a job—is a flaccid cliché. [There are a great many novels/screenplays that deal with Mini-plot inner slice of life conflict with soft Inciting Incidents that do work. *Madame Bovary/Lost in Translation* anyone?] The fatal flaw of the above Story is that the difficulties and successes that the protagonist must contend with (the conflicts) do not escalate. They remain boringly similar from derivative scene to derivative scene and from derivative act to derivative act.

If you had to assign a number from 1 to 10 for each complication in this and its anxiety/conflict level, and tracked the numbers from beginning to end, the result would look something like this…and I'm being generous:

(2) Graduation

(3) Quest to find meaningful work

(4) Not finding meaningful work

(3) Finding a part time job instead

(2) Having success at part time job

(3) Getting promoted at part time job

(3) Finding more success at job

(4) Leaving job to get back to quest for meaning

(5) Failing

(6) Getting the big break

(7) Failing

(3) Resigning oneself to meaningless work, for the sake of meaningful relationships

You'll see just by following the numbers (2, 3, 4, 3, 2, 3, 3, 4, 5, 6, 7, 3) that the Story just kind of slogs along. It goes back over the same old complications too. The stakes are boring as hell. The lead character faces rejection when looking for work until he decides to lower his standards and accept a lesser status job. While at the menial job, he gets the break of a lifetime and successfully takes advantage of it. Then he becomes disillusioned by his success and decides to shuck the entire career and start afresh. Then he goes back to trying to get work in his old career and faces yet more rejection. At last he gets a big break that turns out to be disappointing and then goes back to settle for something in between his dream and punching the clock.

It's not surprising that the above "Story" sounds like the banal professional choices we all make at one or more times in our lives. But just regurgitating dull universal experience does not make for cathartic reading or viewing.

And inevitably if an editor were to tactfully point out that the Story seems a bit undercooked and that the writer should think about committing to a Genre or mixing two or more Genres to ground some finer focused idea/theme…well you probably know how that usually ends. The editor would get a terse reply back. *Thanks for reading, but that's not the way I work…I don't believe in formulaic Genre hackwork.*

But every now and then, an editor will find a pro, someone open enough (or desperate enough) to get back to basics. A writer interested in creating an Inciting Incident at level 10 with conflict/complications that progress from 11 to 100 by Story's end.

Progressive complications move stories forward, never backward. They do so by making life more and more difficult (in positive as well as negative ways) for your lead character. In other words, you cannot have your protagonist stare down the same dilemma in act 3 or act 2 that the character already faced in act 1. You must progressively move from one dilemma to a more trying dilemma to a bigger problem to an even bigger problem etc.

The payoff is when the lead character is faced with the limits of human experience—life and death. *Cool Hand Luke, Sophie's Choice, Network, Unforgiven, Gates of Fire*...walk us to the precipice of human experience and allow us to peer into the abyss. And we don't have to leave our comfortable seats to do it, either. That's called art.

So how can you be sure that your Story does the same?

Ask yourself the simple question...how difficult would it be for my character to reverse his decision? Could he go back to his old life without any repercussions? A few repercussions? Or is there no turning back?

You've hit the *Point of No Return* when no matter what decision the character makes, he will be irrevocably changed by the experience. If he does one thing, he'll put himself in great danger (either physically or psychologically) and if he doesn't, he'll be tormented by his inaction, incapable of functioning the way he used to.

The trick to remember when evaluating the reversibility factor is how difficult will it be for the character to go back in time if they make a certain decision. That is, can they make a decision and not have it affect their worldview? Can they go back to the way things used to be and not suffer any discontent or trauma?

If you re-read the example of the generic submission above, you'll see that no decision that the character makes will change them irrevocably. They can head back in time any time they'd like and not have their worldview changed in any way.

How do you know if you are falling into this same trap? That is, how do you know if you are progressively complicating the life of your character?

I suggest going back to the grading concept above and use the power of ten. Evaluate the difficulty for the character to reverse their decision in each and every scene that you write. With 10 being absolutely irreversible to 1 being an easy switch back. By the way, if your character isn't making any decision in a scene, it's not a scene. It's goofing around. Cut it or revise.

42

THE LITTLE BUDDY OF COMMANDMENT NUMBER TWO

The turning point in a beat, scene, sequence, act, subplot or Story is the moment when new information comes to the fore and a character can't help but react. This is where the rubber meets the road in a Story. Without clearly defined and surprising turning points, the reader/audience will lose interest. Quickly.

I'm writing an entire chapter on turning point and putting it just after Progressive Complications for a reason. Turning points are sort of the little buddies of complication. They are the little choices that a writer makes that drive progressive complications, the nails that put the progressively larger complication building blocks in place in a Story.

There are only two ways you can create a turning point in an event.

The event can turn with:

1. **Character Action**
2. **Revelation**

One of the best ways to tell if your scenes are working is to pinpoint the exact place (the exact beat(s) and the precise place in those beats) when the Story turns. It will be the place when something unexpected happens.

To give you a very obvious example, there is a scene in the screenplay *Zero Dark Thirty* where the female protagonist (Jessica Chastain) has a friendly meeting/dinner date with a colleague (Jennifer Ehle). These are the highest-ranking women in the Islamabad CIA station and it's their infrequent chance to blow off some steam. Our hero is a workaholic and through great effort, she finally pulls herself away from her desk and arrives late for the dinner. There is an awkward moment between the two like the one we all feel when we are reintroduced to a person we don't know well. You can't yell at the acquaintance for being late, but you don't want them to think they can treat you as a second-class citizen either. That sub-textual tension is palpable in the scene as it plays out in the film.

At last the two relax and as they drink a glass of wine together the audience settles in for what they expect will be the typical "girl talk" scene. The audience is expecting these two to commiserate about how shitty it is that they are the only women in the station and how the men treat them poorly and they get no support and blah blah blah. We all like this kind of scene when it's done well, especially after the mini-drama of the protagonist even making it to the dinner itself. As they pick up their wine, we, the audience, are looking forward to a relaxation of physical action in the Storyline and the opportunity to eavesdrop on a juicy conversation.

And we get some of that...but just before the scene goes on too long, while the Jennifer Ehle character is tipping back her second glass of wine, there is a massive explosion. The entire room completely disintegrates. The lights go out, fires erupt etc.

Obviously the scene has completely turned from the action of two people getting to know each other over light dinner conversation to the action of urgency for survival. The two agents have to get the hell out of there before another bomb goes off. The audience is grabbed by the throat and surprised by the revolutionary shift in the scene. The turning point shakes the audience up as they breathlessly go on the ride with the two women as they sort themselves out and find a passageway to safety.

This is an example of a Character Action turning point scene. In an act of terrorism, the major antagonists in the Story, Al Qaeda, have bombed a hotel. This is extra-personal conflict antagonism at a very high level. This kind of turn on big action is one often used for an act climax. It's shocking and changes the entire specter of the Story.

What is an example of a smaller turning point that is not a "big moment" Story event but still emblematic of a character action turning point? There is a wonderful moment in the movie *The Way We Were* that turns the scene with a very subtle action.

Again, the setting is a restaurant/bar. Barbra Streisand plays the lead character Katie Morosky. She's a nice, hardworking Jewish girl from Brooklyn who has entered a blue blood university in New England. She works at the local diner to pay her way through school. She is infatuated with an All American blond blue-eyed young man in her class, Robert Redford's Hubble Gardiner.

In the Story, both Streisand and Redford are studying to be writers. She's the grinder type who busts her ass with every word, sentence and paragraph… relentlessly editing her work intellectually. He's a natural. He doesn't sweat. He seemingly sits down, the gods descend, and he bangs out brilliant short stories.

She hates him for it but also can't help but be attracted to him. Why has God given such gifts to someone so privileged by birth?

So one night…it's late…Streisand has just finished her nightly shift and she's walking back to her campus dorm room. Up ahead, she sees Redford, sitting alone outside a restaurant with a pitcher of beer. He's too much of a temptation. She needs to keep focused. And she's embarrassed too for being such a grind and loser poor girl from the neighborhood. So she crosses the street so that she doesn't have to walk by him.

As she clicks her heels on the opposite sidewalk, Redford calls out to her.

> *The problem with some people is they work too hard.*

He gets her to cross the street. You can tell he thinks she's the greatest thing on earth and he's just drunk enough to let her know that. But he's as insecure and pathetic as she is. He sees himself as a huge fraud, someone given so much for doing far too little. His gifts have not been earned like Streisand's. He's just one of the lucky ones and he finds his life and the life of his friends rather absurd. She's the real deal.

To gain her admiration he tells her that he's just sold a short Story. He knows that she's the only one who would be impressed by such a thing and he gets her to share a beer with him in celebration.

After some flirty chitchat, Streisand begs off. She's gotta get back and do her homework. But before she can get away, Redford tells her to stop. The audience thinks maybe he's going to kiss her and declare his love for her. But instead he takes another action that tells the audience everything they need to know about him.

He sticks out his leg and tells her, *Put your foot here*. She does. He ties her shoelace very tightly and says:

> *Go get 'em, Katie.*

This is also a scene that turns on character action. The big action of the scene is Redford's character tying the shoe of Streisand's character instead of telling her how he feels about her. He sends her on her way content that there is someone wonderful in the world to take on the big battles that he is too cowardly to fight himself. He's fine resting on his freely given gifts, getting drunk and feeling superior to everyone else because he "sees through" the bullshit. He will never take up the sword like this woman will and he accepts that about himself.

This scene occurs in the first fifteen minutes of the movie and it pays off in a huge way by the end. It leads to an end that is both surprising and inevitable.

Okay, so if those are two examples of scenes that turn on action, what are examples of scenes that turn on revelation?

There is a wonderful small scene in *Chinatown* that is a perfect example of revelation.

Jack Nicholson plays Jake Gittes. He's caught up in the investigation of the murder of a wealthy man in Los Angeles. He's at the home of the victim, waiting to interview his widow. As he waits in the backyard garden, there is a Chinese gardener tending a lush natural pool of water. He's pulling out sod that surrounds the pool and notices Gittes looking at him perplexed.

Gittes has actually spotted something in the water and is focusing his attention on whatever it is, but the gardener thinks he's questioning him about why he's pulling up the sod.

Bad for the glass. the gardener says in rough English.

Huh? says Gittes.

Salt water, bad for the glass.

Yeah, bad for the glass. Gittes repeats.

Gittes then asks the gardener to fish out what he's sighted in the pool. The gardener does so, handing him a broken set of spectacles.

The beat ends as the widow (Faye Dunaway) enters, greeting Gittes in dressage gear.

This small scene turns on two seemingly irrelevant revelations that will later have a huge impact on the Story. Gittes doesn't know at the time how the victim was killed (he drowned). And again, this scene, like the one in *The Way We Were* comes very early in the movie and seems sort of off-handed. But the revelations in this exchange between two people who work for the powerful (a private investigator and a gardener) are the key to the entire murder mystery.

The turning point revelations are that the pool in the backyard garden is saltwater and that there was a pair of the murdered man's glasses at the bottom of the pool.

Gittes eventually pulls those two pieces of information together and solves the case.

One last example of revelation turning a scene comes from *The Great Gatsby*.

One day, Gatsby invites his neighbor Nick Carraway for lunch in the city. Carraway arrives and finds Gatsby sitting with an elderly gentleman. He joins the two men. Carraway notices that the man has a set of cuff links made of human molar teeth and that there's something quite peculiar about the relationship between the Oxford educated Gatsby and this rather common figure. At last the man rises to take his leave and Caraway asks Gatsby who the man was.

Why, that's the man who fixed the 1908 World Series…

This revelation that Gatsby is closely associated with an organized crime figure turns the scene and the overall Story. We don't need to know anything more about how Gatsby has found his fortune. He openly consorts with gangsters.

Character action and revelation are the only ways to turn scenes.

When you edit your work, put each of your scenes under a microscope and see where you've turned your scenes and by what method you've done so. If they turn on *action, action, action, action* and you infrequently use *revelation*, guess what? The reader/audience will get frustrated. Your book or screenplay will seem "overly plotted, making it hard to suspend disbelief."

Similarly if you turn all of your scenes with *revelation, revelation, revelation,* your Story will seem, and most likely will be, melodramatic. It will feel like a telenovela/soap opera because there is no let up on new information. Either way, if you do not regulate your turning points, your work will lack narrative drive… that magic stuff that keeps people turning pages.

The key is to find a compelling mix between how your beats, scenes, sequences and acts turn. If your act 1 crisis scene turns on revelation, you might want to consider turning your act 1 climax scene on action and vice versa. If you hear comments from others like "something just doesn't feel right" about your Story, it could be a turning point problem.

Taking an analytical approach to your work when you put on your editor hat is very important. It will help you find out what the problems are in your Story so that you can fix them. It's like a weird noise in your car. You need to find out what the problem is before you can fix it. This is what the analytical/editor mind is all about.

43

COMMANDMENT NUMBER THREE

Thou must have a **crisis**.

The crisis in a beat, a scene, a sequence, an act, a subplot and the global Genre boils down to a question.

In all of the units of Story...after the Inciting Incident...the protagonist faces complication(s)...the Story turning points then lead to definable dilemmas. These dilemmas must coalesce into a question that offers a choice between two options.

Confronted with another character's direct action (or extra-personal action like the bomb in *Zero Dark Thirty*) or by the revelation of new information, will the protagonist do this? Or will the protagonist do that?

The crisis is the time when your protagonist must make a decision. And the choice that he makes will determine whether he'll get closer to or further away from his objects of desire (both external and internal). Often a particular choice will move a character closer to one object of desire while moving him further away from the other...

If the writer is choosing an ironic ending to his Story, it stands to reason that if the protagonist gets closer to his external object of desire, the likelihood is that he'll move further away from his internal object of desire. And vice versa.

Crises are questions that arise just after a scene turns.

That is, once the turn occurs in a unit of Story through an action or a revelation, that change in circumstance raises a question. That question is the crisis.

For example:

- A man walking down the street falls into a manhole. (A coincidental Inciting Incident)
- When he regains his senses, he discovers that he's waist deep in water. (A complication)

- The water begins to rush around him and he struggles to hold his ground. (A second complication)
- He loses his footing and he's moved along in the underground current. (A third complication that escalates the reversibility factor...he won't be able to go back through the same manhole that he fell through...he's quickly reached the point of no return.)
- As he funnels through the pipe, gulping as much air as he can, he discovers that the pipe is getting narrower and that it will eventually reach a circumference that he will not be able to pass through. He'll eventually plug the hole (a turning point on revelation) and then the water will overwhelm him and he will drown (escalation of complication to the limits of human experience).
- He feels along the surface of the pipe to try and find a hold of some sort to stop his forward progress. He finds a crossbar and successfully grabs it. This grabbing of the crossbar is an **active** turning point that changes the direction of the value in the scene, in this case moving it from imminent death to life. The character has actively turned his world around.
- But the water keeps rushing over him, pulling him away from his hold. He understands that there is a limited amount of time that he can stay in this position. As he catches his breath his eyes now adjust to the darkness. He sees that there is a beam of light that shines about twenty feet away from him downstream. He suspects this beam of light comes from another manhole, like the one he fell through. This **revelation** is a second turning point in the scene that increases his chance for survival.
- These two beat turning points (grabbing the cross bar and seeing the light) lead to the scene's *crisis*.
- Should he let go of the crossbar and ride the water twenty feet to the next manhole to take the chance that he'll be able to grab hold of its exit ladder to the street? Or should he stay put, wait for the rush of water to slow and then carefully make his way to the next manhole? He remembers that it was a very busy walkway he fell through and undoubtedly someone saw him fall into the hole. Are the chances that someone did see him fall and went to find help to fish him out better than him taking the risk to ride the water to the next manhole exit?

This question is *the crisis* point of the scene.

The way the protagonist answers this question will show the reader/viewer what kind of person he is. The character's actions, not his words, define him. Compelling *crisis* questions and the way they are answered are the way to reveal character.

If you remember the old Batman TV shows or other kids' programs from the 50s 60s and 70s, you'll recognize the *crisis* point rather easily. This was the point in the show just before a commercial or just before the episode ended. Writing those kinds of crises is a technique called the cliffhanger. It leaves the audience with a question that they will desperately want answered. And used with great skill, cliffhangers increase the narrative velocity of your Story. But trundled out too often, cliffhangers become irritating and cliché.

The *crisis* is that point when the protagonist must do something.

And remember choosing to do nothing is doing something too.

If the man in the hole decides to stay put and wait for help ... that choice says a lot about him.

- He believes in the basic goodness of humanity...that anyone who sees a person fall into a hole would immediately drop what they were doing and run for help.
- He's confident in his strength to hold on to the crossbar for as long as it takes for someone to arrive. Every bit of energy he expels to stay on the crossbar will drain him of energy to reach up to the next manhole and pull him up.

If on the other hand he decides to let go and make a grab for the next manhole that says a lot about him too.

- This character is self-reliant to the point that he'll risk his own life depending upon himself instead of believing in other powers coming to his aid.
- He knows that for every second he spends waiting for help, it will drain him of energy to help himself. And he'd rather bet on himself than someone else to save his own life.

As you can see, both of these options are "bad" choices. They could both result in his death. The character acting on the option that is the least bad choice is what will define him to the reader.

So the two turns of the scene, the action to grab the crossbar and the revelation that there is a manhole twenty feel away, lead to the two pronged crisis questions—*Should I stay? Or should I go?*

If there is an easy way out or an obvious path for your lead character at a crisis, you are making a major mistake. You will lose your reader or your viewer right then and there.

Why?

We live day-to-day, month-to-month and year-to-year, making small, medium and large choices in our lives. The simple choices we make automatically. They are not interesting. We do not want to revisit them in our precious downtime in a Story. Unless she's a diabetic who has already lost her left leg to the disease, having your lead character decide whether or not she puts sugar in her coffee is not a choice any of us wants to read about.

We want to see the hard choices and we want to see where they lead for your characters. None of us can go back in time and change difficult decisions we've made in our lives. So we go to Story to evaluate whether or not we made the right choice. We either find comfort from stories that show us that we've done the right thing. Or on the other side, when we make a mistake, in a Story we get to experience the path of a different course. Risk Free! A new map to help us find our courage.

We go to Story to experience life at the edge, where we've been shaken in our boots in our own lives.

This is what stories are for…to reassure us that we've made the right decision in our own lives or to help us recognize our mistakes, learn from them and find the courage to change.

So the crisis choices in your Story cannot be easy, or we'll fall asleep.

What defines humanity is our ability to think and choose. A muskrat doesn't face existential dilemmas. He doesn't worry about whether or not he should kill a rat and eat it. He just does that automatically. But human beings are blessed and cursed with the ability to choose, to discern complex moral issues and to define their place on the earth by the choices they make. Life is an ever-escalating process of making choices.

All crises, of course, are not created equal. You need to build to the end of the line. They all are not life and death, but they all must be the best bad choice variety or of the irreconcilably good variety. It is the escalation of crises in your Story from reversible to irreversible that "raises the stakes" and not only gives your Story narrative momentum, but deep meaning.

So when you are stuck looking at any of your units of the Story form (beat, scene, sequence, act, subplot, global Story) get out your magnifying glass and analyze the effectiveness of your crises. Are they building from meaningful but not irreversible to life changing and irreversible?

Track them.

If your crises are banal and pointless, so will your Story be banal and pointless.

Before I dive into *climax*, which is the moment when a character acts on his crisis choice, it's worth taking a closer look at the two types of Story crises, the best bad choice and the choice between irreconcilable goods.

44

THE BEST BAD CHOICE CRISIS

We face two critical *crisis* kinds of decisions in our lives.

These decisions define who we are as human beings. We do not live in an evil/good, joy/misery, sated/starving kind of world. Never have. Never will. Because we don't—we always fall on a spectrum within the confines of each of these values—we rely on stories to help us figure out how to choose between two bad choices or two irreconcilably good choices.

These two qualities of dilemma that define us flesh and blood human beings also define characters.

When you are considering how best to create the appropriate *crisis* question for your character, think in terms of the best bad choice or a choice between irreconcilable goods.

What do I mean by "The Best Bad Choice?" Here are two examples, one from the made up world and one from real life.

You've seen the movie *Rocky*? If you haven't it's a very simple setup. The lead character of the movie is a Philadelphia mook named Rocky Balboa, a boxer with a lot of heart but a rapidly fading twinkle of talent. At the beginning of Sylvester Stallone's screenplay, Rocky's at that place we can all appreciate. He's accepted his station in life. He makes enough scratch from the local black hand as an enforcer to live the way he sees himself deserving to live... in a flop house with a sweat and bloodstained mattress propped on cinderblocks with two cans left of a six pack of beer and half eaten slab of processed meat in the fridge.

Rocky still gets in the ring and even sometimes wins, but he's really just ... as my father used to say "getting Monday into Tuesday ... Tuesday into Wednesday ... and so on." Stallone lets us soak up this sad life for a good chunk of pages before he gives us all what we know is coming. The Inciting Incident of the performance Genre in every boxing

Golden ticket

novel/movie/short Story is the opportunity for THE BIG FIGHT. Rocky gets picked to fight the heavyweight champion of the world.

Not because he earned it, but because of his silly pugilistic moniker… *The Italian Stallion*. This is an example of a coincidental Inciting Incident, like winning the lottery.

The chance to fight the big fight is what we all say we want, isn't it?

> *If Random House just took my novel on as a lark… they wouldn't even have to give me an advance… I'd bust my butt, promote it like hell and make it a success… I'd show them how wrong they are to dismiss my work…*

We say to ourselves that given a lock, an opportunity, we'd be our best selves and kick some serious ass.

Would we though?

Stallone knew that giving his fictional character the chance that we all want would seriously invest us in Rocky's life. Even a ballet dancer or billionaire would relate to this guy.

So where does the *Best Bad Choice* come in here? Rocky has no bad choice right? The Gods have intervened and given him something he always dreamed of… what could be bad about that?

Stallone has Rocky explain his situation to the arthritic, pockmarked old Irish gym rat played by Burgess Meredith, a man who has come to see Rocky to ask for the shot to train him. By the way, there's nothing wrong with archetypes/stereotypes if you do them well (specificity please)… and who doesn't love the old battle-scarred sensei? Even though Meredith's "Mick" shamed Rocky by taking away his locker at the gym, Rocky knows that he did it because Mick always expected more of him. Mick thought Rocky had "moxie" before he became a bum.

When Mick comes to Rocky's dump to offer his services, Rocky takes a long look at his situation. Rocky's no Einstein (are any of us?), but he's not stupid either. He has two bad choices.

The first choice is to fight the champ and get the crap kicked out of him. The champ is the greatest fighter of all time and could very likely kill him with one precise blow to his head. At the very least Rocky will be humiliated. He'll become a barroom joke… not just in Philadelphia but all over the world. That's his first choice—humiliation.

The second choice is seemingly not so bad. He could beg off, tell the champ he appreciates the shot, but he's just not at his level. There would be no shame in turning down an unwinnable fight would there? Rocky would be able to keep threatening welshers for his mafia boss and he could stay in his flop for the rest of his life. And he'd have a great Story to tell people about how he turned down the greatest fighter of all time… No one would blame him for choosing to run away.

Really, only one person—two actually—would find that choice cowardly.

The first choice, fighting, could lead to literal death. But Rocky also knows that running away, the second bad choice, would be spiritual death. He'd end up hating himself even more than he already does. Shame is at stake versus honor. (Shame/honor is the core global value at stake for the performance Genre.)

What's even better is that Stallone makes Rocky face himself thirty years in the future, in the form of Mick. Rocky knows that Mick knows the balance sheet of both choices here. Because even though Stallone never literally states it in the screenplay, the reader/viewer knows that Mick made the choice to quit decades before. This is why Rocky and Mick are the perfect match to take on a power as great as the champ.

They're both in it for redemption. And trust me, there is not a fighter in the world who wants to step into a ring with someone looking for redemption. [The External Performance Genre's shame/honor welded to the Internal Morality Genre/ Redemption Plot is irresistible.]

The best bad choice for Rocky is to fight.

He can take a physical beating, but he won't be able to live with himself with a psychological one. He'll always be a bum, but at least he'll be an honorable one. Mick knows Rocky's situation too. It's why he dragged his ass to Rocky's dump in the first place. This best bad choice crisis comes at the end of the Beginning Hook of the screenplay, and it sets up the rest of the movie perfectly.

What's an example of the best bad choice for nonfiction?

A while back, two men in powerful positions in the U.S., one a member of Congress and one a Governor were faced with the same *Best Bad Choice* situation. Both men, as men seem to do over and over again, lost themselves in their intoxicating positions of being highly respected members of government.

A great number of people relied on these men, sacrificed for these men and believed in them. But if you had to boil down to the single other human being on the planet who believed in them the most, you'd have to say their life partners—

their wives—sacrificed the most for them. I'm sure their wives were not and still aren't saints and that the relationships had all of the deeply serious challenges that any committed one does. But the fact is that there's just one rule in a committed relationship that is unassailable.

You must remain faithful. You cannot cheat.

Both men cheated, one with a prostitute and one online. They both made a terrible decision, one that they most likely continued to make over and over again until they got caught. (I'm no psychologist, but it's pretty obvious that everyday people, not sociopaths, do stupid things more out of self-sabotage than animus.)

One chose to call a press conference, admitted that he'd been with a prostitute and eventually resigned as the Governor, probably destroying his political career for the rest of his life in the process. The other said his computer had been hacked and denied that he did anything inappropriate. Eventually after overwhelming evidence that the man claiming victimhood was lying, he finally admitted that he not only did what he said he didn't do, but that he lied about it…twice…once to his wife and then to the world.

Both men had to face a real life *Best Bad Choice*… admit a character defect and take the consequences or lie and maybe get away with it. One man's bad choice was truly better than the other's, wasn't it? The guy who came clean right off the bat? You have more sympathy for that guy, don't you? You're more likely to give that guy a break than the other one, aren't you?

This is the stuff of humanity and by association art. You must understand the concept of the best bad choice and artfully place your characters in these kinds of situations and have them choose. The choices they make will tell the reader/viewer/listener what kind of character they are.

What your characters say they are is not who they are… What they do is the key.

45

THE IRRECONCILABLE GOODS CRISIS

Now the Yang to the *Best Bad Choice* Yin is choosing between *Irreconcilable Goods.*

Making a choice between two "good" things sounds pretty great right? No matter what you pick, a positive will come to the world. But don't Stories require conflict? How can a choice between two good things, not just drive a Story forward but actually create a catharsis?

The key word, of course, is "irreconcilable." Choosing one good precludes the other. What's good for someone else is a different kind of good for you and what's good for you is a different kind of good for someone else.

But any good is just as good as another good, right?

No, it isn't.

One of my favorite movies, *Kramer vs. Kramer,* starts with a double "best bad choice" scenario but then is all about irreconcilable goods.

Wife Kramer (an impossible part played brilliantly by Meryl Streep) is at a crisis point with Husband Kramer (played by Dustin Hoffman). Only problem is that they have a four-year-old little boy.

Is staying with her husband—a narcissist of the highest order who cares little for her and barely registers the existence of their son—until her boy is grown worse than denying her inner self? Wife Kramer thinks staying is worse. She's gotta go. That's best bad choice number one.

Now should she take the little boy with her? She's an emotional wreck and has no idea of what she's going to do with her life or how. So wouldn't it be better to leave the boy with the father until she gets squared away? Wife Kramer thinks leaving the boy is the best bad choice. That's best bad choice number two.

This movie is so brilliantly written that everything I've just described happens in the first sixty seconds...

Now left to care for the little guy after his hysterical wife flies the coop, Hoffman's character has to make a series of irreconcilably good choices.

He can hire a full-time nanny and stay on his career track as an up and coming advertising exec. Or he can take the kid to school, pick him up, make his dinner, clean up after him, discipline him, read him stories, and answer endless ridiculous and often impossible questions from his maddening four-year-old point of view.

Hiring a third-party caregiver would be good for Kramer personally and it would be good for his kid too. All of his hard work making something of himself will most likely lead to professional recognition, more money, etc. And because of the money etc. his son will have privileges and opportunities in life that the older Kramer didn't have when he was a boy.

He'll be a great role model for his son...hard work pays off, stay focused!

But does his son really need that kind of role model when he's four years old?

Doesn't he just want his mom and dad there when he bangs his head on the coffee table?

So the other good choice would be to put the brakes on his career, take a lesser paying job, and make it to every school play. He'll teach his son how to draw just like his old man does for a living. He'll get angry at his son for bullying the next door neighbor and then he'll stand behind his boy when he knocks on the door to apologize...

That would be a good choice too, right?

His son would learn that money and titles aren't really that important if it means that a man can't eat dinner with his family. Having someone to cry with about losing his mommy (or wife) trumps a key to the executive washroom.

Of this stuff are "irreconcilable goods" conflicts made. I saw this movie before I became a man, as I'm sure a lot of men of my generation did. Go to any playground today. Guess what you'll see. A bunch of dads with their kids. Stories change people.

46

COMMANDMENT NUMBER FOUR

You must have a climax in every unit of your Story. Because the climax is the truth of character.

It is the precise moment in your beat, scene, sequence, act, subplot and global Story when your character acts on his/her crisis choice. And as we all know, choices and actions tell the truth about our character(s). We may make a choice to do one thing, but when the moment actually comes, we often act differently.

Seriously, this kind of stuff happens every single day to us. Our friend may tell us that she'll back us up and stand with us at a meeting to discuss what to do about our school's lunch program…but when the meeting commences, our friend often (sadly most often) remains silent.

Our friend's crisis choice that she so passionately told us about before the meeting (she was going to stand up with us to change something that would require a lot of work and risk the majority group's disapproval) is all well and good, but it is not a reflection of her character.

Only her actions reflect her character. Her silence at the meeting tells us who she really is (fearful and cowardly when in a group). That moment of truth is the climax of the scene and it changes the way we view her character from that point forward.

A climax is the active answer to the question raised by a crisis.

It's the choice the character makes between the best bad one or between irreconcilable goods. This is the big reveal of character. Not who he says he is, but who he really is.

Also it's important to remember that when the protagonist makes a choice and acts on that choice, that climax must be on stage. That is, it has to happen on the page or on the screen, not in some previous scene or moment that another character reports. To rob the reader or viewer of the crucial moment of truth for a protagonist will devastate them. It will make them so angry that they will probably never read anything you write ever again. You've promised them page after page that you are going to give them a great scene where the protagonist faces an impossible choice. You've got to deliver it. Seriously.

With that said, secondary characters can choose and act off stage and then the results of those choices and actions can be reported as revelations later on. Protagonists, though, must make their choices and actions ON STAGE!

As with crises, climaxes move from minor to medium to large to life changing. In a Story with both External and Internal Genre dimensions, if faced with the similar crisis in the Beginning Hook and the Ending Payoff, what your protagonist chooses at the beginning of your Story and what your character chooses at the end of your Story should be opposite choices.

What I mean is this: Do you think Rick in *Casablanca* would choose to give up his long-lost love at the beginning of the Story? No way. At the beginning of *Casablanca*, Rick is a self obsessed sad sack who won't stick his neck out for anybody. By the end, he's a hero, a character willing to sacrifice himself for the greater good of humanity. What happens between the beginning and the end is a progressive escalation of crises and climaxes in Rick's life that make him change his worldview. This is what's known as the internal arc of the character and is determined by your choice of Internal Genre.

It is true that some of the External Genres don't require an internal arc...like a master detective murder mystery or a James Bond action adventure, but they still require external crises and climaxes aplenty.

You've probably heard a million times that a character must "arc." What that means (again some Genres do not require an internal character arc) is that the lead character in a Story cannot remain the same person he/she was at the end of the novel/movie as they were at the beginning.

The Internal Content Genres are those that move a character and his status or worldview or morality from one place to another by Story's end. And the global Story's climax delivers the catharsis inherent in such a journey.

Many commercial writers find this "protagonists must arc" rule silly. And extremely talented action writers disregard it all of the time. Don't people face threats in their lives, overcome them, and then return to stasis? Didn't Donald Trump build a fortune, lose most of it, and then regain it? Isn't he the same person he was in 2014 as he was in 1980? Probably he is.

But I would posit that Donald Trump (the public Donald Trump, who knows, he may be a philosopher king in private) is not a three dimensional character. He could be the basis of an action hero, or amateur detective murder mystery (lead characters in long form Storytelling that do not arc) like a John Connor or a Lara Croft or a Miss Marple or Sherlock Holmes or Columbo. But as a fully fleshed out lead character in a literary novel or a thriller or any of the other Genres that require a compelling subconscious as well as conscious object of desire? Not so much.

What the character arc is crucial for is to achieve a cathartic global Story climax. When I say catharsis, I mean an overwhelming emotional reaction from the audience...tears, indescribable joy…the kind of experience that keeps us coming back to the movies, to books, to plays. If you're a writer and you tell me you have no interest in bringing the audience to catharsis, you're lying.

This is not to thumb the nose at the action Genre or the murder mystery or any of the other External Content Genres. Because these Genres have been so thoroughly mined over the centuries, creating a surprising action Story or inscrutable murder mystery Story is practically impossible. It takes a tremendous skill and imagination to breathe new life into these classic Genres. They are as difficult to successfully execute as writing a book that wins the Booker prize. For my money, they are harder to write.

But back to climax:

What do I mean by progressively complicated climaxes?

Let's look at the protagonist in *The Silence of the Lambs*, Clarice Starling, and track some of the climax moments she must face in the novel. By the way, the film adaptation of *The Silence of the Lambs* is dead solid perfect. You know why? Because Ted Tally, the screenwriter, and Jonathan Demme basically "shot the book." They recognized how perfectly constructed the novel was, so they didn't ruin it with "interpretation." You can watch the movie and get the same effect as reading the book. Doing both is one of the rare pleasures in life…especially for Story addicts like myself.

All right, let's track some scenes:

The *crisis* in the very first scene of the book (chapter 1) is a best bad choice situation.

Clarice Starling is given the opportunity to interview the madman Hannibal Lecter. Just being in a room with the guy will open her up to serious darkness. It's no small decision. Her choices are that she can decline the opportunity and protect herself and stay on course to become a garden-variety FBI agent. Or she can take the job and earn brownie points with the man she's trying to impress, the head of Behavioral Science Jack Crawford.

The *climax* of this first scene is that she decides to take the job.

It's an exciting active choice that shows Starling is no coward, but it is in no way a decision that will change Starling's worldview. Is it a huge climax? No. It's a big choice though and one that has just enough oomph to keep the reader turning pages wondering what is going to happen next…

Now the *crisis* in the third scene of the novel's Middle Build (chapter 13) is another best bad decision, but the stakes here are much higher than in the first scene.

Starling must decide whether she should confront Jack Crawford about his behavior toward her at the crime scene in Potter, West Virginia. When the two were there to fingerprint a victim of serial killer Buffalo Bill, Crawford asked to speak with the sheriff privately…out of her hearing range…as if she were too delicate for "manly talk."

Crawford left Starling to stand with a gaggle of low-level cops as if she were a little girl and he, her father, was going in to speak to the principal. The disrespect stings and it hurts her ability to get the townspeople to take her seriously as an FBI agent. She suspects that Crawford is using her.

As she is doing the job of an FBI agent, even though she's an FBI trainee, Starling wants to be treated as such. But if she confronts Crawford about his behavior, she may lose him as her mentor. He may not want to have the kind of honest personal relationship with her that she needs and he could dump her from the investigation. On the other hand, if she doesn't confront him about the disrespect, he will probably continue to treat her as a trained dog instead of a colleague with something to contribute.

So the crisis is *confront and risk banishment* or *let it go and guarantee servitude*.

The *climax* of the scene is that Starling chooses to confront Crawford.

Here is a perfect example of "showing, not telling." Harris never describes Starling as "courageous." Instead he has her act courageously.

And then Harris has Crawford react to her courage too. He apologizes, in his way, by saying *"duly noted, Starling."* Just enough for her to get satisfaction, but not enough to lower his position.

This moment may seem small, but it is a *climax* of one of the novel's subplots as well as the climax of the third scene of the Middle Build. The subplot in this case is an Internal Genre Status Admiration plot. This moment not only moves the serial killer thriller and disillusionment plots forward (Harris' External and Internal global Genre choices), it represents a large change in Starling's status. Her ultimate goal (external object of desire) is to work with Crawford permanently as a certified FBI agent. This moment shows that she's progressed to a place where her superior has acknowledged that she is worthy of respect.

Just to track the progression of *climaxes* here. In chapter 1 of *The Silence of the Lambs,* we have a climax that propels the entire action of the novel...Starling decides to take the job. By the Middle Build, we have a climax that shows Starling has not only done the job well, but is now respected as someone capable of doing the job the rest of her life.

Harris' *climax* progression is natural and organic...seamless.

For fun, let's examine where Harris escalates the *crisis* and *climax* even more to what is often called *The Point of No Return. The Point of No Return* is the critical moment of irreversibility for the protagonist...that place where she'll never be the same, no matter what choice she makes in the crisis.

At the beginning of the novel, Starling decides to expose herself to a brilliant manipulator. She does this rather subconsciously. That is, she doesn't really think too much about the fact that she's serving her own mind up on a plate to the cannibal Hannibal Lecter.

She's jacked up with ambition to join the venerable FBI, so she acts with blind belief in the institution and its stewards, without deeply thinking about the consequences of her decisions. (Sound familiar?) That sentence could describe a freshman in College or a new CEO coming into IBM or us joining a fancy country club.

At the height of the Middle Build, Starling faces a *crisis* that will make her come out of her fog and confront the reality of just what she's gotten herself into. She's progressed from life as normal to life as extraordinary to living without much self-knowledge subconsciously to consciously facing the truth about herself. She's coping with the prospect of her actions or inactions leading to end of the line of human experience...DEATH.

Here's the situation:

Buffalo Bill has abducted another woman and is planning to skin her to create the final piece for his "woman suit." Induced by Crawford, Starling goes to talk to Lecter to convince him to help them stop Buffalo Bill. But Lecter won't speak to Starling unless he gets a *quid pro quo*. He won't help her, unless she opens herself up to Lecter's own special brand of psychoanalysis.

He wants to get inside her mind.

I'm going to analyze this crisis as an irreconcilable goods situation. Starling can either reject the *quid pro quo* and save her inner most thoughts and self and subconscious desires from being toyed with. Good for her. Or she can accept Lecter's terms and perhaps save a woman from certain death. Good for the woman and the rest of society. If she decides to agree, though, she'll essentially be letting the devil into her mind.

This is a major moment of truth and will tell us whether Starling has the stuff of the hero.

At the beginning of the novel, if Starling had faced this same dilemma, chances are she would have chosen to keep her mind to herself. But because she's progressed so far in her quest to become an FBI agent by the time of this critical meeting, she's vulnerable to this ultimatum. There is no turning back once Lecter gets inside her mind.

She'll never be able to get him out.

As you'll see if you take a look at ***The Story Grid for The Silence of the Lambs,*** Harris gives us the point of no return in the middle of his Story. The promise he's making the reader by doing so with half of the telling left, is that he's going to take his Story to the end of the line of human experience.

In terms of the Story's values, Starling has moved from **positive life** at the beginning of the Story to the **negative of unconsciousness** at the end of the Inciting Incident of the global Story to now comprehending that she's in a life or death situation. If she does not act, someone will die. Now the Story value is clearly in the **negative death** arena. But with this big scene coming so early, Harris is promising that the value will go more negative still. He is going to drive it down to the fate even worse than death, the place of **damnation**.

Harris is making a promise in the Middle Build of the Story that is so attractive, the reader won't be able to stop reading. What's even better is that he delivers on that promise so assuredly by the novel's Ending Payoff.

47

COMMANDMENT NUMBER FIVE

The fifth and final element of Story form is the least respected and often forgotten. But it's indispensable.

The resolution of a beat, scene, sequence, act, subplot or global Story is crucial for the reader or viewer to fully metabolize the Story. Many writers dash these moments off in epilogues or one or two sentence updates at the end of a climactic scene.

One exception, of course, is the innovative ending of *Animal House,* which was perfect for that movie because the viewer just needed some time to enjoy the outrageous climax and the wonderful music. Having a scene where the Deltas all met at a diner later that evening to talk about what they were going to do in the future would have been ridiculous. Instead the director John Landis created stills with biographical updates for each of the characters one by one, resolving their stories with a little bit of fallout action from the panic at the Homecoming parade and then a cutaway to a photo and bio. Just like they do in college "class notes" magazines years and decades after.

The ending of *Animal House* was a perfect resolution (easy, funny, smart and with just enough tag moments to bring the viewer down from the hilarious climax). But like all things that have been done over and over again, the photo-montage movie resolution has lost its effectiveness with each new repetition. The most recent I can remember was the movie *Argo*. The trick, as is the trick in not creating cliché moments in the other four Story commandments, is to not settle for the first idea that comes into your head.

Dig deep inside yourself and create something new, something fresh that we have not read or seen before. That takes a lot of time, but it's worth the effort.

So how does a resolution scene work? That is, how does it move from one pole of a value to the other? Isn't it really just a summing up of what has already taken place?

One way to approach a resolution is to create a fable or a metaphor to reinforce the way in which the climax changed the character or characters in the Story. Some of the best fables come from old war stories.

Here's an example of a perfect resolution scene from a longer chapter from Steven Pressfield's book *The Warrior Ethos*:

> *A Roman general was leading his legions toward the enemy in a swampy country. He knew that the next day's battle would be fought on a certain plain because it was the only dry, flat place for miles. He pushed his army all night, marching them through a frightening and formidable swamp, so that they reached the battle site before the fore and could claim the high ground. In the aftermath of victory, the general called his troops together and asked them, "Brothers, when did we win the battle?"*
>
> *One captain replied, "Sir, when the infantry attacked."*
>
> *Another said, "Sir, we won when the cavalry broke through."*
>
> *"No," said the general. "We won the battle the night before—when our men marched through that swamp and took the high ground."*

This is a perfect example of a compelling resolution. In this hundred odd word little Story, the reader walks with an army of thousands, trudges through a harrowing swamp only to be faced with a bloody battle with no sleep. The values at stake are life/death, victory/defeat, honor/dishonor etc. They are all in the negative at the beginning.

But despite the army's exhaustion, they win the battle and end the scene on a positive.

So the Story turns here from what the reader believes could be annihilation (How can one expect to fight hand to hand with no rest the night before?) to victory. The values move from negative to positive. That's the surface external war Genre Storyline for the scene. And it climaxes in victory.

The internal revelation Storyline though is not resolved by the external climax. And yes there is an internal struggle in this Story…the struggle to keep one's shit together before battle and how best to do that. So the resolution of this little Story must "tag" and resolve the Internal Genre.

The reader/listener would be left wanting if the internal lesson wasn't resolved. Without the general calling his victorious drunken mates together and having a little Socratic dialogue at the end in the resolution scene, the internal "revelation plot" and its value shift from negative to positive (ignorance to knowledge) would be lost on the reader. The takeaway is—the way to keep one's head is to think clearly about strategy and tactics. That little lesson makes the chaos of war digestible. It reveals that science and reason can save lives...especially in the preparations for combat.

What's really great about this tiny Story is that the resolution seems obvious once it's stated.

The general reminds his men of the work they put in before the fight. Of course they won the battle because they seized the high ground before the enemy could. Everyone knows it's far easier to win a battle from a higher position. Running downhill is far easier than it is fighting while charging uphill. But because the value at stake in the external Storyline is so dire (being killed in a nasty battle) and the reader's anticipation of the climax of the external Storyline is so great, the reader forgets, if only momentarily, the internal conflict within the characters.

Fighting the internal enemy and winning that battle is the key to defeating the external enemy is the payoff resolution of the Story. Doing the inner work of war is the way to hold off the terror of its commencement.

Thus the resolution of this Story…"we won the battle the night before…" really tags the entire scene, reinforcing the substance of the Inciting Incident (a battle must be fought), the progressive complications (swamps and fatigue), the crisis (do we burn energy for a tactical advantage or rest and fight uphill?), and the climax (they take the tactical advantage).

But didn't Pressfield just repeat some ancient mini-tale? He didn't invent this Story, did he?

Here's a little secret. I've read a LOT of ancient war stories and histories. I can't recall reading this mini-Story in any of the classics. It doesn't mean it's not there, of course. Pressfield has read far more in this arena than I have. But it may not be any one place.

What I think Pressfield did here was what Homer and Thucydides did way back in the pre-digital age. Pressfield opened his mind to all of the reading and work he'd done in his forty plus years of studying writing and ancient history and came up with that Roman general anecdote. Pressfield the writer took all that he read before and created something unique and fresh and true. In less than a hundred words.

Pressfield came up with that resolution. And he came up with the rest of it too. Somehow a guy in Los Angeles in 2011 was able to create a mini-Story using the fable form (a form that was not prevalent in ancient times by the way) that rings true for ancient warriors and of U.S. Special Forces today. And he did it so effectively that *The Warrior Ethos* is now mandatory reading for the U.S. Marine Corps and for first year midshipmen at the U.S. Naval Academy.

Resolutions and turning them masterfully so that they are unexpected, yet on reflection obvious, is what takes a very good Story from entertaining to memorable.

So, don't dash off resolution scenes. Don't settle for "summing up" what happened previously in the climax. The reader already knows what happened. What the resolution moment does is tells the reader exactly what the climax of the Story MEANS. How the worldview has shifted.

Another trick to keep in mind is if your global Story rests on a massive internal shift in your lead character, the resolution scene should resolve the external changes in that character. If your maturation plot is the global Story climax, the resolution scene should revolve around a subplot External Genre. Likewise, like the Pressfield example above, if your global Story rests on a massive external shift like WAR, then the resolution scene should resolve the internal changes in your character.

In *The Silence of the Lambs*, the external climax scene of the global Story is Clarice Starling killing Buffalo Bill. So for his resolution scene(s), Harris does not dwell on the external Storyline. There isn't a big recap of the action from Starling's FBI colleagues...we already know what happened. The external climax is firmly established—Buffalo Bill is dead and Starling killed him. Instead Harris focuses on the internal change to Starling after she attains her conscious object of desire.

The resolution scenes do not go over her being patted on the back etc. reviewing exactly how she figured out everything and found Buffalo Bill's lair.

It ends with Starling accepting the fact that she did not get her subconscious object of desire (safety and protection and rewards from an esteemed social institution). We watch her settle into a new worldview shift. She's moved from blind belief in the righteousness in strict hierarchical law and the order of institutions (FBI) to disillusionment. Even though the External Genre has moved from negative to positive (the killer is dead), Starling's view of the world has gone from naively positive to justified negative.

PART FIVE

THE UNITS OF STORY

48

THE BEAT

The beat is the smallest unit of Story.

And as the smallest, it is often given short shrift by prose writers. In many cases, beats are ignored and left to the exigencies of the subconscious. What I mean by that is that beats are so small (atomic in some instances) that we often leave them unexamined in our quest to finely tune the mechanics of scenes, sequences, acts, secondary plot lines and global stories. And that's okay for the novelist.

Dwelling on the beat in the first drafts of your novel is a mistake. You will most certainly lose the forest for the trees if you obsess about each and every beat. If a scene works, then by association so do the beats that make up the scene. If the scene doesn't work, then having wonderful beats within it will not save it. I recommend that tinkering with beats be best left to the final finish work just prior to publication or production.

But with that said, looking hard at every beat in a Story, while taxing, creates rich subtext. Slight tweaks of beats can highlight image systems and hammer home your controlling idea/theme. Should you spend hours deliberating the use of one word? It depends on the beat within the scene and the importance of that scene to the overarching Story of course. Obviously, you are going to spend a lot of time on every beat in your Story's global climax scene.

Carefully weighing and pruning your language is exactly what you do when you examine beats. My answer is to not even think about parsing beats until you have a very accomplished draft in place. Robert McKee is soon to release a book purely dedicated to DIALOGUE, which I've had the privilege to edit. I suggest you take a look at that book for further delineation about beat craft. It's comprehensive.

In the performing arts, much more so than in prose writing, beats are the central focus. Beats are the actors' medium.

It is within the moment-to-moment beats that actors make specific choices to portray their idea of their characters. Acting is a very difficult skill as it requires the delivery of memorized text in a simulated and at the same time "real" situation—one actor speaking to another is real, even if the text is pre-programmed.

So what is a beat?

A beat is an identifiable moment of change. And like all units of Story, the writer must have the raw materials to create a stable beat. There is an Inciting Incident, a complication, a crisis, a climax and a resolution inside each and every beat.

1. The Inciting Incident is when two characters, each with their own agendas, take the stage or come onto the page.
2. The complication is a clear understanding that their agendas are in conflict. That is, one wants something from the other one that the other does not want to give.
3. The crisis is a question that arises within each character. Do I do this? Or do I do that?
4. The climax of the beat is the active choice that the two characters individually make in response to the crisis.
5. The resolution is the fallout from the choices as evidenced in the reactions of the characters.

I think you can see how this can get mind-trippy.

The beat is the moment when one character realizes that the active choice he/she is making is not working on the other character. He's not successful getting the other person to do what he wants, so he changes the action to try and get it another way. Perhaps scolding doesn't work, so the character changes his approach and tries to woo the other one instead.

For example, in the movie *Tootsie*, there are pitch perfect beats galore.

I saw *Tootsie* decades ago, but there was one moment that was so perfectly executed and so in character that I still use it as the best example of a beat...a definable moment with an Inciting Incident, a complication, a crisis, a climax and a resolution that changes everything.

In the movie, Bill Murray plays playwright, Jeff. He's thrown together a birthday party for his actor friend and roommate Michael Dorsey played by Dustin

Hoffman. Up until this moment, the viewer has only heard about "Jeff" from dialogue between Dorsey and his agent, played by the wonderful Sidney Pollack who also directed the movie. Dorsey has told his agent that he needs a job so that he can raise enough money to put on his friend Jeff's play at a regional summer stock theater. The name of the play is *Return to Love Canal*. For those of you who don't remember, Love Canal was a place in New York that had been built on top of toxic waste. The people who moved into Love Canal got terribly ill (this is all true) and many contracted cancer because of the exposure. It was a big Story in the 1970s and a real tragedy.

So Dorsey's friend Jeff has decided that he will write a play about people who were exposed to horribly toxic substances, who then make the ridiculous decision that they should move back in.

The very title of the play sounds like the work of a very self-important person.

At first exposure, Murray as Jeff seems like a really thoughtful, good friend to Michael. He's put together the party and we watch as Dorsey makes his way around the crowd. It seems that Jeff is just a good egg…no more no less.

Then later on, the camera moves to Murray/Jeff holding court at the kitchen table. He's got a crowd of five people gathered around him and he's telling them his philosophy of theater. He tells them that he wants to have a theater that's only open when it's raining. And then Sidney Pollack cuts the action. That's one beat.

Pollack picks up the action again and now there are only three people listening to Murray/Jeff. Murray/Jeff goes on to further explain that he doesn't want people to tell him how great his work is, he wants them to come out of his plays and say to him.

"I saw your play…what happened?"

Pollack cuts the scene again. That's another beat.

Pollack picks up the action again and now it's just Murray/Jeff and his girlfriend rubbing his shoulders.

Let's walk through the next beat, which is my aforementioned favorite.

1. The **Inciting Incident** is the party.
2. After Murray/Jeff's speech, he's lost his audience. **A complication**.

   Jeff's agenda is to enthrall the guests of his friend's birthday party enough that they will eventually support him either financially or just show up for one of his plays. His bullshit has been working but now it's worn off, which raises the crisis question…

3. The **crisis** question is what can I do to get the attention back on me?

   But remember, the people at the party have their own agenda. They are at this birthday party to see Dorsey and are most likely Dorsey's primary friends, not Jeff's. They find Jeff kind of fascinating at first and he's one of those people you meet at a party who holds your attention and makes you forget the fact that you are at a party. Guys like Jeff relieve the people around them from having to be "on." They don't want to be "on." This guy is "on" so their wants are being met. At first.

   Then Murray/Jeff begins to repeat himself and is starting to bore them. So from the point of view of the partygoers, the Inciting Incident is the party, the complication is that the conversation is getting boring, the crisis is what they should they do about it? Should they leave the circle and have to be "on" somewhere else? Or stay the course and be bored? They leave.

4. Murray/Jeff realizes this has happened. So, he needs to change to get back his audience. That moment of change is the moment the beat changes.

5. The **climax** of the beat is not verbal in this instance. I doubt it was even written into the script. Rather it's a physical motion that the actor Bill Murray uses to keep the scene moving forward.

   Just as he senses that he's lost his audience, Jeff/Murray violently swats at an invisible fly. This action is a desperate attempt to get focus back to him.

   The aggressive move changes the dynamic of the moment and the Story value from **Friendly to Dangerous**. Murray/Jeff doesn't get what he wants (no one is coming back to listen to him), so he strikes out.

And thus another beat begins. That's acting.

This is the example of a very clean and discernible beat. Before the fly-swatting incident, the environment is one way...after the fly swatting incident, things are another way. The beat change was driven by conflict. Murray/Jeff was not getting what he wanted and so he changed his action to get what he wanted. This choice says everything we really need to know about Jeff/Murray. This is a selfish guy who needs constant stroking and support to create his "art." If he doesn't get it, then he will strike out.

The beat is so well done that it brings a very large laugh. The laugh comes from the audience understanding intuitively the dynamic at play and Murray's violent action breaks that artifice. We recognize this kind of thing from our own lives. This moment, entirely invented by Murray, is what is meant by an actor making a specific choice. An active choice (not in the screenplay) that is universally understood by the audience propels the beat and the scene forward.

But you can't put actor moments like that in a novel, right?

Actually you can. Here's a sentence from *The Great Gatsby* that comprises an entire beat.

> *The Carraways are something of a clan, and we have a tradition that we're descended from the Dukes of Buccleuch, but the actual founder of my line was my grandfather's brother, who came here in fifty-one, sent a substitute to the Civil War, and started the wholesale hardware business that my father carries on today.*[7]

The **Inciting Incident** of this beat is the intention of the first person narrator to tell the reader about himself. The narrator begins by telling us about the world he lives in. "The Carraways are something of a clan, and we have a tradition that we're descended from the Dukes of Buccleuch…" Having Nick Carraway, his narrator, state that his family is like a "clan" connotes deep Scottish roots and allows Fitzgerald to establish what kind of people will inhabit the Story. The bloodline is so deep that it extends back to Dukes in Scotland… These are "some high class people" is the narrator's intended message.

But the use of the phrase "something of a clan" raises **a complication**.

The narrator intuitively knows that he may lose his audience if he comes off as too insular or snobby, so he hedges his statement with the word "something," which tells the reader that he's detached from this family attitude. Which raises the **crisis question** of what to do about disabusing the reader of the notion that the narrator is not "like them."

The narrator's object of desire is to get the reader on his side—be willing to listen to him and his Story for quite some time—which results in **a climactic decision** to play down his lineage.

He states that he is from blue blood, but then sensing that this revelation may turn off the average reader, he changes his approach and his action by then confessing that "the actual founder of my line was my grandfather's brother, who came here in '51 (meaning 1851…not exactly a founding father of the revolution), sent a substitute to the Civil War (used money to get out of his Patriotic duty… perhaps this is a line of cowards?) and started the wholesale hardware business (not pedigreed money, money that had to be earned) that my father carries on today."

---

7 *Fitzgerald, F. Scott. The Great Gatsby (p. 3). Simon & Schuster, Inc.. Kindle Edition.*

The **resolution** of the beat is the narrator's confession that he's basically the son of a guy who runs a hardware store. This confession pulls the reader into Carraway's Story. The message to the reader is "I live in a high class world, but I'm not really like those kind of people...Being of salt of the earth lineage, I'm capable of seeing through it..."

So the turning point is the shift from hoity toity "you should listen to what I have to say because I'm a high class guy" to "I may seem to be high class, but the reality of my life is much more in keeping with the average hardworking American Joe..." Fitzgerald accomplishes this shift by having his narrator use an action, **to confess**.

Do you see how brilliantly Fitzgerald created a beat with this one sentence? The first person Storyteller's Inciting Incident is the need for them to tell you something, followed by the complication that perhaps he'll turn off readers who cannot relate to the setting of the Story, giving rise to the crisis of how to get the reader back, leading to the climactic action of confession, and the resolution of getting the broadest possible audience back to hear more of the Story.

What's more, the word choices Fitzgerald makes just could not be any better.

49

THE SCENE

The scene is the basic building block of a Story.

While the beat is the actor's medium, and as such can be "saved" by a skilled actor, even Meryl Streep can't save a poorly written scene. There is just no hiding for a writer when it comes to a scene. It either works or it doesn't. There is either a very clear shift in value from the beginning to the end—a change—or there isn't. If there is no change, no value at stake, no movement, the scene doesn't work. And if a writer's scenes don't work, no matter how well he can craft a sentence, his Story won't work.

I promise you this. If you put aside everything else that you read in this book, hold on to this one kernel of truth. Scenes are the place to focus.

Spend your time dreaming up scenes, writing them down, working them until you are blue in the face. Invest Malcolm Gladwell's golden ten-thousand-hour labor law in learning how to write a scene and you'll always be able to put food on the table. You will be a writer.

You can learn the other stuff easily—in fact it will probably come very naturally—if you can bang out a compelling scene with confidence. You'll get work as a script doctor or an editor or an advertising copywriter or a how-to ghostwriter if you can write a scene that grabs a reader by the throat and surprises them. And the more efficiently you can do so, the better.

While it can be broken down into its component beats, the scene is the most obvious mini-Story. They are the things that stay ever present when we talk about a great movie or great novel. *Remember what happened after character A saw character B with another woman?*

The structure of a scene is straightforward. A scene must move from one value state to another. From a positive expression of a value like "love" to a negative expression of a that value "hate." Or from a negative expression of a value "injustice" to a positive expression of a value "justice." Page upon page of prose without a turn from one value state to another is not a scene.

Just having two characters meet and talk does not make a scene. It's just talk.

The driving force of the scene is conflict. One character is in pursuit of one thing and one or more other characters are in pursuit of another. Only one desire can be fulfilled. So the two forces conflict. One will win and one will lose. Scenes are battles built on conflict. Stories are wars that take values to the end of the line or, at the very least, approach the end of the line.

Scenes can turn on very black and white terms—good/bad, life/death, truth/lie etc.

While long form stories can never deliver much entertainment or emotional impact by just flip-flopping between a positive Story value and its negative opposite, a scene can. In fact, it must. These black and white value shifts are usually the obligatory scenes for the External Content Genres. You'll find these straightforward, easy to understand scenes the most difficult to innovate.

Pure action scenes, for example, move between the simple value of life versus death. The character either lives or dies. These are the James Bond "Hero at the Mercy of the Villain" scenes that we all adore:

> BOND: "Do you expect me to talk?"
>
> GOLDFINGER: stops on the steps and looks down, both hands in his pockets.
>
> GOLDFINGER: "No, Mister Bond. I expect you to die!"

Life/death is the only value at stake in many big action scenes and because it is so simple and understandable, these scenes are some of the most difficult to write. How can you innovative a scene that has been written millions of times?

Can you outdo the action scenes in *The Iliad* or *The Odyssey* or *Beowulf* or *The Terminator* or *North by Northwest*? Maybe not, but think about what fun it would be to try. What is very important to recognize is the size of the mountain you are trying to climb for every scene you write. Besting Homer or James Cameron is a very steep task. Better bring extra oxygen and know that this ain't gonna be done in an afternoon.

You cannot just throw off the first thing that comes to your mind when you are creating an action scene, or any other scene for that matter. Well, you can, but it will be derivative and cliché. I guarantee it.

The reason why you can't settle for the first thing that comes to mind, though, is that the first thing that comes to anyone's mind is all the stuff that's been pumped into your brain since seeing your first cartoon.

This is not to say that you should drive yourself crazy on your first draft and not use these first cliché scenes as mile markers for your Story. It is to say that you can and should use them to give you a sense of the kind of scene you need to drop in, but you cannot be satisfied with the first thing that comes into your mind. The first thing that comes into your mind has been written before.

It's called a memory.

For example, if I'm going to write a thriller, I'll definitely need a scene where the hero/protagonist of the Story is at the mercy of the villain. This is the obligatory scene that all thrillers must have. If the reader/viewer doesn't get this scene, they won't like your book/movie. Simple as that.

My first attempt to craft this scene would go something like this:

> *Our hero is tied to a wall at the four points of his body. The villain begins to crank the rope until our hero is stretched to his limit. One additional crank and our hero's tendons and muscles in his shoulders and hips will pop.*
>
> *But our hero has figured out that if he can just break his own thumb, he'll be able to slip out of the restraint on his most powerful arm.*
>
> *VILLAIN: "Your wife called...I told her you were tied up..."*
>
> *HERO: "That's very funny...Why don't you come over here and say that to my face."*
>
> *Villain walks over to hero. Hero breaks his thumb and gets villain in a headlock with his one strong arm. He chokes villain to death and then unties himself and escapes.*

On just a cursory look at this construction, you'll see that it's basically a mash up of every action movie scene from *Die Hard* to *Taken* to *Goldfinger*.

That's okay for your first draft.

Let the cliché sit on the page while you move forward. You'll definitely come back to it later on when you have your critical editor cap on your head. But for your first draft, write cliché after cliché. It's okay. No one is going to see this draft but you. What you need in a first draft are the types of scenes you'll need and the general order in which they'll fall.

Just don't write scenes that don't go anywhere. They all must have Inciting Incidents (hero caught by villain), progressive complications (tied to a wall… rope pulled to breaking point), crisis (do I try and buy some time or do I break my thumb and try and free myself? Best Bad Choice), climax (breaks thumb), resolution (hero tricks villain, kills him and escapes). The scene moves from death to life. It works.

It's far from great, but it works.

The most important thing to remember about writing a scene is that it has to TURN. It has to move from one state of being to another. It can be a subtle turn, but it must turn in a meaningful way.

When you get stuck, think about the overall state of your protagonist's quest for his objects of desire (both external and internal). Has his quest moved closer to success or failure from the beginning to the end of the scene? It must move from positive to negative or negative to positive or positive to double positive or negative to double negative etc.

If your scene does not move, it has to be reworked so that it does. If you find that you are pulling your hair out trying to turn the scene and it just won't turn, there's a good reason why it won't. You don't need it in your Story. It's undoubtedly a Shoe Leather/Stage Business scene that just moves your character physically from one space to another.

Cut that stuff. You don't need it and it's boring.

What's great about finding these bits in your first draft is that you can just highlight and delete knowing that the reader or viewer will fill in that stage business inside their own minds. They don't want to read the part when your lead character goes to dinner with a friend who tells him all about what's been going on back home for two thousand words.

They want to see the friend pick up a steak knife and try and kill your protagonist. Or they want the friend to brilliantly undermine your protagonist's confidence. A scene must have conflict. And someone must win or lose.

Later on, when we lay out *The Story Grid Spreadsheet* (the micro editorial view), I'll show you how to track the turns in your scenes so that you'll be easily able to pinpoint the duds and fix them.

50

THE SEQUENCE

Sequences give the reader a sense of "critical moments in life." That is, they, like all the other units of Story, have beginnings, middles and ends.

To look at it another way, sequences are large stages in the global Story journey.

Like the beat and the scene and ultimately the act, the subplot and the global Story, the sequence must have the five form elements (Inciting Incident, progressive complications, crisis, climax, and resolution) but it does not have the "major shift" reversals of the Story's core value like the act or global plot. More on these major shifts later on.

Sequence events can be summed up with phrases like "GETTING THE JOB" or "WINNING THE RACE" or "COURTING THE PRINCESS" or "FIRST KISS" or "BUYING THE HOUSE."

More specifically, a sequence is a collection of scenes (or even one) that adds up to more than the sum of their parts but less the major reversal of a Story's core value that occurs in the act. That means that the change that occurs in the sequence is greater in scale than any preceding single scene but not as great as the change that occurs in an act.

For example in the novel and film *Misery*, there are some very definable sequences. I'll work from William Goldman's amazing screenplay adaptation of one of Stephen King's best works. Here are the first seven scenes of the screenplay.

1. The first scene of the movie lasts one minute twenty seconds. James Caan (playing protagonist Paul Sheldon) finishes writing a novel and partakes in his ritual single cigarette and bottle of champagne.

2. The second scene is two minutes forty-five seconds long. Paul leaves his hotel to head home and deliver the novel to his agent but crashes his car in a blizzard.

3. The third scene is a flashback to Paul deciding that he's going to forego the commercial route that has made him so successful and write a real novel. This scene lasts one minute five seconds.

4. The fourth scene finds Paul unconscious. A large figure pulls him out of his wrecked car, throws him over its shoulder and trudges into the woods. This scene is one minute twenty seconds.

5. The fifth scene finds Paul awake in bed. He's being taken care of by Annie Wilkes, played by Kathy Bates. The scene is one minute five seconds.

6. In the sixth scene Annie tells Paul why she did not take him to a hospital. They are snowed in. This scene is one minute five seconds.

7. In the seventh scene Annie explains to Paul just how badly he is hurt. This scene lasts one minute fifteen seconds.

(I've given you the screen time to illustrate just how economic Goldman is with his Storytelling. These scenes are practically the same length, a technique that builds a visual rhythm.)

These first seven scenes comprise three distinct sequences.

The first sequence (scenes 1 and 2) could be called SUCCESSFUL WRITER CRASHES HIS CAR. We know he's successful by the tony ski lodge environment he's in and his choice of champagne to celebrate the completion of his work.

- The Inciting Incident of sequence one is the completion of the novel.
- Progressive complications of sequence one are the weather conditions he faces upon departure.
- The crisis of sequence one is whether he should disregard the storm and press forward homeward bound? Or should he stay put and risk getting stuck in the mountains with nothing to do? This is the crisis' best bad choice question.
- The climax of sequence one is his decision to go.
- The resolution of sequence one is his wrecking the car and being completely incapacitated.

What's so wonderful about this sequence, beyond its economy, is that it results in an irreversible change. The lead character cannot undo the fact that he recklessly drove into the heart of a snowstorm. If the sequence were expanded and the writer decided to wait out the storm until morning and then drive home and then the rest of the events of the Story played out...not only would it alter the tenor of the Storytelling, it would drastically influence the viewer/reader's understanding of the character.

Paul Sheldon takes big chances. He's not a guy who's going to vacillate.

The second sequence is just one scene (and yes a skilled writer can pull off a sequence with one scene). It is the third scene flashback when the viewer/reader is informed of the Sheldon's decision to change his career path. It could be called WRITER STOPS PLAYING TO THE CROWD.

The third sequence is the WRITER GETS RESCUED BY RECLUSE sequence, made up of scenes 4 through 7.

- The Inciting Incident of this sequence is the Annie character played by Kathy Bates pulling Paul Sheldon out of the car.
- The progressive complications are Paul's discovery that 1) while he's safe, he's not in a hospital, 2) his injuries are such that he's at the mercy of a rather strange and powerfully built woman, and 3) the woman has loaded him up with narcotics that keep the pain at bay but are dangerously addictive.
- The crisis question Paul must answer is another best bad choice. Should he use his star power and demand that this woman get him immediate evacuation? Or should he humor her and hope that she comes to her senses?
- The climax is in his ultimate decision to humor her.
- The resolution is that she pushes him deeper and deeper into relying on the pain medication.

Sequences are crucial building blocks of Story, but I recommend that writers focus on scenes in their first draft. Looking at and defining sequences is a great idea, once you have something in hand and you are evaluating how successfully you brought the Story to life. To obsess about them before you have a rough draft is very often a mistake. Sequence analysis is an editorial craft, and as such, should be saved for editing, not initial creation.

If you get stuck and you have no idea where your Story went off tracks, chances are you are either missing or over delivering sequences in the Story. Over delivering on a sequence means that you have too many supporting scenes. One or two can be eliminated entirely without losing any narrative consistency.

Remember that readers and viewers are very discerning and sophisticated (just think about how much Story the average person consumes each day from the newspaper to websites, emails, television shows, books, heart to heart talks with their friends etc.). That old chestnut LESS IS MORE absolutely applies in Storytelling. You want to give the reader just enough to follow the through-line of your Story without overloading them with scenes they've already anticipated in their own minds.

For example, Stephen King and William Goldman knew that a sequence such as ANNIE LEAVES HER HOME FOR A WALK AND DISCOVERS A CAR WRECKED ON THE HIGHWAY is not necessary for MISERY. When Annie appears, the reader intuitively knows that that sequence has happened off stage. If you have that kind of "shoe leather" in your book or screenplay, you will lose the attention of your reader/viewer. And once you lose their attention, it's almost impossible to get it back.

The time to really look hard at sequences is in the third or fourth draft, after you're convinced that your scene by scene, your act by act, your subplot by subplot and your global plot is sound. After you have those marks checked off, it is a very good idea to go back yet again and define the sequences of your scenes. You'll undoubtedly find places to hone and cut.

51

THE ACT

There is a song by the 1980s new wave band *The Godfathers* that I always remember when someone asks me how best to describe an act. It is simply titled, *Birth, School, Work, Death*.

The act is a major life stage in a Story.

The act could be a self-sustaining Story in and of itself. There is no shortage of one-act plays. But in long form Storytelling, acts are the major events that change the Story irrevocably. Again, what that means is that the protagonist's life is changed permanently. Like the beat, scene and sequence, the act must have a clear Inciting Incident, progressive complications, crisis, climax and resolution. And if you were to home in on these particular moments in an act, you would be able to identify the specific sequence, scene and beat that comprises the act's component parts. Beats build scenes, scenes build sequences and sequences build acts.

The act brings explosive change.

As such, acts are often very satisfying in that they bring a very strong Story rush to the reader/audience. But in the long form Story, they must leave the reader/audience wanting more. Even in the final act's resolution (which serves as the resolution for the global Story too) a well-turned Story leaves the reader/audience wanting to hear another Story about the same characters. Hence the sequel, prequel phenomenon we inhabit today.

Long form episodic television series like *Breaking Bad* or *Mad Men* are divided essentially into acts. Each episode is a critical moment/developmental stage in the life of the protagonist, Walter White or Donald Draper, or one of the major secondary characters. We keep coming back to the shows because we want to know how a fundamental change that occurred in one episode will play out in the next.

Acts completely change the global Story, either positively or negatively. Again, the climactic action in an act must be irreversible. That is there is no turning back. Someone dies. Someone gets pregnant. An alien lands on the earth… these are the climactic moments in acts.

The characters and by extension the audience, must be surprised by the action or revelation from the act climax. The values at stake in an act also move the Story's global values. That is, if the Story is a serial killer thriller, its act climaxes must shift on life or death circumstances. The protagonist is either close to bringing the antagonist to justice or the antagonist has the hero on the ropes in a seemingly inescapable situation.

Act climaxes escalate—move closer and closer to the limits of human experience—the further along you move into the global Story. They must progressively complicate, moving from "big" to "huge" to "shocking."

For example, if the first act climax of *Chinatown* was the revelation that Evelyn Mulwray was raped by her father, the viewer would not really be prepared for that level of shock. The viewer has yet to fully attach to the character, so the information that she was raped would not resonate. The writer, Robert Towne, knew that a revelation of that size had to be saved for the ending of the Story. And he puts it exactly where it needs to be...at the penultimate act climax.

Instead Towne ended the first act with the scene when the real Mrs. Mulwray arrives at Jake Gittes' offices.

A mysterious imposter played by Diane Ladd had hired Gittes in an early scene to track the movements of Hollis Mulwray. The real Mrs. Mulwray played by Faye Dunaway arrives at Gittes' offices to tell him that she never hired him to tail her husband, and that the work he's been doing is going to cost him his entire business. She is going to sue him and destroy his livelihood.

This is a perfect end to the Beginning Hook of the Story, a great reversal that turns on both revelation (I'm not the woman who hired you) and action (my lawyer is going to destroy you).

This act 1 climax is irreversible.

Gittes can't go back to the life he had before the real Mrs. Mulwray came into his life. His business is now at risk. His future is in danger and he's not the sort of person who stands idly by when he is threatened. Towne knew that the perfect way of getting his character Gittes to react was by threatening him. Gittes fights back.

How Gittes reacts to the threat defines him, as it does for all of us. His ire propels us into the next act…wondering how the hell is this going to sort itself out?

Plus, at the end of this first act, Towne has made the Story personal to Gittes, a major obligatory element in a crime thriller. Gittes is now the "victim" in his own eyes. And Jake Gittes is not anyone's Patsy. He's going to press forward no matter what.

This characteristic is exactly why the central evil/antagonist in *Chinatown*, Noah Cross, sets Gittes up in the first place. We discover later on that Noah Cross, Evelyn Mulwray's father, essentially owns the Los Angeles Police Department. And we're told that Gittes used to be a cop before he became a private eye. While we never do learn why Gittes left the force, he does confess that his butting in to someone else's business and the tragic end of that interference had something to do with his leaving the LAPD.

Here's the scene just after Gittes gets his nose sliced open:

> EVELYN: "(working on him So why does it bother you to talk about it... Chinatown..."
>
> GITTES: "Bothers everybody who works there — but to me — It was — Gittes shrugs."
>
> EVELYN: "Hold still — why?"
>
> GITTES: "You can't always tell what's going on there —"
>
> EVELYN: "... No — why was it"
>
> GITTES: "I thought I was keeping someone from being hurt and actually I ended up making sure they were hurt."

The antagonist of the Story, Noah Cross, played with relish by John Huston, will not be denied. So when his former partner Hollis Mulwray (his daughter Evelyn's husband) tries to safeguard a young girl from him, Cross undoubtedly asked his cronies in the LAPD which Private Detective he should hire to find the girl.

They recommended Gittes because he is a monomaniac. The cops explain to Cross that Gittes threw away his police career in *Chinatown* just to take a case to the end of the line. Cross, being a brilliant epitome of evil, understands that if he makes the mission to find the girl personal for Gittes, there is little chance he'll fail in finding her. Cross makes it personal for Gittes by using his own daughter to unwittingly bait him. Cross hired the imposter to get Gittes to take the case knowing full well that his real daughter would confront Gittes after she discovered his investigation. [What is so incredible about the above information is that Towne never puts it on the page…it's information that the audience fills in themselves long after they've seen the actual movie.]

The theme/controlling idea of *Chinatown* is simply "evil reigns." No matter who we are and no matter how smart or tough we are, we cannot outsmart or out muscle evil. We are fated to either give in to evil figures like Noah Cross or we are fated to fight against tyranny pointlessly and ineffectively for the rest of our lives. Humanity is repugnant and dirty. Evil has won, always has won and always will win. Principled people with good intentions not only fail to bring justice to the world, by their very naiveté they empower tyrants.

Chinatown's Director Roman Polanski barely survived the Holocaust. Battling demons of his own, he unleashed them all in this effort.

While Towne's screenplay is a masterpiece, the controlling idea/theme of the movie is pure Polanski. What is so striking about *Chinatown*, a commercial Story with one of the most disturbing down endings of all time, is that Polanski's vision was so perfectly put onto the screen, in such a compelling way, that the dark message made sense. It satisfied the viewer. Polanski's art was so perfectly expressed; it made the average Joe willingly submit himself to confronting the very dark underbelly of humanity. That is remarkable.

Chinatown, like *The Silence of the Lambs*, is that very rare commercial Story with a deeply resonant and meaningful controlling idea/theme that is so perfectly crafted, it makes us confront the darkest realities of our being.

52

THE SUBPLOT

Subplot is the next level up from act in the long form Story.

Subplots are the added attractions for a Story and are best used to amplify the theme/controlling idea more aggressively or to counterbalance the global Story with irony.

A quick example would be the love Story in *The Sound of Music* between Liesl and her Austrian messenger boy Rolfe who ends up joining the Nazi Party. While the introduction of the young love is wonderfully engaging in the form of the song "Sixteen Going on Seventeen" in the Beginning Hook of the Story, by the end of the film that delightful innocence has been corrupted by the Nazis. This subplot would be an example of amplifying the theme...*Only a family that sticks together can defeat tyranny.*

Deciding when and where you need to employ a particular subplot is dependent upon the global Story you are trying to tell. Love Story subplots aid just about all of the External Content Genres (war, crime, thriller, performance, etc.).

And an action subplot in a global maturation/coming of age Story (like *Saturday Night Fever*'s gang fight subplot) can raise the temperature of a Global Internal Content Genre. If Tony Manero (played by John Travolta) was never physically threatened by his neighborhood, only spiritually threatened, I doubt his departure to Manhattan in the final scene would have much resonance.

Subplots have all of the same things that all units of Story have (Inciting Incidents, progressive complications, crisis, climax and resolution). But unlike the Global Story requirement that all of the big moments be on stage—witnessed by the reader/viewer—subplot's critical scenes (crisis, climax and resolution) often, by necessity, occur off stage. They can be announced or implied as having occurred off stage in dialogue to dynamically turn scenes. The details of these reported offstage events are often left mysterious, to be filled in by the reader/viewer's mind.

In the *Chinatown* example from the previous chapter on the act, the scenes from the Noah Cross subplot of his orchestrating the hiring of Jake Gittes to find his "granddaughter" are not on the page at all. The reader/viewer only discovers this subplot with the revelation close to the very end of the movie that the woman who was hired to portray Evelyn Mulwray (the Diane Ladd character) at the beginning of the movie has been murdered. Whoever the bad guy is must have hired her and then when Gittes tracked her down, had her murdered.

For another example, let's go back to William Goldman's screenplay adaptation of Stephen King's *Misery*. You'll recall that there is a crime Story subplot in addition to the abduction thriller global Story.

In the movie, Richard Farnsworth plays Buster, the local Sheriff of the Colorado town where writer Paul Sheldon crashes his car. Throughout the film, we see small snippets of Buster gathering information about the disappearance of Sheldon but we don't see all of the crime Story business on stage.

Goldman trusts that the viewer will piece together all of what Buster is up to. He understands that showing all of the investigation steps would not only slog down the pace of the global Story, it would disrespect the audience's intelligence. The audience already knows how a crime investigation ensues from having read and/or watched thousands of hours of crime fiction. So Goldman wisely lets the viewer do that work for him.

Instead he uses the climactic moment of his subplot crime Story…the discovery of the identity of the criminal…as a way to progressively complicate the climactic act of his global thriller Story.

Obviously the climax of his subplot (being it crime and external and active) is the perfect choice to put on stage. It moves his last act of the global thriller Story to the ultimate high. Just when we think someone is going to help Paul Sheldon... Buster shows up at Annie Wilke's house just about certain that she's up to no good...the viewer's hopes are dashed.

When Annie Wilkes kills Buster, all hope the viewer has that a third party will save Paul Sheldon is lost. The final confrontation between the antagonist (Annie) and the victim (Paul) is now one on one. The only person who can save Paul….is Paul. And his chances of doing so phy.sically are impossible. The only way he'll be able to do it is by using his mind.

Misery has one of the best "hero at the mercy of the villain" scenes ever written. The way Sheldon gets out of the jam is by using Annie's cheesy love of romance against her.

Let's go back to the love Story, as it is the most often used Genre for subplots. The reason it is used so often is that it's ideal to soften a particularly violent or horrific global Story (war, horror, thriller).

For example, all love stories must have the obligatory "Lovers Kiss" scene which is the critical moment of electricity that tells the characters their lives will be meaningless in the absence of the other. After the kiss, there is no going back to the life they enjoyed or endured before meeting.

Now if your global plot is a love Story, this obligatory scene (of course that does not mean that the way you write this scene is conventional or derivative) must be ON STAGE. That is, it must be an active scene in which the viewers/readers "watch" the two lovers kiss. [The novel *Atonement* by Ian McEwan and its film adaptation by Christopher Hampton both had the lovers kiss directly on stage. In this case, the war Story serves as subplot to the global love Story.]

But, if you are using love Story as a subplot to another global Genre, like a thriller, you may or may not have to put the "Lovers Kiss" obligatory scene on stage. For example, in *Die Hard* we know that John McClain, the lead character played by Bruce Willis, and his wife have already had their Lovers Kiss scene before the movie even began. The love Story subplot supports the action…the only reason McClain is in the building in the first place is to win back the love of his life. We know that these two people are meant to be together and that Willis will do anything to get Bonnie Bedelia to invite him back to their house for Christmas. If it means having to stop a group of terrorist/criminals to prove his love to her, so be it.

We don't need the backstory Lovers Kiss scene in the movie because the very circumstances of the thriller's setup have already done that work. This is an example of a subplot that picks up a Story in the middle of things. And that is absolutely fine to do for a subplot…and global plot too. Preferable even.

Whether or not to put obligatory/conventional scenes on stage for subplots is a very difficult decision. Putting them in just to show that you know they are required isn't a big enough reason to do so.

Often, writers use an obligatory scene from a subplot as a way to pay off a major global Story change. That is, they present what the reader will initially believe is a scene they've seen a million times before and turn it such that the climax actually reveals a huge change in the global Story. The payoff of the crime subplot in *Misery* is a prime example of that. We expect the criminal to be brought to justice in a conventional crime Story. Not only does that not happen, but the lead investigator is suddenly killed.

I suggest that the writer put all of his energy into crafting the global plot first before making decisions about where and when to pay off the subplots. Oftentimes, the writer subconsciously drops in subplot while concentrating on the global Story. Pay attention to these ideas as they are usually spot on!

It's been my experience that subplots are usually the work of the writer's subconscious. They somehow find themselves woven perfectly into a global Story without the writer even realizing they've done so. You can really drive yourself crazy over thinking the choices you've made with your subplots. I suggest you don't go overboard with subplot analysis unless you really have to.

Also, you need to remember that by Global Story climax, you need to have paid off all of the plots—the global and the subplots. To do so, obviously is not easy. But when it's done well, like in *Misery,* the payoffs are far more than the sum of their parts.

If you are having difficulty after you've gone through your first draft and have found that the climax of the global Story is just not mind-blowing...take a deep breath. Before you dump the whole global baby out with the bathwater, go back and look at your subplots. You may have omitted a key scene (left it off stage) in one of the subplots and failed to pay it off. That could be the big problem at the end of your Story. The solution to that problem is to figure out a way to combine the subplot climax and resolution with the climax and resolution of your global Story.

In *The Silence of the Lambs,* Thomas Harris uses multiple love stories as subplots in his global thriller—the Crawford/Bella love Story, the buddy friendship love Story between Starling and Ardelia Mapp, the father/daughter dynamic between Crawford/Starling, the budding romance between Starling and the scientist Pilcher at the Smithsonian, and of course the strange sadomasochistic May/December thing between Starling/Lecter.

Harris did not load in so much love Story by accident. He knew that to create killers like Buffalo Bill and Hannibal Lecter and put their gruesome actions on stage, he needed to counterbalance the Story with the opposite of their contempt for humanity...love for it.

53

THE GLOBAL STORY

As per our *Foolscap Global Story* Grid, Global Story has the same five elements as each of its component parts—an Inciting Incident, progressive complications, crisis, climax and resolution. Ideally, you "the editor" should be able to pinpoint exactly what beats, scenes, sequences, acts, and subplots in your Story combine to satisfy these requirements.

For example, your global Inciting Incident could be a positive shift in your External Content Genre that occurs in the third beat of the second scene in the first sequence of the first act of your global plot and a negative shift in the Internal Genre that occurs in the third beat of the second scene in the first sequence of the first act of the secondary subplot of your global plot.

But should you plan this stuff out before you begin writing your first draft?

Absolutely not! Don't do it. Seriously, you'll drive yourself crazy.

If you do, you will get an acute case of *Paralysis by Analysis*. Trust me, I battle *P by A* on every single thing I do. It's just the way my brain works when I face a particular problem. Maybe yours does too.

The trick is to combine just enough analysis to get you started (the *Foolscap Global Story Grid*), something to push you through to a first draft. Then and only then, when you have a pound of rough pages, should you dive into the hypercritical editorial pool. And once in that water, it should be your goal to stay in it for the least amount of time necessary to solve your Story problems. Use the macro analysis of the *Foolscap Global Story Grid* and the micro analysis of *The Story Grid Spreadsheet* (that's up next) to find out what problems you have. And then go about fixing them.

And you should refrain from ever speaking in the Story lexicon (Inciting Incident, progressive complications, blah

blah blah) to anyone who has any interest in reading your Story. You will bore them to tears and you will come off as quite mad. The exception of course is with fellow *Story Grid* nerds. Then you can go to town.

Remember that the first rule when editing a book is to DO NO HARM. Most of the books I've edited in my career never required the depths of detailed analysis that you could potentially mine from *The Story Grid*.

Could I have put the full *Story Grid* to bear on each and every one of them? Sure. But that is not the editor's job. The editor's job is to help the writer find peace with their work while also doing what's necessary to make the Story "work" as well as it possibly can.

Without driving the writer crazy!

If you are the writer and the editor (and you should be both) do your best to balance both forces within yourself. Allow the writer in you to have freedom. When you're writing don't think about all of this *Story Grid* editorial stuff. After you've set yourself a writing task (the lovers meet scene, for example) just write down whatever comes out. And then move on to the next assignment without editing the thing you just banged out.

Only after you have a full draft of something do you want to turn over the reins to your editor self.

Just as you gave your writer self freedom without harsh criticism while he was working, so you should allow your analytical/somewhat nutty inside baseball editor to do what he does without criticism too. Balancing the two sides of yourself is the goal.

When you feel like you're being too loosey goosey when you're editing, you probably are. And likewise, if you feel like you're being too tight and analytical when you are writing, you probably are. Listen to that stuff and clamp down or pull back as necessary.

But lastly, when you're noodling a new project, don't complicate for the sake of theory. Don't map out all sixty-four of your scenes in detail before you write them. Give yourself just enough guidance to keep your pen moving. No more, no less.

But when you have a draft, it's time to figure out what's working and what's not working. Then improve what's working and fix what's not.

The tool that will show you exactly where you need to focus is up next. I call it *The Story Grid Spreadsheet*.

PART SIX

THE STORY GRID SPREADSHEET

54

WHERE EDITORS BEGIN

Now that we've reviewed the five fundamentals of Story form (Inciting Incident, Progressive Complications, Crisis, Climax and Resolution) and the six units of Story (Beat, Scene, Sequence, Act, Subplot and Global Story), let's take a step back to the very beginning.

What does an editor do the minute a manuscript that he's commissioned lands on his desk?

Let's assume he's already read it.

The Story isn't working quite yet.

It's close, but it's vaguely disappointing.

There is no easy fix that comes into his mind. He knows that he'll have to do a comprehensive analysis of the work before he'll be able to give the right diagnosis and provide suggestions capable of helping the writer fix the problems.

The first editorial stage is to pull up a fresh *Story Grid Spreadsheet* and fill it in. This is no small task, but it is crucial to take a book that doesn't work to one that does.

As we are leading up to ***The Story Grid for The Silence of the Lambs***, let's create *The Story Grid Spreadsheet* for it too. So in the next few chapters, we'll walk through the data points on *The Story Grid Spreadsheet* column-by-column and row-by-row. These data points, when combined with *The Foolscap Global Story Grid,* will ultimately generate that very strange-looking infographic I shared with you at the very beginning of the book.

By the time we're through, you'll be able to walk through *The Story Grid* from left to right, from top to bottom and everywhere in between and intuit exactly how Thomas Harris created such an amazing Story.

We'll get there, I promise. It's the Ending Payoff of this book.

I have to confess at this very moment my blood is pumping. I'm excited. For a Story nerd, there is nothing more appealing than figuring out how a master writer put together his masterpiece.

55

TRACKING THE GLOBAL STORY

Scene, Word Count, Story Event

Once you have a first draft, you'll need to inspect each of the units of your Story and make sure you've used the right materials. Just like a building, you'll want to make sure that your Story will stand up to the test of time. This is what *The Story Grid* is all about. It's an editorial tool above all else.

What is also appealing about creating *The Story Grid* for your Story is that it requires you to use a completely different part of your brain. You can give your creative side a rest and dive completely into the analytics. For each and every scene you've written in your book, you'll now take inventory of what exactly you have in hand by writing down critical information in each column of *The Story Grid Spreadsheet*.

It's crucial to be very meticulous about the notations because the spreadsheet will be invaluable in pinpointing places where you went off course, missed a crucial scene or beat, and/or made minor continuity mistakes.

Spend the time making your notes in *The Story Grid Spreadsheet* succinct. But err on the side of being comprehensive in your first round. Trust me, you'll go through this spreadsheet so many times that, by the end of the process, you'll be able to boil down each scene in your book to a phrase.

And if you can't, you'll know the scene is too obtuse…not clear…in need of an overhaul.

Here's another major word of advice.

Don't stop and fix an obvious problem until you've completed the entire spreadsheet!

It is just about impossible to toggle between your creative side (writing the Story) and your analytical side (editing your

Story) simultaneously. You need to separate Church and State. The Writer and the Editor. When the Writer is doing his work, the Editor has to be on vacation...and when the Editor is doing his work, the Writer has to be on vacation.

You, the Editor, need to see the work as a whole, every single piece, before you'll be able to tackle revisions. If you revise before you've done a complete analysis, you'll find that your first instinct solutions will not work when viewed globally. That is, you may come up with a great idea to fix chapter 3, but if you actually do that revision, you may up fouling up the foundation for your best work in chapter 1 and your best work in chapter 18.

So don't do it, no matter how easy a fix you think it is, or how dreadfully terrible the scene is.

Not writing while you are editing is going to be as hard as it is to not revise your work while you're writing. But you can't give the Writer a working plan to fix all of the novel's problems as the Editor until you've digested the entire *Story Grid Spreadsheet*, put it together with the *Foolscap Global Story Grid* and mapped out the final *Story Grid.* After you've done all of that work, the problems AND THE SOLUTIONS TO THOSE PROBLEMS will be evident.

You must resist the temptation to revise before you have all of this work done. Seriously. If you don't, you'll add months if not years to your workload or you'll abandon it completely because you'll come to the conclusion that your work is unsalvageable. It's not!

THE EDITOR STAGE ONE

If you have a pile of pages completed and you are putting your editor hat on for the first time, the very first thing to do is to write out your list of fifty-odd scenes/chapters. In order to figure out what's going on in the Story, you need to know where everything is.

So when I take on a new editing job, I'll first sit down with the manuscript and a stapler. I'll go page by page and separate the entire book into its component scenes. There are usually between fifty and seventy scenes in a novel. So I'll have a pile of fifty to seventy packets.

I'll then turn on my computer and pull up a fresh Excel spreadsheet. As I will be analyzing *The Silence of the Lambs*, I'll label the file "*The Story Grid Spreadsheet for The Silence of the Lambs."* I've gone through *The Silence of the Lambs* and determined that Harris' sixty-one chapters break down to sixty-four scenes. Harris wisely chose to make each of his chapters a scene, with the exception of three chapters, which comprise two scenes stitched together.

Now on my spreadsheet, in the very first column, at the top I'll type **SCENE** and underneath, I'll write from 1 to 64 row to row.

Next to the **SCENE** column, I'll create another column called **WORD COUNT.** For this column, I'll simply add up the number of words for every single scene. For example, the first scene is the first chapter in *The Silence of the Lambs* and it runs for 1,690 words, so I'll type 1,690 in the corresponding cell for scene 1.

It's a grind to do this for every scene, but keeping track of the word count is invaluable. It will allow you as the editor to compare and contrast how you, the writer emphasized or deemphasized a particular scene just by its very length, and where you should trim and/or revise to best effect. It's not a lot of fun to run your cursor over a big patch of text just to get the word count number, but when you have the entire word count on a single spreadsheet, scene by scene, you've got some vital information.

When you the editor first finished reading the draft, you may have had a suspicion that a very minor scene went on far too long, while a critical scene was too short. Saying that you have a suspicion to a writer is one thing. Telling them exactly what scenes you are referring to and their respective word counts is far more helpful.

Actually showing the writer that, for example, his "getting a haircut" scene took six thousand words, while his "contemplating suicide" scene took less than one thousand is far more persuasive to get him to cut the haircut and pump up the suicide. There is no arguing when you have pinpointed information.

It should take you a full workday, perhaps two or three when you are just getting started, to complete these first two columns. I'd suggest that you assign yourself this task on Day One of Editing and no matter how long the process takes you, knock off for the day when you complete the work.

Editing requires very concentrated attention. When you get tired, you screw up. Just like writing. So until you're in the Editing groove, give yourself ample time to complete *The Story Grid* tasks.

THE EDITOR STAGE TWO

After you've filled in your scene numbers and word counts, it's time to fill in the next column on *The Story Grid Spreadsheet,* the **STORY EVENT** column. I recommend you read *A Practical Handbook for the Actor,* which was written by a group of actors from the Atlantic Theater Company to help you nail Story Events. I keep the book handy at all times.

The trick to filling out the **STORY EVENT** column is to reduce each scene to its essence, either a single sentence or a phrase that will tell you the gist of what has occurred in the scene. It's a great way to build a shorthand language with the writer too. You can refer to *The killer prepares* scene and know exactly where in the novel it takes place.

I also suggest that once you've completed this column you go out and buy a stack of 3 x 5 index cards and write down each scene on one card, along with its corresponding sequential number and word count. This is a technique I used back in college when I struggled through organic chemistry. On one side of the card, I'd draw you the structural diagram for a particular compound like Benzene, and on the other, I'd write the word Benzene. I'd walk around with a stack of these in my backpack at all times. So on my way to odd jobs or to the canteen for dinner, I'd be able to quiz myself and keep everything straight.

You can make notes about each of these scenes in your downtime and you'll be surprised at the kind of subconscious work your mind will be doing just lugging the cards around. Try it.

When you are first running through the book scene by scene, and coming up with the Story events for each, it could take anywhere from a day to a week or more of work. Don't kill yourself over getting the perfect description for every Story event. You'll end up tweaking just about all of them by the time you're through generating the full *Story Grid.*

Don't grind too hard now. Write down just enough so that you'll remember the scene as a unit. So later on, when you're thinking about the sequence of your Story, you'll think in terms of "The break-up scene" or "The battle for Constantinople scene" instead of the myriads of beats and details that will go into each.

Here's how I did it:

The first scene/chapter in *The Silence of the Lambs* can be summed up as **"FBI Section Chief Jack Crawford summons FBI trainee Clarice Starling and recruits her for 'an interesting errand.'"** And here is how the beginning of your *Story Grid Spreadsheet* will look:

SCENE	WORD COUNT	STORY EVENT
1	1,690	FBI Section Chief Jack Crawford summons FBI trainee Clarice Starling to recruit her for an 'interesting errand.'

Now it is simply a matter of going through the entire manuscript and generating a list of all of the scenes in their particular order with their word counts and their particular Story events.

If you discover (and you will) that one or more of your scenes do not have events, you'll find that these are the sorts of expositional passages that can be cut in your next draft. But for now, simply write down the core of activity. That is, "John walks to town" or "Susan thinks about ice cream" can be written in the Story Event column as placeholders. They aren't really events. They're stage business/ exposition. You'll fix them later.

Don't freak out if your scenes don't seem all that exciting yet. Even those shoe leather scenes that aren't really scenes are important to keep in that first draft. They are important because there is probably critical exposition in these passages that must be woven into the Story.

There will be plenty of time to evaluate the effectiveness of each scene's event later on. You didn't nail it perfectly on the first draft (who does?) but don't throw these "not working" scenes away or try and fix them yet. You need to see the full picture as an editor to make specific decisions later on.

Let's move forward.

So after a full workweek, we've got the first three columns together for our *Story Grid Spreadsheet*.

When I finished my spreadsheet's first three columns, I knew that *The Silence of the Lambs* is sixty-four scenes comprised of 96,299 words. I now knew its core component parts. That is a huge step forward.

Now it's time to break these sixty-four scenes down further to see just how and where Thomas Harris not only delivered the five commandments of Story form for each, but how he solved the knotty problem of abiding by all of the conventions and obligatory scenes of his chosen Genres.

56

TRACKING THE SCENE

Value Shift, Polarity Shift, Turning Point

The next three columns on *The Story Grid Spreadsheet* pinpoint the mechanics of each scene.

Essentially, the **VALUE SHIFT**, **POLARITY SHIFT** and **TURNING POINT** columns will tell you how each scene has moved the Story forward. You'll identify what value is at stake at the beginning of the scene and the value by the end of the scene. Then you'll determine whether that value has shifted from positive to negative or negative to positive. Lastly, you'll determine the precise moment in the scene when that shift occurred, the Turning Point.

These three columns will give you the perspective necessary to track the success of your Story form. That is whether your Inciting Incidents, progressive complications, crises, climaxes and resolutions in each scene are clearly defined. If you have to struggle to determine what value is at stake in your scene or if there was no discernable moment in the scene when it shifted from positive to negative or negative to positive, you'll know that you have more work to do on that scene.

Before I lay out these three columns for the sixty-four scenes in *The Silence of the Lambs*, some definitions and refreshers of fundamental Story principles are in order:

Story Value: These are human experiences that can shift in quality from positive to negative or negative to positive from moment to moment. For example happy/sad, wisdom/stupidity, love/hate, freedom/slavery, innocence/experience, etc. Every scene must turn a Story value or it is not a scene. It must start someplace (happy) and end somewhere else (sad) or there is no movement, no change and the Story stops dead in its tracks.

Polarity Shift: The polarity shift is simply shorthand for the value valence change from +/- or -/+. Remember that change can occur in a scene that moves from good to great or bad to worse too. +/++ and -/-- are perfectly valid polarity shifts and are essential to building the thriller's progressive complications. Choosing when to escalate the complications in your overall Story can make or break it from one that "works" to "doesn't work."

Turning Point: the precise beat when the value in the scene shifts from positive to negative or negative to positive etc. Turning points can either happen through action (a bomb blows up) or revelation. ("I'm you're father, Luke.")

You can see the Value Shift, Polarity Shift and Turning Point columns for *The Silence of the Lambs* in the long spreadsheet at the end of this part of the book. You'll notice that I've categorized the turning points as either turning on "action" or "revelation."

Tracking the quality of the turning points is important, as it will give you a sense of flow and continuity of your Story. If you are turning your scenes the same way over and over again, it would be good to know that, right?

Repetitious turns will turn off a reader or viewer subconsciously. They won't know exactly why they're losing the ability to suspend their disbelief in your Story, but they will.

No matter how great the scene is, if it is the tenth straight scene that turns on revelation, you will bore your audience. You've got to mix it up and surprise the reader at every opportunity. So if they are expecting some big revelation to happen, it's best to throw down some action. And vice versa.

THE EDITOR STAGE THREE

Now it's time for you to go through all of your scenes and evaluate your value shifts, polarity shifts and turning points. Take your time doing so and be brutally honest with yourself. This process could take as long as two weeks to complete. Set yourself a reasonable goal each day. *Today I will evaluate ten scenes.*

Remember that we all have a tendency to protect ourselves from criticism by writing down "what we intended to do" as opposed to "what we really did" on the page. And we become more and more susceptible to that temptation when we've been slaving in the analytical mines all day. So take your time and do this piecemeal. And again, don't rewrite now. Wait until you've finished your *Story Grid* before you set yourself to that task.

It's okay if you want to write down what you intended to do as well as what you actually did if that will allow you to be truthful. What you don't want to do is write down what is not on the page. Remember that no one in the universe will look at your *Story Grid Spreadsheet*. Nor would they really understand what it means anyway. The last thing you want to do is lie to yourself about what is actually on the page. You need to remind yourself that you are going to fix the problems in due course. This is the time to find the problems, not to sweep them under the rug.

So if you find that your first ten scenes do not turn or there is no clear value at stake, but a whole slew of values, or that you've used the same polarity shift over and over again, don't sweat it. Just barrel through and write down the truth of every scene in your first draft and leave the "solution" stage for another time.

FINDING THE PROBLEMS IS THE EDITOR'S #1 JOB

This first draft spreadsheet round is all about finding the problems.

It's not about solving the problems.

The only way to solve all of the problems in your draft is to have them all clearly listed in front of you. So you must force yourself to keep the Writer on vacation and also don't overwork the Editor. Pace yourself. You may not think that you are getting anywhere, but you are. When you finish *The Story Grid Spreadsheet*, you'll be able to go through it over and over again and mine seriously valuable insight. But if your spreadsheet is not complete or there are intentions and not actualities listed in it, it will do you little good. It will be more of an excuse list than a helpful tool.

Think of *The Story Grid Spreadsheet* like a knife. You must hone it and keep it razor sharp so that when you need to cut or re-envision a scene, you'll know exactly where to do it and more importantly WHY to do it. The How of doing it will also come to you over time. Not now, but when you least expect it. Let the writer deal with the How later. You'll be amazed by how smart that guy is.

57

TRACKING CONTINUITY

Point of View, Period/Time, Duration, Location Onstage Characters, Offstage Characters

The last six columns in *The Story Grid Spreadsheet* concern Story continuity.

These are important to track so that you keep all of the setting, time, and character entrances and exits in sync. On the screen, continuity glitches can take the viewer right out of the experience. We've all seen movies where a character is smoking a long cigarette in one scene. And then the shot cuts to another character and then back to the cigarette smoker who is now holding a drink with no cigarette in sight. Those continuity glitches aren't just distracting; they ruin the viewer's ability to suspend their disbelief. The same thing can happen in a novel or play.

The Story Grid Spreadsheet is the place to keep track of all of the little details that can sabotage the finest of stories.

Again, this is pure analytical labor. It takes serious concentration. So, I'd suggest doing only a limited amount of this work per day. Set a goal to do ten scenes and then shut it down and walk the dog. You can get seriously hinky if you try and knock off these details in a day. Take your time. The more accurate the spreadsheet is, the more helpful it will be.

Here are the column headings with brief descriptions:

Point of View is the vantage point from which the reader/viewer sees the fictional world. You'll see that Thomas Harris uses nine different points of view in *The Silence of the Lambs*.

Here is a chart of all nine along with the number of scenes each has in the novel.

	Number of Scenes			
	BH	MB	EP	TOTAL
Starling POV	10	17	5.5	32.5
Crawford POV	2	5	3	10
Catherine Martin POV	0	3	0	3
Authorial POV	0	2	2	4
Buffalo Bill/Jame Gumb POV	0	2	2.5	4.5
Hannibal Lecter POV	0	4	1	5
Senator Martin POV	0	1	0	1
Police/FBI/Paramedic POV	0	2	1	3
Ardelia Mapp POV	0	0	1	1
	12	36	16	64

Where Harris chose to switch points of view were critical decisions. The way you choose to approach point of view is no less crucial. Track them and you'll be able to experiment. If you don't track them, you won't know how you handled this crucial Storytelling device from scene to scene. And that is just silly not to know.

Period/Time is simply the time of day, hour, weekday, month or year that the scene is taking place. For example, late afternoon, Thursday February 6 is a very specific period and time designation. The more specific you are with the period and time in each of your scenes, the better. If you are unable to pinpoint exactly when the scene you've written has taken place, you need to figure that out. If you don't know, the reader certainly won't either.

Why would you ever want to lose a reader because they are confused about the time in a scene? Thomas Harris embedded all of the information necessary to map out the exact time and day of his Story. I figured it out. You have to be able to do it too.

Duration describes the approximate length of time the scene took to occur. If it's a meeting, chances are it won't last longer than fifteen minutes. If it's a long chase action scene, the duration could be much longer. You need to choose how long your scene will play out. Again, specificity and variety are keys to holding a reader's interest. One meeting scene after another will bore them to tears. And action scene, action scene, action scene will suck the life out of them.

Location is literally where the scene is taking place. Again be as specific as possible.

Onstage Characters column is a literal list of all of the characters present in the scene. It's important to have a keen understanding of who is on stage in every single scene. If someone never appears on stage and is just referred to, that choice will have a very big impact on how the reader imagines them. I also track the total number of players on stage and place the number next to the list in a separate column. Again we don't want the same characters over and over again in the same combinations. We want variety.

Offstage Characters are the people who are not in the scene but are referred to by the people on stage. This is especially important when tracking "speeches in praise of villains" in thrillers and in establishing relationships between characters. If your onstage characters never refer to any offstage characters, the scene will not feel authentic. The first thing we all do in a conversation is refer to other people. If your characters don't do that in your Story, they will not come off as "real." I also track the total number of players mentioned off stage in the scene and place the number next to the list.

58

THE STORY GRID SPREADSHEET FOR *THE SILENCE OF THE LAMBS*

SCENE	WORD COUNT	STORY EVENT	VALUE SHIFT	POLARITY SHIFT	TURNING POINT	POINT OF VIEW
1	1690	FBI trainee Clarice Starling is summoned by FBI Section Chief Jack Crawford and recruited for "an interesting errand."	Ignored to Chosen	-/+	Action Crawford gives Starling a job	Omniscient Intracranial Clarice Starling Her thoughts in Italics
2	1821	After his clumsy advances are rebuffed, Dr. Frederick Chilton torments Starling as he ushers her underground to meet Dr. Hannibal Lecter.	Chosen for Merit to Used as Bait to Chosen	+/-	Revelation The reality of FBI Life vs. Fantasy and Lecter's ferocity	Omniscient Intracranial Clarice Starling Her thoughts in Italics
3	2923	Starling meets Lecter, who is amused by her but contemptuous until she proves her mettle, then he gives her a valentine.	Unwanted to Welcomed	-/+	Revelation Lecter knows Starling better than she knows herself. How will he use that knowledge?	Omniscient Intracranial Clarice Starling Her thoughts in Italics
4	1003	Starling seizes the opportunity to dig deeper into the Lecter case, but is rebuffed by Crawford when she offers to help. (Speech in praise of the villian Lecter inside of the Raspail case file)	Encouraged to Discouraged	+/-	Action Crawford says "no."	Omniscient Intracranial Clarice Starling Her thoughts in Italics
5	525	Crawford tends his comatose and dying wife and then reassures himself that he is not dying. In fact he is well.	Death to Life	-/+	Revelation Crawford lives in death	Omniscient Jack Crawford
6	1637	In a note, Crawford praises Starling's Lecter report and rewards her with clearance to follow up on the Raspail car clue from Lecter but she fails to track down the whereabouts of the car. (Obligatory Investigation and red herring scene)	Success to Failure	+/-	Revelation Car was destroyed	Omniscient Intracranial Clarice Starling Her thoughts in Italics

PERIOD/TIME	DURATION	LOCATION	ONSTAGE CHARACTERS	NUMBER	OFFSTAGE CHARACTERS	NUMBER
Thursday Morning 6-Feb	Fifteen Minutes	Bottom Floor, half buried in earth FBI Academy Quantico,Virginia In suite of offices	FBI Trainee Clarice Starling Section Chief of the FBI's Behavioral Sciences Dept. Jack Crawford	2	"people who do not ask for favors" "Berry's stuff" "my father was a marshal" "thirty-two known serial murderers" Serial Killer Psychiatrist Dr. Hannibal Lecter "Hannibal the Cannibal" Serial Killer "Buffalo Bill" Director of the Baltimore State Hospital for the Criminally Insane Dr. Chilton Prince Andrew Will Graham Red Dragon Francis Dolarhyde Picaso Nurse "The Director"	13
Friday 11:30 a.m. 7-Feb	Fifteen Minutes	Baltimore State Hospital for the Criminally Insane	58-year-old Dr. Frederick Chilton Clarice Starling Alan (orderly outside Chilton's office...) Barney (subterranean orderly) A voice (Miggs)	5	"a lot of detectives" Dr. Lecter Special Agent Jack Crawford Office girls Nurse Lecter mangled Doctors Aldo Ray	7
Friday 11:45 a.m. 7-Feb "Valentine's Day is only a week away"	Thirty Minutes	Baltimore State Hospital for the Criminally Insane	Clarice Starling, trainee Hannibal Lecter Barney Miggs	4	Jack Crawford Frederick Chilton, Ph.D. Alan Reporter Miggs (Multiple) Will Graham Buffalo Bill Benjamin Raspail How many women has Buffalo Bill "used?" (Five) "your mother" West Virginia Starlings or Okie Starlings? "his face" Census taker	17
Friday Afternoon into Late Evening 7-Feb	Eight Hours	Outside Hospital Back to Quantico	Clarice Starling Jack Crawford Ardelia Mapp	3	Lecter Raspail President of Baltimore Philharmonic Conductor of Baltimore Philharmonic Raspail's Family Other Lecter victim families Everett Yow Miggs	8
Friday Evening 7-Feb (2 days since she spoke)	Five Minutes	Crawford Home Arlington, Virginia	53-year-old Jack Crawford Bella	2	Day nurse	1
Monday Morning 10-Feb to Wednesday 12-Feb 4:00 p.m.	Two and a Half Days	FBI Academy Quantico, Virginia	Clarice Starling John Brigham, firearms instructor Lomax Bardwell A foreman at Sipper Salvage Ardelia Mapp Dr. Chilton's Secretary	6	Jack Crawford The Director Raspail Personnel at the Baltimore County Courthouse A Friendly Clerk Buddy Sipper	10

SCENE	WORD COUNT	STORY EVENT	VALUE SHIFT	POLARITY SHIFT	TURNING POINT	POINT OF VIEW
7	682	Crawford tells Starling about Miggs' death and then schools her with the "ass u me" deconstruction. Gives her the opportunity to follow the Raspail clue further.	Discouraged to Encouraged	-/+	Action Crawford gives new assignment	Omniscient Intracranial Clarice Starling
8	70	Letter poem from Lecter, "Sorry about Bella, Jack." to Jack Crawford of condolence for Bella	Dismissive to Concerned	+/-	Revelation Lecter knows about Bella but not from Starling	Omniscient Jack Crawford
9	3620	Starling and Yow go to storage unit Starling finds Lecter's "valentines"and the head in the jar	Progress to Breakthrough	+/++	Revelation Head in Jar	Omniscient Intracranial Clarice Starling Her thoughts in Italics
10	662	News team monitoring police channel shows up before cops after Starling calls in "the head in the jar". While Starling prevents them from getting inside her aggression doing so is filmed and she becomes the "story".	Stymied to Victorious	+/-	Action Starling stops Media	Omniscient
11	1505	Starling goes to see Lecter after securing the mini storage area by calling for backup. "Why don't you ask me about Buffalo Bill?" Lecter admits to killing Raspail and eating his sweetbreads. Lecter asks for a view and says he'll help with BB if Crawford agrees to give it to him. Buffalo Bill has a two story house.	Confident to Confused to Informed	+/-/+	Action Gets Lecter to Talk	Omniscient Intracranial Clarice Starling Her thoughts in Italics
12	1758	Starling in school, pulled out, given a gun and told to meet Crawford at a Quantico airstrip. She's going to help fingerprint BB's latest "floater". Crawford gives her the BB case file to read on the plane.	Humiliated to Proud	-/+	Action Starling gets called up to the Majors	Omniscient Intracranial Clarice Starling Her thoughts in Italics
13	2165	Starling reads the BB file, killed at least 5 in last 10 months, skinned post mortem dumps them in River…lots of exposition Crawford goes over where they are headed.	Glamour to Grotesquery	+/-	Revelation The Killer File	Omniscient Intracranial Clarice Starling Her thoughts in Italics
14	3776	Potter, West Virginia fingerprinting	Clueless to Evidence	-/+	Revelation moth in mouth	Omniscient Intracranial Clarice Starling Her thoughts in Italics

PERIOD/TIME	DURATION	LOCATION	ONSTAGE CHARACTERS	NUMBER	OFFSTAGE CHARACTERS	NUMBER
					Lecter Dr. Chilton The Coroner The District Attorney	
Wednesday 12-Feb 4:00 p.m.	Fifteen Minutes	FBI Academy Quantico, Virginia	Jack Crawford Clarice Starling	2	Miggs Lecter Chilton Overnight Orderly Raspail Everett Yow	6
Wednesday 12-Feb 4:15 p.m.	One Minute	FBI Academy Quantico, Virginia	Jack Crawford	1	Hannibal Lecter	1
Saturday 15-Feb Evening, Dark	Three Hours	Baltimore Split City Mini-Storage (Baltimore City split from Baltimore County in 1851)	Clarice Starling Everett Yow	2	Raspail Bernard Gary Miggs Starling's Father Starling's Brother	5
Saturday 15-Feb Evening, Dark	Twenty Minutes		Jonette Johnson Clarice Starling Everett Yow Assistant Cameraman. Harry Cameraman	5	Authorities WEYE Mobile unit	2
Saturday 15-Feb Later that Evening	Thirty Minutes	Baltimore State Hospital for the Criminally Insane	Clarice Starling Hannibal Lecter	2	Buffalo Bill Miggs Raspail Klaus (R's Lover) Jack Crawford	5
Monday 17-Feb Morning	One Hour	FBI Academy Quantico, Virginia to Airborne on Blue Canoe	Clarice Starling Brigham. gunnery sergeant	2	Jonetta Johnston Hannibal Lecter National Tattler Melvin Purvis Ardelia Mapp Jack Crawford Buffalo Bill Marine Jimmy Price Bella Gramm and Rudman	11
Monday 17-Feb Morning	Forty-Five Minutes	Airborne to Potter West Virginia	Clarice Starling Jack Crawford	2	Will Graham (Crawford's last protégé) Jimmy Price Buffalo Bill The Bimmel Girl from Belvedere Ohio The next one he grabbed The one after has never been identified The Varner woman The Kittridge girl from Pittsburgh	8
Monday 17-Feb Early afternoon	Three Hours	Potter Funeral Home	Clarice Starling Jack Crawford Sheriff's Deputy Dr. Akin two young, one old deputy two state troopers Chief Deputy deputy Sheriffs and troopers Oscar "Jess"	14	Someone from DA's office Sheriff Perkins Mrs. Perkins Field services commander from Charleston Some officers from CIS "Claxton" Buffalo Bill Mountain midwife "her" "her folks"	25

SCENE	WORD COUNT	STORY EVENT	VALUE SHIFT	POLARITY SHIFT	TURNING POINT	POINT OF VIEW
15	1160	Crawford and Starling talk about the case, Starling is dropped at Smithsonian to get information about bug cocoon. Before she leaves Crawford explains why he disrespected her at Potter, WV proving that he cares about her feelings.	Respect to Intimacy	+/++	Action Crawford tells Starling why	Omniscient Clarice Starling NO THOUGHTS IN ITALICS
16	2287	Starling gets information about bug cocoon.	Capable to Incisive	++/+++	Revelation Cocoon was homegrown, not indigenous to U.S.	Omniscient Intracranial Clarice Starling Her thoughts in Italics
17	999	Catherine Baker Martin is abducted.	Progress to Failure	+++/---	Revelation The woman's mother is U.S. Senator	Omniscient Catherine Baker Martin
18	330	Procedures for Senate Member Family abduction authorial exposition	N/A	N/A	N/A	Omniscient Reportage
19	344	Crawford gets call from FBI Director and they talk about what to do next. Senator sends a lear jet to pick up Crawford and take him to Memphis.	Contained to Unbounded	--/---	Revelation Six/Seven Days before she's dead	Omniscient Jack Crawford
20	2576	Starling learns of abduction. Left out of Memphis trip. Called back in after a day cooling her jets in class at Quantico.	Outside to Inside	-/+	Action Crawford calls Starling back onto the case	Omniscient Intracranial Clarice Starling Her thoughts in Italics

PERIOD/TIME	DURATION	LOCATION	ONSTAGE CHARACTERS	NUMBER	OFFSTAGE CHARACTERS	NUMBER
					Granny women, wise women, Herb healers Dr. Lecter Lamar "the girl from Akron" Billy Petrie Jabbo Franklin Bubba Franklin Duke Keomuka Satellite Monroe Game warden Dorothy FBI switchboard wire room across Country Major wire rooms in the East 3 officers from WVA CSI	
Monday 17-Feb Evening	Twenty Minutes	Car ride to FBI headquarters	Jeff (Crawford Driver) Jack Crawford Clarice Starling	3	Hannibal Lecter Buffalo Bill Mengel case Jane Doe J. Edgar Hoover	5
Monday 17-Feb Evening to Early Morning Tuesday 18-Feb	Four Hours	Smithsonian Museum of Natural History	Guard at Smithsonian Clarice Starling Noble Pilcher Albert Roden Ardelia Mapp	5	Jack Crawford Smithsonian chairman Buffalo Bill The Black Witch Moth	4
Early Morning Tuesday 18-Feb	Fifteen Minutes	East Memphis Tennessee Stonehinge Villas	Catherine Baker Martin Her Best Boyfriend Buffalo Bill/Jame Gumb	3	Mom Junior U.S. Senator from Tennessee	2
2:45 a.m. Tuesday 18-Feb to 6:30 a.m.	Four Hours	Memphis FBI Washington D.C.	N/A	N/A	Memphis Special Agent in Charge Senator Ruth Martin FBI technicians The Reactive Squad The Hostage Rescue Team Catherine Baker Martin	6
6:30 a.m. Tuesday 18-Feb	Three minutes	Crawford's Car at a rest stop Arlington, VA	Jack Crawford Director of FBI (Alpha 4) (Tommy)	2	Catherine Martin Phil Adler from White House President Senator Martin Bella	5
7:50 a.m. Tuesday 18-Feb	Twelve Hours	FBI Academy Quantico, Virginia to Smithsonian	Clarice Starling Gracie Pitman Crawford's Secretary Ardelia Mapp Jack Crawford	5	Ardelia Mapp Burroughs Stafford Jack Crawford Catherine Martin Buffalo Bill Dr. Alan Bloom of U of Chicago Francis Dolarhyde Garrett Hobbs Stevie Wonder Emily Dickinson Albert Roden Hot Bobby Lowrance Starling's Father brothers and sister memory of her mother Jeff (Crawford's driver)	16

SCENE	WORD COUNT	STORY EVENT	VALUE SHIFT	POLARITY SHIFT	TURNING POINT	POINT OF VIEW
21	1121	Starling hears from Crawford that Buffalo Bill killed Klaus (bug in his throat too) and not Raspail, like Lecter said…Starling has to talk to Lecter again.	Being Useful to Being Used	+/-	Revelation There was a cocoon in Klaus' throat	Omniscient Intracranial Clarice Starling Her thoughts in Italics
22	1440	Crawford explains that Lecter must know who Buffalo Bill is and that he's playing a very long game	A tool to a Colleague	-/+	Action Crawford sends Starling back to talk to Lecter again	Omniscient Intracranial Clarice Starling Her thoughts in Italics
23	934	Jame Gumb singing in shower tucking penis and testicles behind legs.	Life to Death	+/-	Revelation The killer's state of mind	Omniscient Reportage
24	770	Starling meets with Chilton again before gaining entry to Lecter.	Vulnerable to In control	-/+	Action Starling humiliates Chilton to get what she wants	Omniscient Intracranial Clarice Starling Her thoughts in Italics
25	2654	Starling interviews Lecter.	In control to Vulnerable	+/-	Action Quid Pro Quo Revelation He wants a vest with tits on it.	Omniscient Clarice Starling NO THOUGHTS IN ITALICS
26	1202	Catherine Martin in the hole washing	Captive to Prey	-/--	Revelation fingernail from another woman in the hole	Omniscient Catherine Martin
27	707	Starling calls Crawford outside the Maximum Security after her Lecter meeting.	In control to Being used	+/-	Action Starling confronts Crawford about being used	Omniscient Intracranial Clarice Starling Her thoughts in Italics
28	2609	Another Lecter/Starling Interview Faustian bargain soul for worldly gain	Vulnerable to Powerful	-/+	Revelation BB was turned down for sex change	Omniscient Clarice Starling
29	1264	Lecter gets cell cleaned. Remembers Raspail's story about Jame Gumb.	A Break to a Breakthrough	+/++	Revelation Identity of Jame Gumb and relationship to Raspail Action Lecter's routine changed	Omniscient Intracranial Lecter His thoughts in Italics
30	1231	Chilton confronts Lecter in his cell, threatens him, then facilitates his escape	Contained to Released	++/--	Action Chilton switches the deal Lecter will be sent to Tennessee	Omniscient Intracranial Lecter His thoughts in Italics

PERIOD/TIME	DURATION	LOCATION	ONSTAGE CHARACTERS	NUMBER	OFFSTAGE CHARACTERS	NUMBER
Tuesday 18-Feb Evening	One Hour	Smithsonian	Smithsonian Guard Clarice Starling Jack Crawford Jerry Burroughs Klaus (head) Bobby	6	Catherine Martin Dr. Angel Raspail Buffalo Bill Hannibal Lecter	5
Tuesday 18-Feb Evening	Thirty-Seven Minutes (37 miles to hospital from Smithsonian)	Surveillance Van to Baltimore State Hospital for the Criminally Insane	Clarice Starling Jack Crawford Jeff (Crawford's driver)	3	Hannibal Lecter Raspail Klaus Will Graham Alan Bloom Buffalo Bill Catherine Martin Senator Martin Night nurse Frederick Chilton	10
Tuesday 18-Feb Evening	Twenty-Five Minutes	Jame Gumb House	Jame Gumb Dog, Precious person in well	3	Fats Waller	1
Tuesday 18-Feb Evening 10:00 p.m.	Ten Minutes	Baltimore State Hospital for the Criminally Insane	Clarice Starling Frederick Chilton Alonzo	3	Hannibal Lecter Baltimore D.A.	2
Tuesday 18-Feb Evening	Ten Minutes	Baltimore State Hospital for the Criminally Insane	Alonzo Clarice Starling Barney the orderly Hannibal Lecter	4	Jane Austen Catherine Martin the Late Miggs Jack Crawford Sammie the new Miggs Eldridge Cleaver Senator Martin	7
Tuesday 18-Feb Evening	Twenty Minutes	Jame Gumb House Basement	Catherine Martin Jame Gumb Precious	3	Senator Martin	1
Wednesday 19-Feb 2:00 a.m.	Five Minutes	Orderlies' Lounge Baltimore State Hospital for the Criminally Insane	Clarice Starling Jack Crawford	2	Kimberly Jane Emberg Hannibal Lecter Catherine Martin Buffalo Bill Alonzo Barney, the orderly	6
Wednesday 19-Feb Early a.m.	Forty-Five Minutes	Baltimore State Hospital for the Criminally Insane	Hannibal Lecter Clarice Starling Barney, the orderly	3	Buffalo Bill Frederick Chilton	2
Wednesday 19-Feb Daybreak	Fifteen Minutes	Baltimore State Hospital for the Criminally Insane	Hannibal Lecter Barney, the orderly	3	Raspail Jame Gumb Klaus	3
Wednesday 19-Feb Daybreak	Fifteen Minutes	Baltimore State Hospital for the Criminally Insane	Frederick Chilton Hannibal Lecter	2	Starling Jack Crawford Klaus Bella Crawford Senator Martin Buffalo Bill	6

SCENE	WORD COUNT	STORY EVENT	VALUE SHIFT	POLARITY SHIFT	TURNING POINT	POINT OF VIEW
31	1594	Crawford tries to get transsexual info from Johns Hopkins. Gives doctor an hour then finds out about Chilton's ploy and Lecter's departure for Tennessee. Tells Director to let them go. TURNING POINT Crawford knows that someone will die at Lector's hand if he's taken out of Baltimore. Let's them go because he needs Lecter to solve case.	Failure to Win to Setback	-/+/-	Action Crawford tells FBI to let Lecter go.	Omniscient Crawford Intracranial His thoughts in Italics
32	481	Lecter put on the plane to Tennessee.	Locked up to Outside	+/-	Action Barney taken off Lecter detail	Omniscient Reportage
33	556	Starling gets news from Crawford about Chilton's screw up at Howard Johnson's. She sews the frayed part of her blazer. She won't have a problem getting to her gun like her father had.	Outside to Inside	-/+	Action Starling fixes coat	Omniscient Starling Intracranial Her thoughts in Italics
34	3033	Crawford picks up Starling.	Protégé to Colleague	+/++	Action Starling gets Lecter's stuff from his cell	Omniscient Crawford Intracranial
35	1695	Senator Martin interviews Lecter in Tennessee	Cold to Hot	-/+	Revelation BB is Billy Rubin	Omniscient Senator Martin Intracranial Thoughts in Italics
36	1126	Jame Gumb considers his moths in his basement black room with night vision goggles.	Contemplative to Active Gumb will kill the next day	+/-	Revelation Harvest in 24 to 48 hours	Omniscient Jame Gumb Intracranial
37	4085	Starling goes to Catherine Martin's house to find out about her. *not letting rage and frustration keep you from thinking...*	Wanted to Unwanted	+/-	Revelation Catherine had acid and dirty pictures Action Starling told to go back to DC	Omniscient Starling Intracranial Thoughts in Italics
38	3014	Starling meets with Lecter at old courthouse.	Out to Back in	-/+	Revelation He covets	Omniscient Starling Intracranial Her thoughts in Italics

PERIOD/TIME	DURATION	LOCATION	ONSTAGE CHARACTERS	NUMBER	OFFSTAGE CHARACTERS	NUMBER
Wednesday 19-Feb Morning	Thirty Minutes	Gender Identity Clinic Johns Hopkins Office	Jack Crawford Dr. Danielson Jeff the driver	3	Alan Bloom Buffalo Bill Catherine Martin Senator Martin the Director Chilton Attorney General of Maryland Governor of Maryland Hannibal Lecter	9
Wednesday 19-Feb Morning	Fifteen Minutes	Tarmac in Baltimore	Frderick Chilton State Troopers Barney, the orderly Hannibal Lecter	4	Guards in Tennessee Sammie	2
Wednesday 19-Feb Morning	Ten Minutes	Bad Motel Near Hospital for the Criminally Insane Bedroom	Starling	1	Frederick Chilton Jack Crawford Starling's mother The crow from her childhood	4
Wednesday 19-Feb Morning	Ten Minutes	Walking outside Hospital	Jack Crawford Clarice Starling Jeff Barney	4	Frederick Chilton Catherine Martin Senator Martin Jimmy Hoffa Tylenol Killer Lecter Buffalo Bill Klaus Raspail	9
Wednesday 19-Feb Morning	One Hour	Memphis Air National Guard hangar Briefing Room (office)	Senator Martin Jack Crawford Hannibal Lecter Frederick Chilton Brian Gossage	5	Dr. Allan Bloom Catherine Martin Paul Krendler from Justice Major Bachman from the Tennessee Bureau of Investigation Buffalo Bill Hostage Rescue Team Clarice Starling William "Billy" Rubin Benjamin Raspail	9
Wednesday 19-Feb Morning	Fifteen Minutes	Jame Gumb House basement	Jame Gumb Catherine Martin	2	Unknown bodies in basement	1
Wednesday 19-Feb Morning	One Hour	Stonehinge Villas East Memphis Catherine's bedroom	Clarice Starling Tennessee state trooper at apt Senator Martin Paul Krendler Brian Gossage A technician several policemen	7	Catherine Martin Hannibal Lecter Mr. Copley Jack Crawford Billy Rubin Buffalo Bill Frederick Chilton Bella Kimberly from Potter West Virginia three Seans	10
Wednesday 19-Feb Afternoon	One Hour	Old Memphis Courthouse Top Floor	Clarice Starling Hannibal Lecter Vernon Pembry, T.W. guard on Lecter floor Sergeant C.L. Tate three state trooper guards	6	FBI Agent Copley Frederick Chilton Billy Rubin Deputy Assistant Attorney General Krendler Jack Crawford Marcus Aurelius	6

SCENE	WORD COUNT	STORY EVENT	VALUE SHIFT	POLARITY SHIFT	TURNING POINT	POINT OF VIEW
39	2319	Lecter escapes.	Imprisoned to Free	+/-	Revelation Metal in mouth	Omniscient Hannibal Lecter
40	2603	Lecter Escapes II	Imprisoned to Free	-/--	Revelation Pembry's alive	Omniscient Sergeant Tate
41	335	Lecter escapes to airport in ambulance.	Free to Freer	--/---	Action Ambulance goes to Airport	Omniscient Attendant Point of View
42	1821	Crawford explains to Starling and the reader how Lecter did it. Starling is in deep trouble. She'll be recycled if she doesn't stop working the case.	Safety to Risk	+/-	Revelation If Starling keeps working the case she'll be recycled	Omniscient Starling Intracranial Her thoughts in Italics
43	1284	Pilcher explains the significance of the moth…skull on its wings named for two rivers in hell. Customs forms could help her find the importer. Very rare.	Good even Better	+/++	Revelation Moth is very rare someone raised it	Omniscient Starling Intracranial
44	1567	Catherine strategizing how to kill him. She gets the dog close to falling down the well but is unsuccessful.	Capture to Release	+/-	Action Precious doesn't fall into hole	Omniscient Catherine Martin Intracranial Her thoughts in Italics
45	579	Crawford learns that Lecter was bullshitting about "Billy Rubin".	Bad to Worse	-/--	Revelation Lecter leaves message that Billy Rubin is dead end.	Omniscient Crawford Intracranial
46	531	Lecter in St. Louis, Marcus Hotel	Bad to Worse	--/---	Revelation Lecter took car not plane	Omniscient Hannibal Lecter
47	561	Starling comes back and gets help from Mapp.	Bad to it's going to be Okay	-/+	Revelation Starling will beat the hearing	Omniscient Starling Intracranial

PERIOD/TIME	DURATION	LOCATION	ONSTAGE CHARACTERS	NUMBER	OFFSTAGE CHARACTERS	NUMBER
Wednesday 19-Feb 6:00 p.m.	One Hour	Old Memphis Courthouse Top floor	Officer Pembry Office Boyle Hannibal Lecter	3	Frederick Chilton Clarice Starling	2
Wednesday 19-Feb 6:30 p.m.	One Hour	Old Memphis Courthouse Top floor to Bottom	15 Policemen Sergeant Tate 2 Relief Corrections officers Sweeney (collects the tray) Berry Howard Bobby Jacobs Murray Officer Johnny Peterson	10	Hannibal Lecter Pembry Boyle Catherine Martin	4
Wednesday 19-Feb 7:00 p.m.	Fifteen Minutes	Ambulance	Ambulance attendant Ambulance driver Hannibal Lecter	3	N/A	N/A
Wednesday 19-Feb 7:00 p.m.	One Hour	Crawford's House Arlington, VA Study	Clarice Starling Jack Crawford Nurse	3	Bella Copley in Memphis Hannibal Lecter Burroughs Frederick Chilton Krendler Senator Martin Billy Rubin Alan Bloom (never on stage) FBI Assistant Director John Golby The Chief Gunny, John Brigham Catherine Martin Klaus The Pilcher Fellow from Smithsonian Crawford's driver Jeff	15
Wednesday 19-Feb 8:30 p.m.	One Hour	Smithsonian Insect Zoo	Clarice Starling Smithsonian guard Pilcher	3	Wilhelm von Ellenbogen Dr. Roden	2
Wednesday 19-Feb 9:30 p.m.	Fifteen Minutes	Jame Gumb's House in the well	Catherine Baker Martin Precious Jame Gumb	3	Martin's housekeeper, Bea Love	1
Thursday 20-Feb 12:30 a.m.	Ten Minutes	Crawford's House Arlington, VA Study	Jack Crawford	1	Hannibal Lecter Raspail and his motor home Klaus Copley Benson Jerry Burroughs at NCIC bilirubin…Billy Rubin…coloring agent in shit Senator Martin Frederick Chilton Marilyn Sutter Clarice Starling	11
Thursday 20-Feb 12:00 a.m.	Three Hours	Marcus Hotel St. Louis Bedroom	Hannibal Lecter Hotel Clerk	2	Lloyd Wyman Myron and Sadie Fleischer Pavilion Robert J. Brockman Memorial Library	3
Thursday 20-Feb 1:00 a.m.	Thirty Minutes	FBI Academy Quantico, Virginia Bedroom	Ardelia Mapp Clarice Starling	2	Kim Won John Brigham Chimel versus California Schneckloth versus Bustamonte	8

SCENE	WORD COUNT	STORY EVENT	VALUE SHIFT	POLARITY SHIFT	TURNING POINT	POINT OF VIEW
48	485	Bella dies she leans forward then dies. Starling is now the closest relationship Crawford has to a sympathetic human being.	Hope then Death	+/-	Action Bella dies	Omniscient Crawford Intracranial
49	2361	Preparations for the hide harvest. Gumb's mom on video first.	Bad to Worse	--/---	Revelation Gumb is an expert tailor	Omniscient Gumb Intracranial
50	2761	Starling wakes in the middle of the night. Anger pushes down the fear.	Ignorant to Knowing	-/+	Action Starling reviews the case file, can't help herself	Omniscient Starling Intracranial Her thoughts in Italics
51	473	Starling asks Crawford to go to Ohio.	Knowing to Acting	+/++	Action Crawford gives Starling all of his money	Omniscient Crawford Intracranial
52	1499	The procedures to killing Gumb's victims. Martin has taken Precious off stage.	Death to Life	--/++	Action Martin kidnaps precious	Omniscient Gumb Intracranial
53	771	Starling gets permission from Bimmel father to look at Fredrica's room.	Hope to Encouragement	+/++	Action Bimmel's father agrees to show Starling room	Omniscient Starling Intracranial Her thoughts in Italics
54	853	Crawford hears from Johns Hopkins and gets name of killer, Jame Gumb.	Hopeless to Hope	---/+++	Revelation Doctor tells Crawford about Jame Gumb	Omniscient Crawford Point of View his thoughts in Italics
55	2288	Starling figures out that Buffalo Bill sews.	Unknown to Known	-/++	Revelation BB can sew	Omniscient Starling Intracranial Her thoughts in Italics

PERIOD/TIME	DURATION	LOCATION	ONSTAGE CHARACTERS	NUMBER	OFFSTAGE CHARACTERS	NUMBER
					the Katz principle Krendler Hot Bobby Lowrance Gracie	
Thursday 20-Feb 3:00 a.m.	Ten Minutes	Crawford's House Arlington, VA Bed	Jack Crawford Bella	2		
Thursday 20-Feb 3:00 a.m.	One Hour	Gumb's House bed	Jame Gumb Precious	2	Gumb's mother	1
Thursday 20-Feb 5:00 a.m.	One Hour	FBI Academy Quantico, Virginia Starling's bed to laundry room	Clarice Starling Ardelia Mapp Hannibal Lecter's notes	3	Frederick Chilton Senator Martin Krendler Hannibal Lecter Jack Crawford Raspail Catherine Baker Martin Kimberly (one of the victims from WV) Buffalo Bill Burroughs Billy Rubin Bella Barney, the orderly Fredrica Bimmel	14
Thursday 20-Feb 8:00 a.m.	Fifteen Minutes	Steps of an Arlington Funeral Home	Jack Crawford Clarice Starling	2	Jeff Bella Fredrica Bimmel Kimberly Emberg Hannibal Lecter	5
Thursday 20-Feb 9:00 a.m.	Fifteen Minutes	Gumb House	Jame Gumb Catherine Martin Precious	3	Danny Kaye	1
Thursday 20-Feb 12:00 p.m.	Fifteen Minutes	Belvedere Bimmel House Outside in the yard	Clarice Starling Bimmel neighbor Bimmel's father, Gustav	3	Fredrica Bimmel Jack Crawford Catherine Martin Kimberly Emberg the Kidnapper the police	6
Thursday 20-Feb 12:00 p.m.	Ten Minutes	Crawford's FBI Headquarter Office	Jack Crawford FBI Assistant Director John Golby Dr. Danielson	3	Klaus Raspail Phyllis or Bella Frederick Chilton Everett Yow, Raspail's lawyer Burroughs Hannibal Lecter J. Edgar Hoover He Dr. Purvis John Grant of Harrisburg Alan Bloom Hannibal Lecter Jame Gumb	14
Thursday 20-Feb 12:30 p.m.	Fifteen Minutes	Belvedere Bimmel House Frederica bedroom	Clarice Starling Mr. Bimmel New Mrs. Bimmel with baby	3	Fredrica Bimmel Buffalo Bill Kimberly Emberg Catherine Martin	4

SCENE	WORD COUNT	STORY EVENT	VALUE SHIFT	POLARITY SHIFT	TURNING POINT	POINT OF VIEW
56	1784	Phone call tells Starling FBI is on the case. The killer is in Calumet City.	In the game to Out of the game	+/-	Revelation FBI has Gumb in its sights	Omniscient Starling Intracranial Her thoughts in Italics
57	1628	Starling interviews Hubka who gives her "Mrs. Lippman's" family address.	Stagnant to Moving forward	-/+	Revelation Fredrica sewed a lot for Mrs. Lippman	Omniscient Starling Intracranial Her thoughts in Italics
58	508	HOSTAGE RESCUE team in air, ready to go.	Close to Very close	+/++	Action FBI about to knock down door	Omniscient Team Commander Joel Randall Intracranial
59	4000	Starling kills Gumb.	Death to Life	---/+++	Revelation moths goat smell	Omniscient Gumb Intracranial thoughts switches to Starling Intracranial thoughts after the moth giveaway on the back of his robe then back to Gumb Intracranial after Starling smells the goat, the smell of the schizophrenic from the cell next to Lecter Back to Starling Intracranial after the gunshots
60	774	Starling comes home a hero but has to take exams.	Hero to Trainee	+/-	Revelation Washing machine like a great maternal heartbeat	Omniscient Ardelia Mapp's Intracranial

PERIOD/TIME	DURATION	LOCATION	ONSTAGE CHARACTERS	NUMBER	OFFSTAGE CHARACTERS	NUMBER
Thursday 20-Feb 12:45 p.m.	Ten Minutes	Belvedere Bimmel House phone call in entryway	Clarice Starling Burroughs Mrs. Bimmel and baby Mr. Bimmel Fredrica's Mother	5	Buffalo Bill Kimberly Emberg Jack Crawford Jame Gumb aka John Grant Beaver Cleaver Two female Marshals and a nurse Gumb's grandparents Chief gunny Brigham Catherine Martin Senator Martin Hannibal Lecter Starling mother and father Stacy Hubka	13
Thursday 20-Feb 1:00 p.m.	Ten Minutes	Franklin Insurance Agency Belvedere, OH	Clarice Starling Stacy Hubka Boss at Franklin Insurance Agency	3	Cher Bono Fredrica Bimmel Skip Mr. Toad Pam and them, Pam Malavesi Houdini Jame Gumb or John Grant Jaronda Askew Mrs. Burdine Mrs. Lippman	10
Thursday 20-Feb 1:00 p.m.	Ten Minutes	In the Air 24 Passenger Jet over Chicago	Hostage Rescue Team Commander Joel Randall Vernon Eddie Bobby DEA Commander	5	DEA Guys	1
Thursday 20-Feb 4:00 p.m.	Thirty Minutes	Jame Gumb House Belvedere Ohio	Mr. Gumb Mom Gumb Precious Catherine Martin Clarice Starling	5	Precious It Mrs. Lippman Fredrica Bimmel Jack Gordon Catherine's mother Fireman TV crews	8
Friday 21-Feb 12:05 a.m.	Six Hours	Washington National to Van to Quantico	Ardelia Mapp Clarice Starling Jeff. (Crawford's driver) Jack Crawford	4	Bella's Relatives Senator Martin Brigham Krendler Pilcher at Smithsonian	5

SCENE	WORD COUNT	STORY EVENT	VALUE SHIFT	POLARITY SHIFT	TURNING POINT	POINT OF VIEW
61	1011	Starling checks in with Crawford. They watch news.	Protégé to Pro	-/+	Revelation Lecter is long gone	Omniscient Crawford Intracranial
62	1172	The ugly truth about Gumb. Fredrica was his friend even writing him a nice note from the pit.	Sadness to Exploitation	-/--	Revelation Lecter knew it was Gumb from the start. He used the FBI to get his freedom	Omniscient
63	361	Starling plans to go away with Pilcher.	Duty to Fun	-/+	Revelation Starling going away with Pilcher	Omniscient
64	921	Lecter at the Marcus Hotel writing letters.	Duty to Fun	+/-	Revelation Lecter will kill Chilton and will watch Clarice	Omniscient Hannibal Lecter Intracranial
	96299					

PERIOD/TIME	DURATION	LOCATION	ONSTAGE CHARACTERS	NUMBER	OFFSTAGE CHARACTERS	NUMBER
Friday 21-Feb 6:00 a.m.	Twenty Minutes	Crawford's FBI Headquarter Office	Jack Crawford In-Laws Clarice Starling	3	Bella Jame Gumb Catherine Martin a dog (precious) Fredrica Bimmel Stacy Hubka Burdine woman Mrs. Lipman's old address Senator Ruth Martin Ardelia Mapp Stringfellow Hannibal Lecter Brigham the Director	14
Days/weeks later	Days/weeks	Indeterminate	Clarice Starling Jack Crawford	2	Jame Gumb Mother Grandparents Klaus Raspail Hannibal Lecter Everett Yow Clarice Starling Frederick Chilton John Grant Mrs. Lippman Fredrica Bimmel	12
Days/weeks later	Days/weeks	The Old DC-6	Ardelia Mapp Clarice Starling	2	Noble Pilcher Pilcher's sister	2
Days/weeks later	Days/weeks	Marcus Hotel	Hannibal Lecter waiter	2	Barney, the orderly Frederick Chilton Clarice Starling Jack Crawford Noble Pilcher	5

59

FROM MICRO TO MACRO

With sixty-four rows corresponding to sixty-four scenes in the novel *The Silence of the Lambs* and fourteen columns detailing the step-by-step progression of the global Story along with the key values for each scene labeled and all elements of continuity detailed, we've got the micro progression of scenes fully fleshed out. Now is the time to use *The Story Grid Spreadsheet* to help us analyze the novel from the thirty-thousand-foot view, the macro distillation of the *Foolscap Global Story Grid*.

We've now reached:

THE EDITOR STAGE FOUR

Deconstructing the big movements of how Thomas Harris created that rarest of novels—the outrageously successful commercial thriller that stands as one of the pre-eminent novels of the twentieth century will be a lot of fun. Seriously. Somehow Harris wrote a book that was impossible to put down but deeply resonates with the reader long after he's finished reading. I've gone through the book at least fifty times line by line and I always discover something new. While I do not profess to have any insight into the working mind of Thomas Harris or of how he crafts his stories, what I can do is analyze the structure of his work within the traditions and conventions of his chosen Genres.

We're going to do this by going back to our *Foolscap Global Story Grid*. This is the Norm Stahl/Steven Pressfield one piece of paper that outlines an entire novel. So let's now go macro and fill in the foolscap page for *The Silence of the Lambs*.

PART SEVEN

BUILDING THE FOOLSCAP GLOBAL STORY GRID

60

BACK TO GENRE

If you're like me, right now your head is swimming.

You've just spent three or four weeks using a microscope to lay out the elements of a novel, all of its scenes and continuity details, turning points, values etc. Moving from minutiae to the view from thirty thousand feet is a very difficult transition. No matter how many books I've worked on, the moment I've completed *The Story Grid Spreadsheet* brings great joy and soon thereafter great sorrow. Because inevitably, I'll have this really cool document and not really know what to do with it.

Don't panic.

It is in these times that Genre will save you. Remember that Genres manage audience expectations. So if we head back to looking at the big picture by detailing the Genres inherent in our Story, we'll be able to make sure we hit all of our marks. That is, we can make sure that we abided by the conventions and obligatory scenes of our chosen Genres. And once we've made sure we've done that, we can then hone them so that they are extraordinary. But if we don't have a checklist of things to make sure we've done, we'll just get lost in the details of our micro *Story Grid Spreadsheet*.

The *Foolscap Global Story Grid* is that checklist. So let's fill it out and see how Thomas Harris solved all of his Genres requirements.

Let's go back to those very important half dozen questions that the editor must ask himself of every project that crosses his desk. These are the make or break questions that will give him the definitive answer to that crucial question—Works, Doesn't Work?

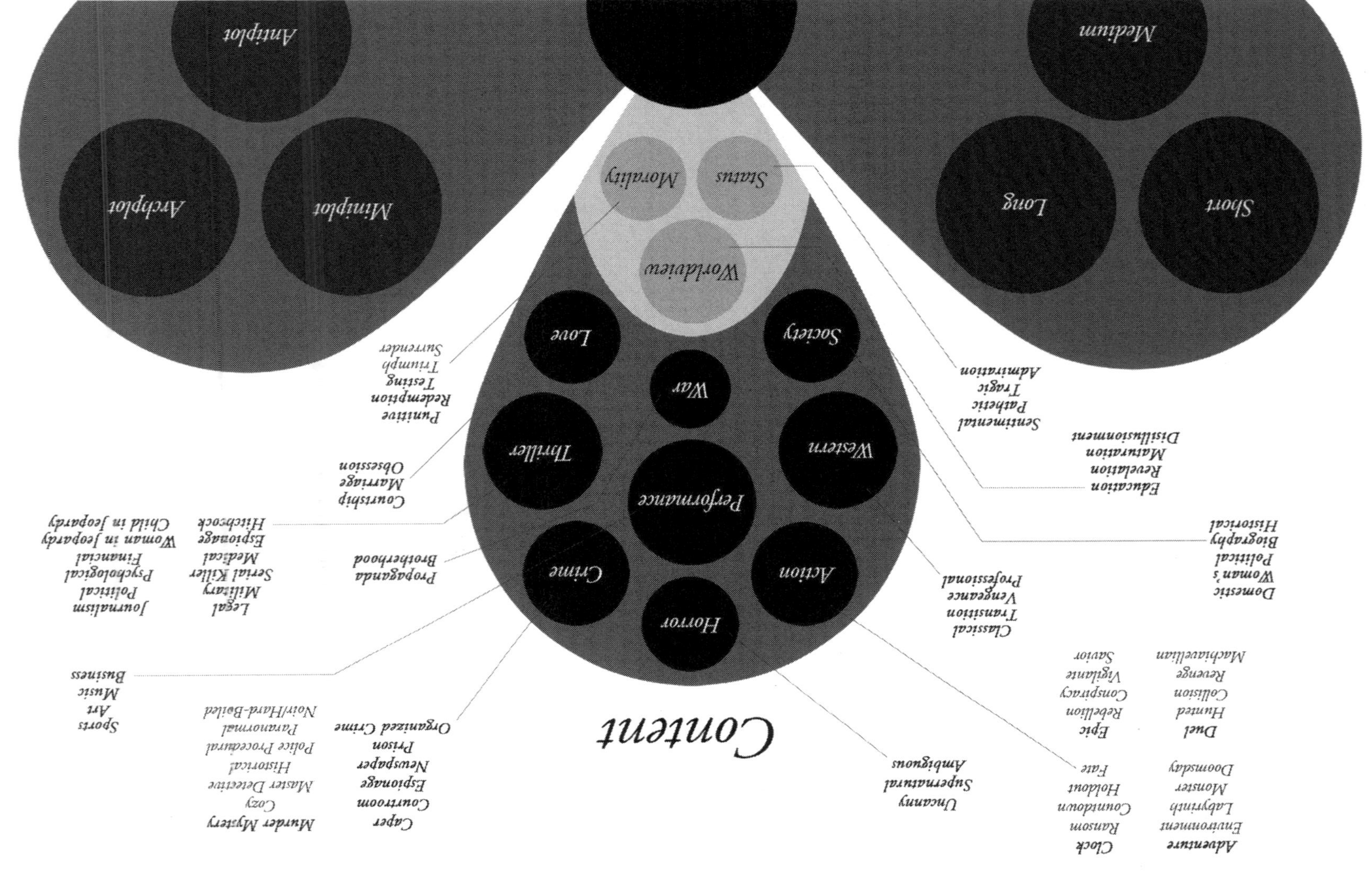
Content
Horror
Crime
Thriller
Love
Performance
War
Action
Western
Society
Worldview
Morality
Status
Archplot
Antiplot
Miniplot
Long
Medium
Short
Adventure
Environment
Labyrinth
Monster
Doomsday
Clock
Ransom
Countdown
Holdout
Fate
Duel
Hunted
Collision
Revenge
Machiavellian
Epic
Rebellion
Conspiracy
Vigilante
Savior
Uncanny
Supernatural
Ambiguous
Caper
Courtroom
Espionage
Newspaper
Prison
Organized Crime
Murder Mystery
Cozy
Master Detective
Historical
Police Procedural
Paranormal
Noir/Hard-Boiled
Sports
Art
Music
Business
Propaganda
Brotherhood
Legal
Military
Serial Killer
Medical
Espionage
Hitchcock
Journalism
Political
Psychological
Financial
Woman in Jeopardy
Child in Jeopardy
Courtship
Marriage
Obsession
Punitive
Redemption
Testing
Triumph
Surrender
Classical
Transition
Vengeance
Professional
Domestic
Woman's
Political
Biography
Historical
Education
Revelation
Maturation
Disillusionment
Sentimental
Pathetic
Tragic
Admiration

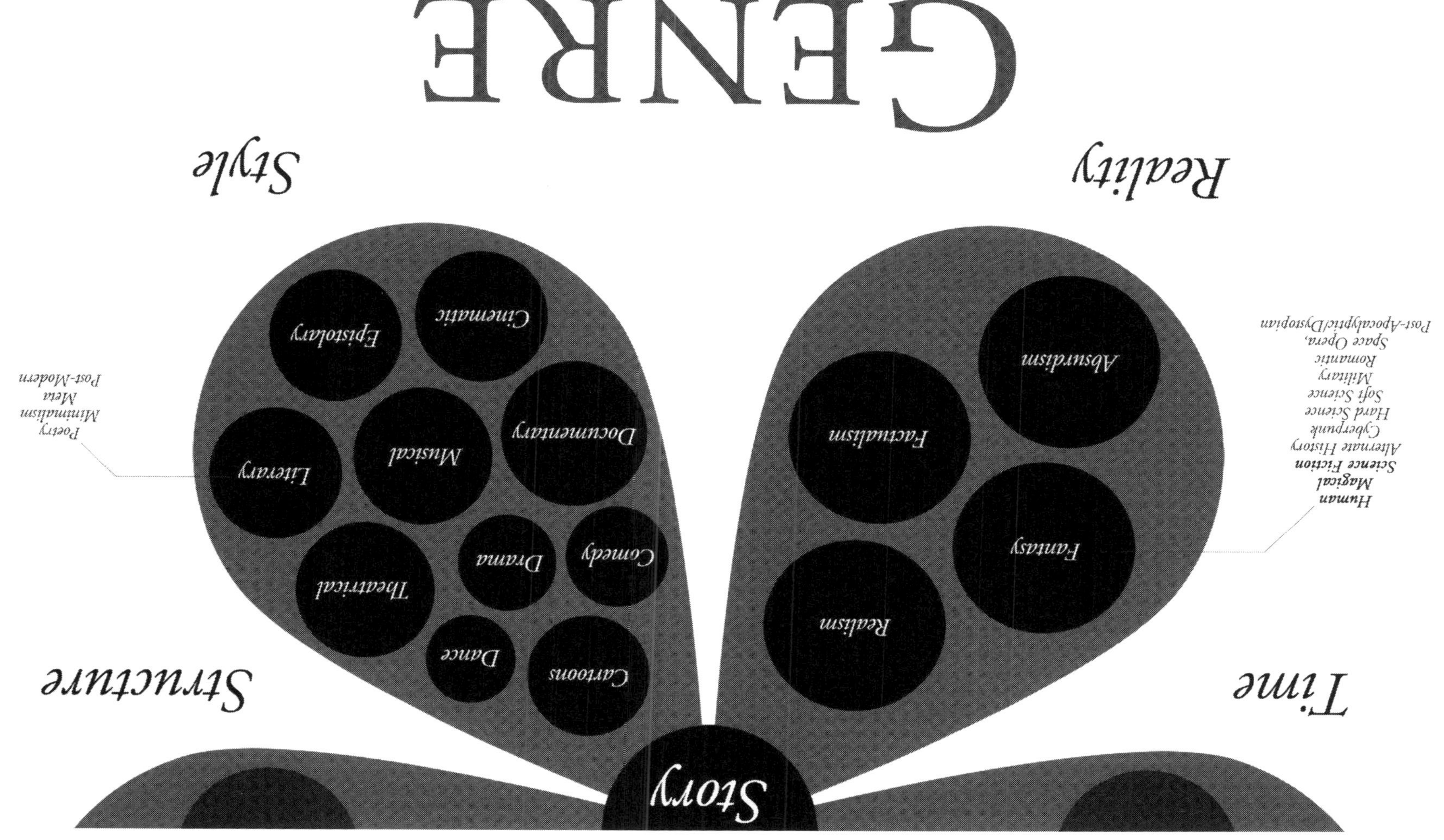
GENRE
Story
Structure
Style
Reality
Time
Cartoons
Dance
Comedy
Drama
Theatrical
Documentary
Musical
Literary
Cinematic
Epistolary
Poetry
Minimalism
Meta
Post-Modern
Realism
Factualism
Fantasy
Absurdism
Human
Magical
Science Fiction
Alternate History
Cyberpunk
Hard Science
Soft Science
Military
Romantic
Space Opera,
Post-Apocalyptic/Dystopian

Here they are again:

1. What's the Genre?
2. What are the conventions and obligatory scenes for that Genre?
3. What's the Point of View?
4. What are the protagonist's objects of desire?
5. What's the controlling idea/theme?
6. What is the Beginning Hook, the Middle Build, and Ending Payoff?

After we've answered these six big questions, we'll be able to build our *Foolscap Global Story Grid* one page—the single page document that gives us our Big Picture. So let's take a deep breath and just start out with answering Genre.

After just one read, an experienced Editor would have no problem (with the exception perhaps of the Internal Content Genre) categorizing *The Silence of the Lambs'* Genres.

Let's run 'em down:

1. **TIME**: Obviously, the novel is long form Storytelling.
2. **REALITY:** From the first page, with its reportorial sensibility and the specificity of its references to a real life law and order institution (FBI) and settings, it's clear we're dealing with the realities of contemporary life. So Realism is the Reality Genre.
3. **STYLE:** As we are dealing with concrete emotional terrain, the Style Genre is Drama.
4. **STRUCTURE:** Structure is classic Arch-plot with a protagonist on a personal quest (Ambitious newbie trying to become FBI agent) and then given an external mission too (interview the craziest killer ever).
5. **CONTENT:**

    A. EXTERNAL: The External Content Genre has all of the markings of the thriller (see the earlier chapters, THE UNIVERSAL APPEAL OF THE THRILLER and THE OBLIGATORY SCENES AND CONVENTIONS OF THE THRILLER) and as it concerns the hunt for a serial killer, the flavor of thriller is serial killer.

B. INTERNAL: I'll get into the Internal Content Genre and why I categorize it as "disillusionment" later on.

Okay, so we know the Genres. We can now fill in our Foolscap.

61

FILLING IN *THE FOOLSCAP*

For fun, let's look at the world through Thomas Harris' eyes and let's pretend that he uses *The Story Grid* to help him organize his thoughts. It's 1982 and he has to make some choices. Again I have no idea how Thomas Harris works nor would I presume to tell him how to work. I'm just looking at the end result and reengineering it through my *Story Grid* methodology.

He's already written a great serial killer thriller called *Red Dragon*, which introduced the piece de resistance of serial killers, Hannibal Lecter.

What's he going to do next?

Harris is a working pro. That is, he makes his living writing. *Red Dragon* was successful enough that his agent and his editor probably plead with him to write a sequel. The publisher backs up the notion with a hefty advance. So Harris is tasked with outdoing *Red Dragon*, the novel that defined the serial killer novel.

What a nightmare!

Congratulations…you've done something very few writers have ever done before…now do it one better!

Harris doesn't panic. He gets out a legal pad of foolscap paper and writes down what he needs to decide. It will look like this:

		FOOLSCAP GLOBAL STORY GRID		
		External Genre:		
G	S	External Value at Stake:		
L	T	Internal Genre:		
O	O	Internal Value at Stake:		
B	R	Obligatory Scenes and Conventions:		
A	Y			
L		Point of View:		
		Objects of Desire:		
		Controlling Idea/Theme:		
B			External	Internal
E			Charge	Charge
G	H	1. Inciting Incident:		
I	O	2. Complication:		
N	O	3. Crisis:		
N	K	4. Climax:		
I		5. Resolution:		
N				
G				
			External	Internal
M	B		Charge	Charge
I	U	1. Inciting Incident:		
D	I	2. Complication:		
D	L	3. Crisis:		
L	D	4. Climax:		
E		5. Resolution:		
			External	Internal
E	P		Charge	Charge
N	A	1. Inciting Incident:		
D	Y	2. Complication:		
I	O	3. Crisis:		
N	F	4. Climax:		
G	F	5. Resolution:		

The first question to answer is easy:

External Genre: **Serial Killer Thriller**

The second question is easy too, as we know the thriller Genre backwards and forwards. The global value at stake in a thriller is a convention—life/death.

External Value at Stake: **Life to Unconsciousness to Death to Damnation**

Now, why did I write down Life to Unconsciousness to Death to Damnation? I did so to remind myself of the progression of negativity of the LIFE value. It moves from LIFE to UNCONSCIOUSNESS to DEATH. But of course, it goes even further. To the end of the line of human experience.

What is that?

It is the fate worse than death…DAMNATION.

The most compelling thrillers take us to the end of the line...the limit of human experience. Thomas Harris knows that his protagonist for his sequel must move through these stages to reach a fresh and personal hell (just like his protagonist Will Graham did in *Red Dragon*). His protagonist must face damnation. [Review the chapter THE POWER OF NEGATIVE THINKING in part 3 for further explanation on value progressions.]

We are just two answers into filling out our Foolscap page and already we know just about everything we'll need to know about the global structure of the new novel. Just by clearly deciding the global Genre and using the value at stake for that Genre as our North Star.

Here's why.

We have to write a BEGINNING HOOK for the novel, then a MIDDLE BUILD, and finally an ENDING PAYOFF. But we can't just willy-nilly shift our global Story Genre in mid-stream from serial killer thriller to love Story and throw out our global life value and substitute it with a global love value.

That would be a recipe for disaster.

The reason why we can't do this is because the major turning points in a Story require turns on the global value of the chosen global Genre. That is, the climax of the Beginning Hook, the climax of the Middle Build and the climax of the Ending Payoff must turn on the Life value for a thriller. For a love Story they must turn on the love value.

Now smaller scenes in the thriller novel (those we fully detailed in our spreadsheet) can certainly turn on other values. But the big moments have to turn on the global value.

Because we know straight off the bat that we're writing a sequel to a serial killer thriller, we know that we have to abide by the serial killer Genre's conventions for the major turning points of the Story.

Harris knows that those conventions insist that he move the lead protagonist from a stable LIFE at the beginning of the Story to a state of cluelessness, UNCONSCIOUSNESS, at the end of the Beginning Hook of his Story.

And then Harris knows that he has to take the protagonist from UNCONSCIOUSNESS at the end of his hook to the threat of DEATH in his Middle Build.

And finally he must take his protagonist from the threat of DEATH at the climax of his Middle Build to the threat of DAMNATION to pay off the entire Story.

This is his goal…to take his protagonist to the limits of external human experience. Some thrillers, most in fact, don't go this far and that's okay. But they have to at least have the threat of damnation if not put it in play. Or they've gone to the limits of human experience in the Story's supporting Internal Genre. Or they simply work without going to the end of the line. They work, but they'd don't push the envelope of the Genre. If you want to transcend the run of the mill stuff in your chosen Genre, you must take the Story to the end of the line.

Harris went for broke with *The Silence of the Lambs*. He chose to take his Story as far as it could go.

Because he knows he's going for broke, Harris moves to the last three quarters of his foolscap page and writes the following in the three blocks designated for his Beginning Hook, Middle Build and Ending Payoff. These notes will remind him of how his scenes must progress.

			External	Internal
B				
E		**Move from Life to Unconsciousness**	Charge	Charge
G	H	1. Inciting Incident:		
I	O	2. Complication:		
N	O	3. Crisis:		
N	K	4. Climax:		
I		5. Resolution:		
N				
G				
			External	Internal
M	B	**Move from Unconsciousness to Death**	Charge	Charge
I	U	1. Inciting Incident:		
D	I	2. Complication:		
D	L	3. Crisis:		
L	D	4. Climax:		
E		5. Resolution:		
			External	Internal
E	P	**Move from Death to Damnation**	Charge	Charge
N	A	1. Inciting Incident:		
D	Y	2. Complication:		
I	O	3. Crisis:		
N	F	4. Climax:		
G	F	5. Resolution:		

On his foolscap, he's reminding himself that the BEGINNING HOOK of his book will move his protagonist from LIFE to UNCONSCIOUSNESS. Then the MIDDLE BUILD must take the character from UNCONSCIOUSNESS to threat of DEATH. And lastly, the ENDING PAYOFF must deliver the limit of human experience moving from the threat of DEATH to the threat of DAMNATION.

So if and when he gets stuck at any place in his novel, Harris will have a concrete reminder of the most important progressions. He'll have something to use to evaluate his scenes. No matter how great a scene, if it gets in the way of moving his lead character from one life value to the next, it has to go.

What is so impressive about Harris is that instead of banging out just another book that mirrored the progressions of *Red Dragon*, he challenged himself to write something completely different. The foolscap he has in hand now is the same as it would have been for *Red Dragon* at the same stage of construction.

But, what Harris chose to do with *The Silence of the Lambs* is to do *Red Dragon* one better. He added a remarkably satisfying Internal Content Genre for his protagonist. Reading *Red Dragon* and then *The Silence of the Lambs* back to back is the equivalent of listening to Glenn Gould's *Goldberg Variations* recorded in 1955 and then listening to the same pieces recorded in 1981. They are both astounding works, but for my money Harris in 1988 and Gould in 1981 are examples of creators moving from exuberant geniuses to seasoned artists.

62

THE INTERNAL CONTENT GENRE OF *THE SILENCE OF THE LAMBS*

Human beings live in two worlds, the external and the internal, on the public stage and inside ourselves. We pursue external objects of desire like a new job or a spouse or if we're in law enforcement, we seek to bring criminals to justice. But we also have internal objects of desire, like respect or redemption or belonging to something bigger than ourselves. But the deepest internal object of desire, the one we admire most in our fellow human beings and in ourselves, is to seek truth.

And truth is defined as a search for those unknowable answers to two questions:

Who am I?

Why am I here?

It is within the Internal Content Genres that we find the pursuit of answers to these ultimately unknowable questions.

The best stories, the ones that we fall head over heels in love with, are those that contend with finding deep internal truth.

Thomas Harris decided, whether consciously or subconsciously matters little, that the way to outdo *Red Dragon* was to put as much emphasis on his Internal Content Genre in *The Silence of the Lambs* as he does his External Content Genre.

Remember that the external Story of life is on the surface.

And two kinds of outside forces drive external events. Harris knew that he had the personal outside forces of the serial killer Buffalo Bill and the extra-personal outside forces of the FBI Behavioral Science Unit to drive his external Story for *The Silence of the Lambs*. His lead protagonist's external Story would move backward or forward according to her moment-to-moment success pursuing her conscious object of desire, her "want."

What's wonderful about Harris' choice of protagonist (beyond the fact that he wisely chose to feature a woman trying to make it in a man's world) is that he does not give her the obvious "want" of most serial killer stories. We don't meet a seasoned/hardened detective faced with a seemingly impossible task. Well, we do, but he's the secondary character Jack Crawford.

Instead of making the charismatic Crawford his lead, Harris introduces us to a version of ourselves, a newbie trainee with a lot of ambition and "on the surface" qualities that seem to be easy to exploit. She's smart, but more importantly, she has the physical qualities that will attract the attentions of Hannibal Lecter. Clarice Starling's "want" at the beginning of the Story is a reflection of her internal need to find the truth. Just as every one of our deep-seated wants is to find truth.

At the beginning of the novel, Clarice Starling just **wants** to become an FBI Agent under Behavioral Science head Jack Crawford.

But when she discovers the errand that Crawford sends her on could help solve the Buffalo Bill case, her want then escalates to contribute to cracking the case itself. She now **wants** to play a big role in catching the serial killer du jour.

That change in want, driven by events arising from conflict, moves the external Story forward. She's now "wanting" something else and we as readers are pulled with her as she chases it. We want it for her too. What this "on the surface" drive sets up is an internal journey too. We the readers might not know the specific internal reasons why it is so important for her to be an FBI agent, but Harris does.

And Harris masterfully takes us deeper and deeper into Starling as a human being. She doesn't know it (and we don't know it either really), but her want to become an FBI Agent has turned into a need to find truth...about the world she inhabits and the truth about herself.

She wants to find the surface truth of the identity of Buffalo Bill, but she also needs to learn the truth of the institution that is tasked with finding him (the FBI Behavioral Sciences Unit) in order to be ultimately successful in her career. Crawford is retiring soon. What will it take for her to get his job someday? Learning the truth about the institution brings up yet another need…to find out the truth of why she needs to be a part of it so badly.

Remember that we look to Story to instruct us how to navigate the world. While we the readers get sucked into the External Genre, Thomas Harris is also telling an underlying Internal Content Genre Story. The "A" Story is the serial killer thriller and the "B" Story is the internal content Story all about Starling, an empathetic stand-in for the reader.

We don't live in one world. We live in two.

The external world (how we live among our fellow man pursuing what we want) and the internal world (how we find peace within ourselves by getting what we need) are the hemispheres of human experience.

Let's get back to Thomas Harris' foolscap and look at how he answered the crucial Internal Content Genre and the value at stake progression:

Internal Genre:
Internal Value at Stake:

Again, Harris knew that he was going to write a sequel to *Red Dragon* and that it would be a serial killer thriller that had **life** as its central global value at stake. I also suspect that he knew that he wanted his lead character to "win" the external challenge—to find the killer. That is, he wanted his protagonist to smite the dragon, to get what she wants externally. He may have toyed with the idea of Buffalo Bill getting away or even killing Clarice Starling and using a part of her body to perfect his woman suit, but I doubt that notion got very far. Having a schizophrenic flayer of women come out on top just doesn't jibe with even the most cynical views of contemporary society. The world is a mess, but it's not so chaotic that you can't walk down the street without the threat of death. At least that's true within the confines of western society's reading public...those people who would actually engage and buy Harris' book.

So if the External Genre ends up as a "win," a positive success, the killer is brought to justice and the protagonist survives, what "B" Story could Harris tell that doesn't end with roses and sunshine?

Remember that one of the reasons we find Story so compelling is that it provides both sides of life in the telling...the positive and the negative. So if the External Genre ends in positive, the Internal Genre should end in the negative. The combination plate of win/lose produces irony. If the writer invests in a deep Internal Content Genre as his "B" Story and chooses to have it succeed or fail in the same way as his External Content Genre, the Story won't work. It will ring untrue. Readers will come away disappointed, even though they don't know exactly why.

The thriller often uses a secondary tragic love Story to counterbalance the positive of getting the criminal. That is, the protagonist falls in love, but then loses the love after the killer discovers the attachment. The villain then kills the protagonist's love interest or his buddy salvation partner etc. The lead character wins by bringing the antagonist to justice, but loses by losing her love.

We've seen this twist a million times. It's not that you can't use love Story to accomplish this goal if you set out to write a thriller, but you're going to have a hell of a time making it fresh and surprising. We're so used to this subplot that most readers will be so far ahead of the Storytelling that they'll abandon the book very early on in the read. They know it's only a matter of time before the bad guy kills the hero's lover/partner/friend.

Harris uses love Story as subplot in *The Silence of the Lambs*, but he uses it as tertiary comic relief more than dramatic revelation—i.e. the nerd at the Smithsonian's flirtation with Clarice Starling. Harris also uses the father/daughter mentor/apprentice love relationship masterfully too, but serious romantic love is not a driving force in the book.

Instead of trying to reinvent the wheel with Starling falling in love as his "B" Story, Harris decided to use his journalist's training to comment on a social institution. He has Starling learn the hard way about the realities of the FBI, bureaucracy, politics, sexism etc. The way he chose to dramatize this education, while also adding deep layers of characterization to his lead character, is to choose the Disillusionment Plot as his Internal Content Genre.

Remember that the disillusionment plot is a movement from a positive belief in the order of the universe, basic fairness etc. (positive) to a darker point of view, one that recognizes the murkiness of life, the real injustice and mendacity that plagues us all. To have no illusions is to understand that a person must have powerful political connections to move up in a large organization. Working one's fingers to the bone is all well and good, but getting to "the top" requires alliances and careful manipulations.

The disillusioned come to the conclusion that there is no treasure at the end of the hard-work rainbow, because there really isn't any rainbow to begin with. What we think we want and how we think we can get there is never what it really turns out to be. To become a pivotal high-ranking FBI agent has as much to do with who your friends are as it does with how hard you work or how talented an agent you are. Harris chose to have Starling learn this needed dark lesson while she pursues her external wants—finding Buffalo Bill.

The value at stake in the Disillusionment plot is the lead character's worldview. What Germans call *Weltanschauung*. I love the German word because, for me, it sounds visceral, in the guts. Generally, the progression of negativity of the *Weltanschauung* value moves from ILLUSION to CONFUSION to DISILLUSION to the negation of the negation DYSTHYMIA (a chronic state of negative/ depression).

But for *The Silence of the Lambs,* I define the progression as a movement from the negative state of naïve positivity of BLIND BELIEF (assuming something without empirical proof) to the positive state of JUSTIFIED BELIEF (coming to trust based on evidence) back to the negative with the rise of DOUBT (counter evidence arising disproving previous data) and culminating in deep negative of DISILLUSION.

For Clarice Starling, her disillusionment plot manifests itself through her illusions about the meritocracy of the FBI. She begins the Story from a positive yet dangerous state of BLIND BELIEF in the power figures and the FBI institution as a whole. At the beginning, she's being played by Jack Crawford to do his dirty work (using her as bait for Hannibal Lecter to help Crawford crack a case) but because she is so blinded by her ambition and ego, she doesn't question Crawford's motives. She wants to believe that Crawford sees something in her, some quality above and beyond her test scores and beauty that leads her to this great opportunity.

After he pulls her in, Crawford then actively manipulates Starling into seeing the FBI as a righteous institution. He rewards her with more authority and respect as she proves herself capable. He confuses her and her confusion/unconsciousness leads her to JUSTIFIED BELIEF that the FBI really is a meritocracy. Harris has Starling transition from BLIND BELIEF to JUSTIFIED BELIEF just as he moves the external value from LIFE to UNCONSCIOUSNESS at the end of the Beginning Hook of the novel.

Later when the FBI and Crawford come under extreme stress after the kidnapping of a senator's daughter though, the real truth about the institution begins to reveal itself to Starling. Her illusions about her place in the world begin to shatter. By the novel's end, she is forced to directly oppose the FBI in order to get what she wants (Buffalo Bill) which also saves her from spiritual damnation.

After all of the machinations within and outside the FBI, at the end of the novel Starling is DISILLUSIONED.

She has a negative worldview. She understands that there are no rules at the FBI beyond self-preservation. She is not at the end of the line in terms of the disillusion value (catatonic depression or Dysthymia), but her worldview has dramatically changed from the beginning of the novel to the end.

While the external content value ends at positive, the life value has been restored (although it is not at the level that it was at the beginning of the novel), the internal value ends at negative. I'll do a much deeper dive into this dual progression and how the two values arc in relation to one another chapter by chapter later on when we build our final *Story Grid*.

So here is how we'll fill in our Foolscap for the Internal Genre:

Internal Genre: **Worldview Disillusionment**

Internal Value at Stake: **Blind Belief to Justified Belief to Doubt to Disillusionment**

And let's add in the Internal Value Progression alongside the external value progression on the rest of our page:

B			External	Internal
E		**Move from Life to Unconsciousness**	Charge	Charge
G	H	1. Inciting Incident:		
I	O	2. Complication:		
N	O	3. Crisis:		
N	K	4. Climax:		
I		5. Resolution:		
N		**Move from Blind Belief to Justified Belief**		
G				

			External	Internal
M	B	**Move from Unconsciousness to Death**	Charge	Charge
I	U	1. Inciting Incident:		
D	I	2. Complication:		
D	L	3. Crisis:		
L	D	4. Climax:		
E		5. Resolution:		
		Move from Justified Belief to Doubt		

			External	Internal
E	P	**Move from Death to Damnation**	Charge	Charge
N	A	1. Inciting Incident:		
D	Y	2. Complication:		
I	O	3. Crisis:		
N	F	4. Climax:		
G	F	5. Resolution:		
		Move from Doubt to Disillusion		

63

THE OBLIGATORY SCENES AND CONVENTIONS OF *THE SILENCE OF THE LAMBS*

So Thomas Harris has his marching orders in terms of his External and Internal Content Genres. What he'll do now is write down the obligatory scenes and conventions of the serial killer thriller in shorthand to remind himself of his "must haves."

Obligatory Scenes and Conventions: **1. Crime/MacGuffin 2. Villain makes it personal 3. Red Herrings 4. Clock 5. Speech in praise of villain 6. Hero at mercy of villain scene 7. False Ending**

Looking at this list of seven, Harris understands that each of these elements should be literally "on stage, on the page" so that the reader is clearly satisfied that they've been delivered. They can't be off stage and reported by a third party.

So, we'll need at least seven scenes to deliver what is expected in a thriller:

- A scene/chapter that establishes the central crime and its inherent MacGuffin (the big "want" of the villain)
- A scene/chapter that establishes that the villain has made his crimes personal in relation to the investigator
- A scene/chapter that establishes at least one false lead/red herring
- A possible scene/chapter that clearly establishes a clock
- A scene/chapter that establishes the gravitas/praises the intelligence and/or power of the villain
- A scene/chapter that puts the hero at the mercy of the villain
- A scene/chapter that is a false ending

These seven scenes are extremely concrete assignments. They break down an extremely intimidating task into clear, doable bits. While you may end up writing twenty versions of each of these scenes before you find the perfect fit for your Story, understanding what these scenes are and why they need to be in your thriller leapfrogs you into action.

Write them down on your one page foolscap so that you never forget their importance. And then make damn sure that you have them in your final manuscript. I'll show you how to do this when you map out the final *Story Grid*. I'll pinpoint exactly where Harris satisfied these conventions…the exact scenes themselves.

64

POINT OF VIEW AND CONTROLLING IDEA IN *THE SILENCE OF THE LAMBS*

Moving down the top of the foolscap, Harris now has to make global decisions about the point of view and generally what his controlling idea/theme will be for the entire novel.

Let's start with Point of View.

This choice is relatively simple for a thriller. I'd suggest either one of two.

You can write a thriller in first person from the lead character's point of view. The effect is literally having your lead character tell the Story to the reader. *I went to see Hannibal Lecter…* for example.

The advantages of first person are the immediate establishment of a tight bond between the reader and a character. Gillian Flynn does this extraordinarily well in *Gone Girl* for both her female and male lead characters.

The limitations of first person, though, are the inability to narrate a scene where your lead character is not present. Some writers get around this limitation by having multiple first person Storylines, like Gillian Flynn does. Others find that a singular and direct approach aids them in creating tension. First person is a perfectly valid, and when done well, an extremely compelling choice. Years ago I worked on a police procedural novel called *Eleven Days* by Donald Harstad, which used first person to perfection.

The alternative to pure first person is to use the wonderful old standby "cheat" called Free Indirect Style. Free Indirect Style evolved in the nineteenth century in France and other places where writers were working out "realism." Gustave Flaubert is often credited with the first very immersive Free Indirect Style in Madame Bovary. Essentially, Free Indirect Style is a way of writing in third person, while also allowing the writer to crawl inside the brain of a character and tell the reader her thoughts. For more on it, re-read the FREE INDIRECT STYLE chapter in part 3.

Harris chose to use Free Indirect Style throughout the novel.

Just to make the Free Indirect Style more clear, I'll refer to this technique in *The Story Grid Spreadsheet* and in the text from this point forward as **Omniscient Intracranial**, which is sort of a wide-angle "mind-reading" vision from a single character's point of view.

Next Harris had to choose whether he should add additional points of view other than his lead character, Clarice Starling. I'm sure he debated these choices innumerable times in his mind, but for my money, I think he came up with a perfect mix when he gave dedicated chapters to Jack Crawford, Jame Gumb, Hannibal Lecter, Catherine Martin, Senator Martin, Ardelia Mapp, and Select Police/FBI/Paramedics. Harris also used straight up third person omniscient a number of times (the journalist's default choice to tell a Story) in order to convey an authoritarian sensibility for exposition. The effect was to drop in essential exposition in the guise of an official report or a journalist's notes. He does this with his journalistic detailing the preparations of the FBI's Hostage Rescue Team for example.

A list of all of the points of view and the number of scenes each point of view has in the Beginning Hook (BH), Middle Build (MB) and Ending Payoff (EP) of the entire novel follows.

Last but certainly not least, Harris may have begun writing *The Silence of the Lambs* with some sort of controlling idea in mind. I don't think it tormented him to the degree that his first Lecter-themed novel, *Red Dragon* did. But remember that I have no idea whatsoever about his writing process. All of my analysis of his work is through the lens of *The Story Grid* and not in any way a nonfiction account of how Mr. Harris writes.

Let's review again exactly what a controlling idea is.

The controlling idea is the takeaway for the reader. It's what the entire Story is all about. And it should be easily expressed in one sentence, describing how and why a change has occurred from the state at the beginning of the Story to the state at the end of the Story. As Harris has decided to counterbalance his external thriller plot with an internal disillusionment plot, he's setting out to leave the reader with a sense of irony.

	Number of Scenes		
	BH	MB	EP
Starling POV	10	17	5.5
Crawford POV	2	5	3
Catherine Martin POV	0	3	0
Authorial POV	0	2	2
Buffalo Bill/Jame Gumb POV	0	2	2.5
Hannibal Lecter POV	0	4	1
Senator Martin POV	0	1	0
Police/FBI/Paramedic POV	0	2	1
Ardelia Mapp POV	0	0	1
	12	36	16

If he had decided just to focus on the External Plot, his controlling idea would be something like "Justice triumphs when the protagonist empathizes with the victims." Remember that Starling doesn't crack and break the Buffalo Bill case until she looks at the world through Fredrica Bimmel's eyes, the first victim of Jame Gumb in Belvedere, Ohio.

But Harris set out to do more than just convey the message that we should pay as much, if not more attention to the victims of violent crime as we do the perpetrators. As a former journalist for the Associated Press and reporter on the police beat in Waco, Texas, Harris was well aware of the human infatuation with evil and of how that curiosity is exploited by tabloid journalism.

That theme was a very big element in *Red Dragon*.

How he chose to create deeper meaning with *The Silence of the Lambs* is by placing as much emphasis on Starling's self-delusion and naiveté as he does on the thriller plot. How she changes from the beginning of the novel and how she comes to a deeper understanding of herself and her place in the world by the end is the heart and soul of the work. It's not just the emphasis on the disillusionment plot that takes the novel into a higher realm; it's the mechanism Harris chose to enlighten Starling that provides an even deeper irony.

At the end of the novel, Starling has saved the life of another person and saved herself from personal damnation. But she did so not by being supported by a righteous human institution, the FBI, but through the help of evil incarnate, Hannibal Lecter. The FBI portrays itself as a force of good, but in the novel, it is in fact the opposite.

The psychopath who literally eats human beings he finds contemptible for seemingly no other reason than sport is in fact the most consistent and forthright character in the entire novel. While he certainly withholds information from her, Lecter does not lie to Starling.

He mentors her far more than Jack Crawford.

And it is through Lecter's help that Starling is not only able to help humanity, but to find the truth about herself. The trick she learns by the end of the novel is not to silence the screams of the lambs within her, but to listen to them.

So what is the overarching controlling idea of *The Silence of the Lambs*? The clue for me is in Harris' choice of title.

Starling has to accept that the shrieks of the lambs within her psyche will never go away. She can live in fear of them and do everything in her power to escape them or she can use them as fuel to compel her in her life's work—seeking justice. On a global thematic scale, I think you can see the lambs as Jesus Christ metaphors. That is, we continually slaughter the truth, the word of Christ, the lamb of God.

We deny the truth of ourselves. We silence innocence.

Lecter, the dark prince, understands that Starling's anger (a dark force) and her deep sense of injustice from her childhood are the very things that will enable her to unearth the truth about Buffalo Bill. Lecter literally asks Starling a number of times in the novel, "What do you do with your anger, Clarice?"

She never verbally answers the question. But she does with her actions.

She uses her anger to drive herself into the abyss…to raise the courage to battle the dragon in his own dark lair. She succeeds on one level, slaying Buffalo Bill, but loses on another.

Her pas de deux with Lecter ultimately ensures the cannibal's escape. Perhaps the controlling idea is this: **Justice prevails when the protagonist engages her inner darkness as passionately as she does her "positive" side.**

Alternatively, **We silence the word of God because the Devil's diction is far more entertaining.**

Or, **Evil silences truth.**

I suspect Thomas Harris understands the irony of a serial killer thriller as "entertainment" far better than we.

65

FINISHING THE FOOLSCAP FOR *THE SILENCE OF THE LAMBS*

To complete the bottom three quarters we need to go back to our *Story Grid Spreadsheet*. Our goal is to pick out the five scenes from the novel that comprise the five cornerstones of Story Form—the Inciting Incident, a progressive complication, the crisis, the climax and the resolution—for the Beginning Hook of the novel. Then, we'll do the same thing for the Middle Build of the book and lastly the Ending Payoff.

Where to begin?

Let's go back and pretend that we're Thomas Harris using *The Story Grid* to lay out his novel before he actually wrote the first draft. How would he approach filling in this section of the *Foolscap Global Story Grid*?

Well, he'll know a few things right off the bat about Beginning Hooks, Middle Builds, and Ending Payoffs. He'll know the values at stake and the kind of transitional scenes he'll need to write to move from the Beginning Hook (BH) to the Middle Build (MB) and from the MB to the Ending Payoff (EP).

1. He'll need a scene at the end of the Beginning Hook that shifts the global value of his External Genre in a major way, while it also shifts the global value of his Internal Genre in a major way, such that there is a clear demarcation in the reader's mind. This doesn't mean that he just slaps a divider in his book and calls it PART TWO. It means that the reader subconsciously understands that "now things are getting serious."

2. He'll need a scene at the end of the Middle Build that shifts the global value of his External Genre in an even bigger way than the transition scene from BH to MB. This scene must also shift the global value of his Internal Genre in an even bigger way than the transition scene from BH to MB.

> There must really be an even clearer demarcation in the reader's mind at the end of this scene. Like a spectator at a Fourth of July Fireworks show, the reader now must subconsciously understand that the grand finale of the novel is on the way. The reader will put the book down at this point, go to the bathroom, refill their glass of preferred beverage and let every person know around him/her to leave him/her alone until they've finished the book.

So let's figure out how Harris solved these two scenes…that is, what chapters from our *Story Grid Spreadsheet* represent these two critical scenes?

From my point of view, scene 12 (which corresponds to chapter 10) is the transitional scene that ends the Beginning Hook and moves to the Middle Build. Let's look at whether or not this scene does what it's supposed to do.

Does it shift the global value of the External Genre (the serial killer thriller value is life) in a major way?

Remember that Harris made a note to himself a while back that reminded him that he had to shift the value from Life to Unconsciousness by the end of the Beginning hook. Does he do that with this scene? The answer is that he actually takes the value a little further than unconsciousness…he takes it to what I call "off stage death."

If he were to have just taken it to unconsciousness, the end of the Beginning Hook would be the discovery that there was some killer out there that no one had any clue was active. Everything that the FBI had thought about the Buffalo Bill case would be completely turned on its ear. I think that moment (life to unconsciousness) comes earlier in the telling and is not a major turning point in the novel. It was the revelation that Hannibal Lecter knew about the head in the jar in the storage unit and that he mostly likely knows the real identity of Buffalo Bill.

So what do I mean by "off-stage death"? This is when the novelist reports of death. He doesn't put it on the page. Harris has Crawford tell Starling about Miggs' death in scene 7 (also chapter 7), which is the first death of the novel. Now in scene 12, we learn that another victim of Buffalo Bill has surfaced. Can you make the argument that this revelation can also be interpreted as information that informs the FBI that what they thought was true isn't? Sure.

The reason why scene 12 is the moment when the value drastically shifts in terms of the life value is that it requires a very large reaction on the part of the central figures in the novel. The Miggs death doesn't, nor does the head in the jar. The Miggs death matters little to the FBI. And the head in the jar seemingly means little too. But the discovery of a body in a river is cause for the private plane to be brought out and to immediately fly to West Virginia to check for fresh clues.

Does it shift the global value of the Internal Genre (the disillusionment Genre's value is worldview) in a major way?

Prior to scene 12, Starling is operating under "blind belief" of the meritocracy inherent in the FBI. She thinks the way the FBI works is that if you do exceptional work, you'll move up. You'll be rewarded with more responsibility. It's the same "blind belief" that we all begin with when we get out of college or start a new job or join the tennis team. We believe that all we have to do is work hard and do great work and we'll be rewarded. Oftentimes, at the beginning of our honeymoon with a particular institution, this blind belief is rewarded. That is, if we do bust our chops, we do get recognized and we do get a pat on the back. It is this pat on the back that moves our attitude from "blind belief" to "justified belief." Our idea that hard work pays off with recognition is proven correct, so we place more trust in the institution. When what we think is true turns out to be true, we trust our rational faculties all the more.

So, Starling sets off at the beginning of the novel with "blind belief" in the FBI. She gets an interesting errand from big shot section head Jack Crawford, interviews Lecter, writes up a stellar report and does a great job. Crawford tells her as much and rewards her with another job, following up the lead that Lecter gave her about the "valentines."

Remember that Crawford didn't agree to let Starling follow up on that clue initially. It was only after her report came in that he agreed. That small detail... denial of unproven skill and then rewarding of proven skill strengthens Starling's belief in the meritocracy of the FBI. Not in a major way, but a very important building block kind of way. If Harris had Crawford give Starling the go-ahead to track down the clue without her first proving herself with her report, the reader would have found that odd...unbelievable even.

So by scene 12, Starling has proven herself twice. She did the great report on Lecter, which got her the chance to follow up the clue. The clue turned out to be the head in the jar at the storage facility in Baltimore, which was another star in her cap. Remember also that she initially failed in her attempt to track down the clue. Crawford lectured her about the failure in his "assume" speech and then he gave her the advice that led to her success. More incremental proof of meritocracy.

So now when the global external value shifts and there is the discovery of a dead body in West Virginia, Starling gets the big call to go with Crawford to fingerprint the dead body.

This is a major shift in the Internal Genre for Starling. Her "blind belief" now moves to "justified belief." She did great work and now she's being brought up to the big leagues. She's going to work with Jack Crawford as his right hand. The progressive build of this promotion to junior FBI agent in training from plebe at the academy is a major shift. And it happens in the transitional scene 12 (chapter 10) when the external value shifts too. This is not a coincidence. It is indispensable Story craft.

So in my estimation, scene 12 is the resolution scene of the Beginning Hook of the novel as well as the Inciting Incident of the Middle Build of the novel. Great how that works out right? Very efficient Storytelling.

Now let's move on to the transitional scene between the Middle Build and the Ending Payoff.

It is scene 50 (chapter 48) when Starling meets Crawford at the funeral home to ask him for his blessing for her to go to Belvedere, Ohio.

Does it shift the global value of the External Genre (the serial killer thriller value is life) in a major way?

Thomas Harris knows that he has to move the global value from life to death to the fate worse than death (damnation) in order to pay off the promise of his chosen global External Genre. It is in scene 50 that this escalation of stakes becomes very clear. The mere fact that it takes place in front of a funeral home after the death of Jack Crawford's wife lets the reader know that there are fates worse than death. Outliving your loved one is certainly one.

From chapter 3, Bella has been slowly withering away, sapping Crawford of life force. While he's a stoic and tight-lipped professional, the reader can sense that he's not going to be of much use once his beloved kicks the bucket. And he's not.

Starling too has been beaten down, pushing her to quit her pursuit of Buffalo Bill.

Political machinations have forced her back to the academy. She's been warned that if she goes near the Buffalo Bill case again, she'll be washed out of the program. And it's also clear that even if she makes it through and gets her badge as a full-fledged FBI agent, chances are that she'll end up in a satellite office in Podunk U.S.A. She's not liked.

But what Starling can't abide is the fact that a woman is not only going to be killed, but her body will be desecrated, flayed and used to make a vest with "tits on it." Deep down she knows that if she does not do everything in her power to try and save the woman, she'll never forgive herself. Forget about the lambs she didn't try and save when she was a girl, how in the hell is she going to live with herself knowing that she did nothing to save another human being?

This is the place where the External Genre moves from death to damnation for this very reason.

If Starling quits and does nothing, a woman will die and she will suffer a fate worse than death. So will Starling. She'll have to live with unimaginable self-hate. Damnation indeed.

So in scene 50 (chapter 48), Starling goes to Crawford and asks him to send her to Ohio to figure out how Buffalo Bill hunts. Crawford, on the verge of an emotional breakdown and also at the end of his career, agrees. Starling is the last best hope.

Does it shift the global value of the Internal Genre (the disillusionment Genre's value is worldview) in a major way?

I think it's obvious by scene 50 (chapter 48) that Starling is no longer a believer in the meritocracy of the FBI. Just to recap, she's been used to titillate a cannibal serial killer. That killer, Hannibal Lecter, turned the tables and used the FBI's stupidity against itself in a way that ensured his escape. He's now at large after slaughtering a number of innocent people. And God knows whether he has designs on visiting Starling in person in the near future. Not only that, but the FBI blames Starling for his escape and only through the intervention of the man who got her into the mess in the first place (Crawford) is she still a viable candidate to get her badge. Barely.

She's moved from "blind belief" in the Beginning Hook, to "justified belief" and "doubt" in the Middle Build, and now she's on a steep dive into "disillusionment" for the Ending Payoff.

What's really great here is that she now knows the truth.

The FBI is bullshit. But, the job is not.

Her mission in life is still to bring justice to the world, to save as many lambs as she can. Now that she no longer confuses the artifice of her mission (the badge) with the actual mission, she's a force to be reckoned with.

She's literally no longer operating under any illusions. She doesn't think she's going to get anything out of her mission to Ohio. In fact, she's pretty certain she'll get recycled for going in the first place. But she does it anyway.

She's now a hero. She sacrifices herself for the sake of others.

You'll notice that both of Harris' transitional scenes that create major Story value shifts are not big action scenes. There is no gunplay or blood.

He trusted his Story to deliver…not spectacle. And boy does it.

Now that we have our two critical Major shifts figured out, all we need to do is walk back through the other scenes that make up the Inciting Incidents, progressive complications, crises, climaxes and resolutions for our Beginning Hook, Middle Build and Ending Payoff and track the polarity shifts in each of these scenes in terms of the two global values at stake, life and worldview.

So now we have a completed *Story Grid Spreadsheet* and a completed *Foolscap Global Story Grid*. Let's put them together to generate the entire *Story Grid* for *The Silence of the Lambs*.

		FOOLSCAP GLOBAL STORY GRID		
		FOR ***THE SILENCE OF THE LAMBS***		
		External Genre: **Serial Killer Thriller**		
G	S	External Value at Stake: **Life to Unconsciousness to Death to Damnation**		
L	T	Internal Genre: **Worldview Disillusionment**		
O	O	Internal Value at Stake: **Blind Belief to Justified Belief to Doubt to Disillusionment**		
B	R	Obligatory Scenes and Conventions: **1. Crime/MacGuffin 2. Villain makes it personal 3. Red Herrings**		
A	Y	**4. Clock 5. Speech in praise of villain 6. Hero at mercy of villain scene 7. False Ending**		
L		Point of View: **Protagonist (FIS)+ Eight Others**		
		Objects of Desire: **Wants to rise in the FBI, Needs to "silence" the torment of abandonment**		
		Controlling Idea/Theme: **Justice prevails when the hero identifies with the vulnerability of the**		
		victims as deeply as she deduces the core pathology of the villain.		
B			External	Internal
E		**Move from Life to Unconsciousness**	Charge	Charge
G	H	1. Inciting Incident: **Starling accepts "errand" to interview Lecter**	+	-
I	O	2. Complication: **Lecter's valentine lead turns into a dead end**	-	+
N	O	3. Crisis: **Does Starling re-engage Lecter after discovering head?**	?	?
N	K	4. Climax: **Starling re-engages**	+	-
I		5. Resolution: **Lecter gives up Buffalo Bill clue.**	+	-
N		**Move from Blind Belief to Justified Belief**		
G				
			External	Internal
M	B	**Move from Unconsciousness to Death**	Charge	Charge
I	U	1. Inciting Incident: **Dead body found in West Virginia**	-	-
D	I	2. Complication: **Starling taken off of the case**	-	-
D	L	3. Crisis: **Should Starling rebel and investigate by herself?**	?	?
L	D	4. Climax: **Starling goes alone to Ohio**	+	+
E		5. Resolution: **Has Crawford's blessing but not the FBI's**	+/-	+
		Move from Justified Belief to Doubt		
			External	Internal
E	P	**Move from Death to Damnation**	Charge	Charge
N	A	1. Inciting Incident: **Clues found in Bimmel's House**	+	+
D	Y	2. Complication: **FBI says it has found Buffalo Bill in Illinois/False Ending**	+	-
I	O	3. Crisis: **Does Starling quit her investigation?**	?	?
N	F	4. Climax: **Starling stays the course**	+	+
G	F	5. Resolution: **Starling slays Buffalo Bill**	+	+
		Move from Doubt to Disillusion		

PART EIGHT

THE STORY GRID

66

PUTTING IT ALL TOGETHER

At long last, now it's time to combine the Macro with the Micro and create *The Story Grid*.

The first thing we need to do is to get out a big piece of graph paper.

I use eleven-inch by seventeen-inch paper that is divided into .25 inch boxes, which will give you sixty-eight boxes from left to right and forty-four boxes from bottom to top. You can also use a spreadsheet program like Excel. Just set it up so that the row and column settings are both at .25 inches.

I turn it so that it is in the horizontal configuration and then count up twenty-two boxes from the bottom which will be just about the middle of the page and draw a thick black line across. This will be the horizontal, or x-axis of our *Story Grid* for *The Silence of the Lambs*.

On the horizontal x-axis we will use one box to designate a scene from *The Silence of the Lambs*. From our *Story Grid Spreadsheet*, we know that there are sixty-four total scenes in the book, so I label from one to sixty-four across the black line from left to right.

Under and above each of the scene numbers, I'll boil down each scene event that I've written on my *Story Grid Spreadsheet* to the shortest possible phrase or sentence that tells me what's happened. I'll then write down the event above or below the horizontal line to designate the value shift of that particular scene.

So if the scene moves from a positive to a negative value charge, I will put the label for that scene beneath the x-axis to indicate that it ends negative. If the scene moves from a negative to a positive charge, I will put the label for that scene above the x-axis to indicate that it ends positive.

What do I glean from the *Foolscap Global Story Grid?* The Beginning Hook, Middle Build and Ending Payoff of the Global Story. So I'll move to scene 12 on my sheet and draw a vertical line straight down from top to bottom and I'll do the same at scene 50. Now I have the whole novel broken down into the three component parts.

67

THE BEGINNING HOOK OF *THE SILENCE OF THE LAMBS*

So, after I've combined the *Spreadsheet* info with the *Foolscap* for the Beginning Hook of the novel, which comprises the first twelve scenes, the horizontal axis should look like the diagram on the next page.

You'll notice a couple of things.

1. Ten of these first twelve scenes are written from Clarice Starling's point of view (again, I've used the information we wrote down in *The Story Grid Spreadsheet*), while two are from the point of view of Jack Crawford. Thomas Harris wisely made sure that the reader will not get too distracted in the Beginning Hook. The reader needs to bond immediately with the protagonist Starling, or the rest of the novel won't work. But Harris also knew that thematically he needed to establish "impending death" early on so that the reader wouldn't shudder and abandon the book when things got bloody. He does this by using Crawford's ailing and comatose wife Bella as the device to signal to the reader that the Story is going to go to the limits of human experience. Bella's unconsciousness lurks over the entire novel until scene 50 when she finally dies and Starling now has her full faculties available to deal with Buffalo Bill. Plus the dying wife element really softens Crawford as Starling's manipulative mentor. Without Bella, Crawford would come off as a real asshole.

2. Scenes 3 and 11 have italicized type describing the events. I've put italic type here to designate the times when Starling and Lecter meet one on one. The Lecter interview scenes are brilliant. But the reader still "sees" the scene through Starling's point of view. To be able to immediately go back and see when they occur and how they evolve shows just how carefully Harris constructed the Story.

3. The Story events in scenes 5 and 8 are shaded boxes. The shaded boxes indicate when Thomas Harris has shifted the point of view to Jack Crawford. So all scenes in the novel that are from the point of view of Jack Crawford will be in shaded boxes.

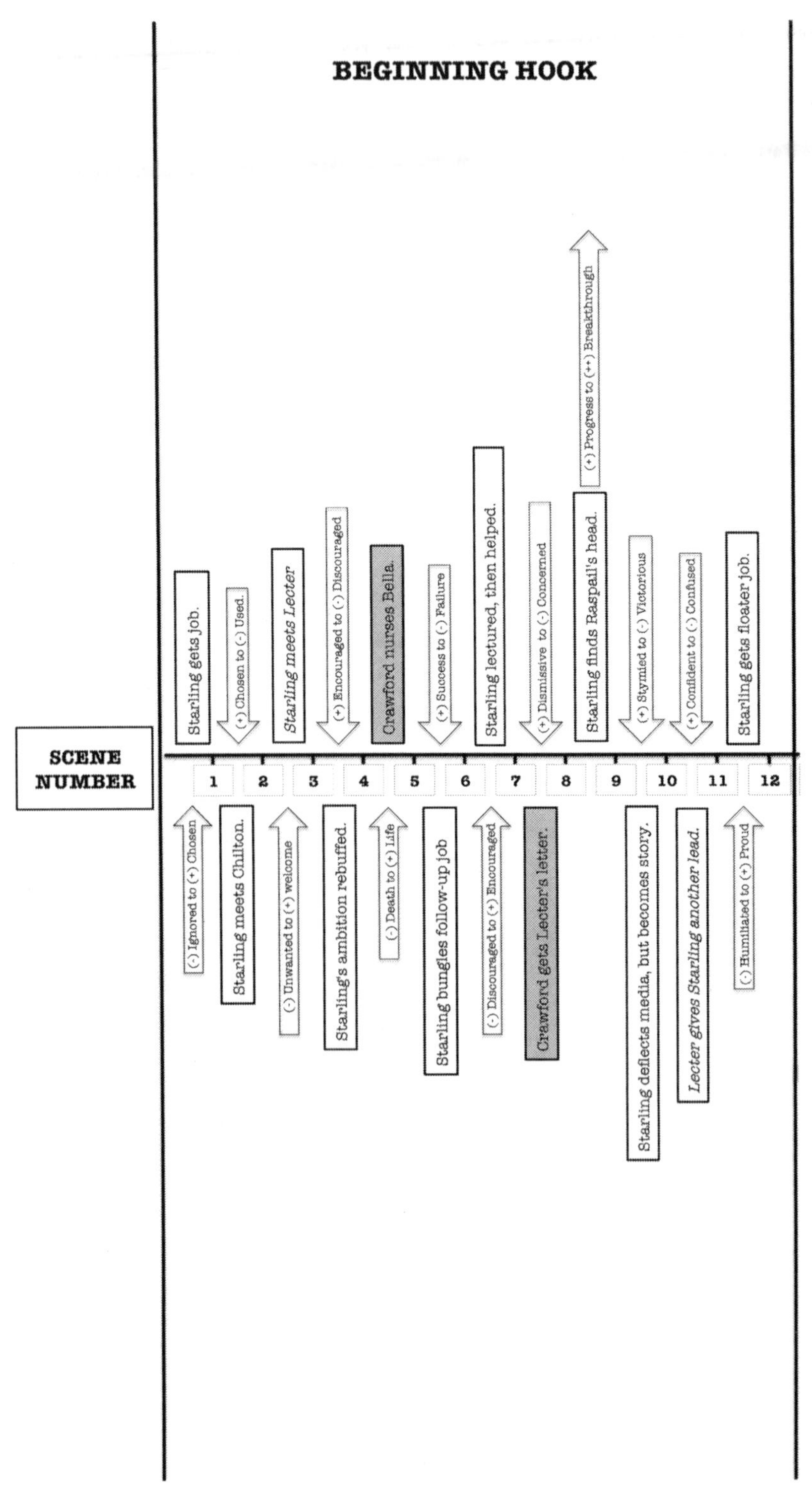

Harris will use eight other points of view. Here is that box again that shows you the others as well as the number of scenes each POV has in the Beginning Hook (BH), Middle Build (MB) and Ending Payoff (EP) of the book.

	Number of Scenes			
	BH	MB	EP	TOTAl
Starling POV	10	17	5.5	32.5
Crawford POV	2	5	3	10
Catherine Martin POV	0	3	0	3
Authorial POV	0	2	2	4
Buffalo Bill/Jame Gumb POV	0	2	2.5	4.5
Hannibal Lecter POV	0	4	1	5
Senator Martin POV	0	1	0	1
Police/FBI/Paramedic POV	0	2	1	3
Ardelia Mapp POV	0	0	1	1
	12	36	16	64

Next up, the vertical line/y-axis

Not only can we track the progression of Story events and shifts in values scene by scene in *The Story Grid,* we can also track the progression of the global Genre values. We do this by moving from scene to scene on our *Story Grid* and evaluating the state of the global value at stake in each scene. Is it positive or negative in relation to the scene that came before it? We'll put a dot on the grid on the vertical y-axis, corresponding to the scene based on the movement of the global value at the end of that scene.

Remember that the serial killer life value in *The Silence of the Lambs* moves from Life to Unconsciousness to Death to the fate worse than death (Damnation) and the disillusionment internal worldview value moves from blind belief to justified belief to doubt to disillusionment. We'll mark those levels of positive and negative on our Story Grid alongside the y-axis so we don't forget.

We can use the vertical axis of our graph paper to track how these global values are moving.

So to begin, let's define the area above the horizontal line as Positive in global value and below the horizontal line as Negative in global value. Let's designate the Life value with a solid line and the Worldview value with a dashed line. With these definitions in mind, let's walk through the progression of global values in the Beginning Hook.

The EXTERNAL GENRE VALUE "LIFE" starts at the most positive for Clarice Starling at the very beginning of the novel. She's got her shit together. As an FBI trainee, she's on her way to reaching her goal of becoming an FBI agent. Then she gets the call to see Jack Crawford.

In scene 1 (chapter 1) Crawford offers her the Inciting Incident "errand" to go and interview the most dangerous serial killer on earth. Now her "LIFE" value is threatened in the negative. She's going to be putting her life in danger, and she has no idea how much danger, so the curve of her Life value descends. She's acting without knowing just exactly what she's gotten herself into, approaching unconsciousness.

Now let's look at the Worldview value.

As Starling's LIFE value in the EXTERNAL PLOT descends toward UNCONSCIOUSNESS, the INTERNAL GENRE VALUE "WORLDVIEW" ascends.

At the beginning of the novel, Starling's worldview is filled with "illusion." She's ignorant of the ways of the professional world and thus vulnerable for manipulation. While some would argue that illusion is a positive outlook on life in that the individual is immersed in the powers of positive thinking, for our purposes, and for Harris', this lack of knowledge is in fact a false positive.

And a false positive is in fact, negative.

I'm defining it as "Blind Belief." And I'm giving it a negative charge.

Justified belief as I'm defining it will be evidence in the righteousness of a blind belief. In this case a particular institution, the FBI. Doubt however will have a negative charge as will ultimately disillusionment.

Let's track the internal value for the Beginning Hook.

At the onset of the Story, Starling is clueless about the ways of the world...as represented by the FBI. She thinks that as long as she does what she's told and does it well, she will move up in the FBI hierarchy. To pinpoint her illusion/naiveté more precisely, I think the notion of "blind belief" is most accurate. She goes on faith that the FBI's fundamental concern is with maintaining law and order. And order means rules, appropriate conduct that must be adhered to in order to become part of the institution. And once inside the institution, Starling believes that there are clear steps that an agent takes in order to rise in the organization.

As the BEGINNING HOOK of the novel progresses, Starling becomes less and less naive just as her life faces more and more threats. Her external moves down the graph, while her internal moves up. She doesn't know that Crawford is using her to get to Lecter until the smarmy Dr. Chilton assaults her with that possibility.

That revelation makes Starling even more confused about exactly what her errand is really about. Her blind belief is now in question. Meanwhile, she's getting a serious lesson in the lack of gravitas her position as an FBI agent in training means. She's losing her illusions and gaining understanding of her place in the world.

At the climax of the BEGINNING HOOK of the novel, you'll see that the two values intersect. The climax comes in scene 12, chapter 10 when Starling is "rewarded" for her intrepid investigation of a clue proffered by Lecter. By following Lecter's lead, she's discovered a severed head of an unknown victim in the storage unit held by one of Lecter's victims.

She's also shown to be a capable agent when faced with media interference. So Crawford pulls her out of the Academy to accompany him on a trip to West Virginia. The fact that Starling is also from West Virginia is certainly not far from his mind either.

Another victim of Buffalo Bill has been found, which moves the life value across the dead zone.

On the worldview dashed line side of things though, Starling, just a newbie trainee, has moved up the ladder. She's now joined the hunt for Buffalo Bill and Harris has completely hooked the reader. Her worldview has now shifted from blind belief to justified belief.

Obviously Crawford's pulling her into a serial killer investigation when she is only a trainee is a huge deal. Even Starling isn't sure why he's is bringing her, but instead of deeply questioning his motives, she puts her head down and resolves to do the best job possible. She's crossed the line from "blind belief" to "justified belief."

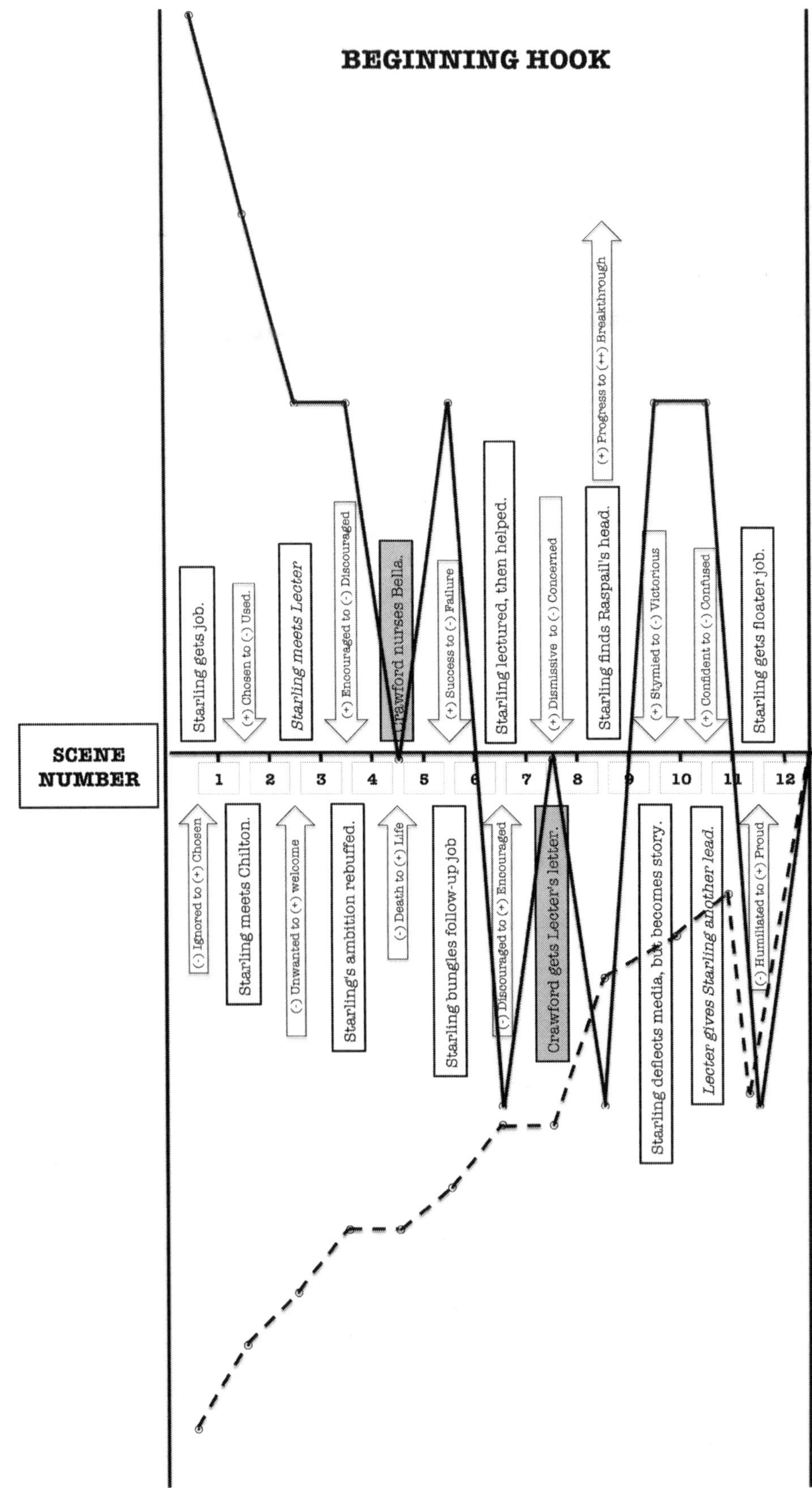
BEGINNING HOOK
SCENE NUMBER
1
2
3
4
5
6
7
8
9
10
11
12
Starling gets job.
(+) Chosen to (-) Used.
Starling meets Lecter
(+) Encouraged to (-) Discouraged
Crawford nurses Bella.
(+) Success to (-) Failure
Starling lectured, then helped.
(+) Dismissive to (-) Concerned
Starling finds Raspail's head.
(+) Progress to (++) Breakthrough
(+) Stymied to (-) Victorious
(+) Confident to (-) Confused
Starling gets floater job.
(-) Ignored to (+) Chosen
Starling meets Chilton.
(-) Unwanted to (+) welcome
Starling's ambition rebuffed.
(-) Death to (+) Life
Starling bungles follow-up job
(-) Discouraged to (+) Encouraged
Crawford gets Lecter's letter.
Starling deflects media, but becomes story.
Lecter gives Starling another lead.
(-) Humiliated to (+) Proud

She's done what she's been told and she's done it well. So, as she expected previously based on blind assumption (Harris even makes a joke about the word "assume"), she's being elevated in the FBI hierarchy based on what she perceives as merit.

Her worldview is now more informed and she's now a believer in the way the FBI works.

Let's take a short time out here and check in on THE MATH of the book. By my calculation, *The Silence of the Lambs* is 96,299 words. The end of the BEGINNING HOOK comes after TEN CHAPTERS/TWELVE SCENES and takes up 18,152 words, or 19% of the entire novel. Not exactly the 25% we use to estimate the length of a novel's beginning in our 25/50/25 principle, but definitely in the general arena that we've been using as our yardstick for long form Story.

68

THE MIDDLE BUILD OF *THE SILENCE OF THE LAMBS*

Next comes the MIDDLE BUILD of the novel, the longest and most challenging section to keep the reader in suspense. You'll not find a finer execution of a Middle Build than *The Silence of the Lambs*.

Using our *Foolscap Global Story Grid* and our *Story Grid Spreadsheet*, I'll do the exact same thing we did for the Beginning Hook of the book for the Middle Build. I'll boil down each scene event that I've written on my *Story Grid Spreadsheet* to the shortest possible phrase or sentence that tells us what's happened. I'll then write down the event above or below the horizontal line to designate the value shift of that particular scene. So if the scene moves from a positive to a negative value charge, I will put the label for that scene beneath the x-axis. If the scene moves from a negative to a positive charge, I will put the label for that scene above the x-axis.

We'll track the movement of the "Life" and "Worldview" values in the y-axis too.

The "Life" value (straight line) will grow ever more negative until the "all is lost" moment when the FBI and by association Starling is the furthest away from identifying and capturing Buffalo Bill. You'll notice that the "all is lost" moment comes just about at midpoint of the entire novel. That is no coincidence!

As for the "Worldview" value (in dashed line), it will rise to its greatest height in scene 27 (chapter 25) when Starling with complete faith in the meritocracy and righteousness of the FBI makes the Faustian bargain with Hannibal Lecter. She'll open up her inner world to him in exchange for his help finding Buffalo Bill. She soon finds out that this decision will haunt her the rest of her life.

The MIDDLE BUILD diagram is on pages 306 and 307.

The Inciting Incident for the MIDDLE BUILD is the discovery of the "floater" in West Virginia. This is the third dead body introduced in the novel. The first you'll remember is the suicide of Miggs and then the floating head at the storage unit. Harris is raising the stakes in the Story with the increase in body count. Having the Buffalo Bill bodies (Miggs was a result of Lecter's work) submerged in fluid is also an apt metaphor for the haziness with which Starling and the FBI see the world. The life value is definitely in the death arena.

In the early stages of the Middle Build, her internal "justified belief" value is gaining in positivity. She's doing great work and being rewarded. Cause and effect are seemingly in sync.

But what's with that dip in scene 14 (chapter 12)?

That dip is Harris creating the perfect progressive complication to get Starling (AND THE READER) to believe in the righteousness of Crawford and the FBI to an almost unassailable level. Harris needs this dip in order to make Starling's later decision to sacrifice her inner peace for the good of the FBI (and for what she thinks her rewards will be for doing so) believable.

She's not an idiot for agreeing to allow Lecter inside her brain. Crawford is manipulating her to do so. She's been victimized by her mentor (Crawford) and the institution that he represents to her, thus making the reader empathetic to her plight.

But if Harris doesn't fortify the "fairness" of Crawford at this point, the reader may not completely empathize with Starling at the crucial moment in the novel for the protagonist (the stand-in for the reader)...the point of no return.

Here is that dip moment again.

When Starling and Crawford are in West Virginia, Crawford disrespects her in front of the local police by barring her from a confidential meeting about the dead girl. Starling takes offense and momentarily questions whether this is a Standard Operating Procedure in the FBI. Do the higher ups use the agents below them in order to amplify their power?

This dip is the representation of her momentary questioning of the core righteousness of the FBI. It's sort of a "wait a minute, am I being played?" inner doubt in Starling. And it's simply brilliant.

When they return from West Virginia after Starling has discovered another crucial bit of evidence (the moth cocoon in the throat of the victim), Starling is emboldened. She confronts Crawford about the disrespect. Crawford cops to it and then gives her a very reasonable and clear explanation about why he dissed her. This moment in the novel jacks up the internal value toward the positive even more for Starling. Her "justified belief" in the meritocracy and order of the FBI is not only restored but is much higher than it had been before.

Harris ends the chapter with these two sentences. "She would have killed for him then. That was one of Crawford's great talents." There is no doubt that Crawford has done this sort of manipulation before…it's one of his best plays in his playbook.

You'll also notice that in scene 13 (chapter 11), Harris satisfies the "speech in praise of the villain" thriller convention in the form of having Starling read and review Buffalo Bill's case file. This killer is brilliant...seemingly impossible to catch...he leaves no clues. We'll make a note of this on our Story Grid and check off the requirement on our *Foolscap Global Story Grid*.

Let's move forward.

Just as Starling is getting traction with Crawford, in scene 17 (chapter 15), Harris raises the stakes again. He moves the life value at stake from investigation of old death to the real threat of future death with the abduction of a senator's daughter, Catherine Martin. In addition, Harris has now thrown in a clock plot to his Story, another popular feature of the thriller. If the FBI doesn't get some breaks, a woman will die. Harris literally establishes the clock at the end of scene 18 (chapter 16) with an exchange between the FBI director and Crawford, "What have we got at best—six or seven days, Jack?"

Why does Harris use a senator's daughter as the victim?

He's setting up Starling's disillusionment plot. It has to make sense. So Harris has set up a dramatic difference between Buffalo Bill's victims. A senator's daughter is going to get a full court press. But what about victims like Fredrica Bimmel? Girls/women from the coal mines just like Starling? They get dehumanized, just bodies in a timeline. They don't matter.

With a senator's daughter at stake, the FBI will be put under serious duress and will be politically vulnerable. And when institutions come under duress, their true characters reveal themselves. Stress threatens the institutions' order and hierarchy. Because institutions are just collectives of human beings with no real soul of their own (unless they are benevolent tyrannies that is), when bad things happen to them, most people run to protect themselves. And they look for sacrificial lambs to offer up if the shit really hits the fan. Fall guys to blame. Harris uses the serious threat of political reprisal as a way to reveal the truth about the FBI. Is it really the roses and sunshine meritocracy filled with stern but benevolent mentors like Jack

Crawford that Starling believes? Or is that myth just a convenient mask that men like Crawford use to cover up the realities of the institution?

If Harris did not use the daughter of a powerful figure as the victim, the motivations of the people within the FBI and the ancillary antagonists like Dr. Chilton would not be as clearly delineated. The "importance" of the victim increases the urgency.

Harris is also using Catherine Martin to show (not tell) how there is a very real difference in value of her life versus the previous victims. The other women who were killed and flayed are referred to more as evidence than they are as human beings. They're pejoratively "the Bimmel Girl," "the Kittridge girl from Pittsburgh," "the next one he grabbed," "the one after," and "the Varner woman."

The subtext here is that what was once a plodding, clinical investigation into the murders of run of the mill every-woman is now the number one priority of the FBI. And it's all because of the serious value of Buffalo Bill's next target. If he'd grabbed a waitress instead of the daughter of a senator, he'd get away with it.

I'll get into this a bit more later on, but what makes Starling so effective as an investigator is her ability to identify with the unnamed, "lesser" victims. And how she comes to that realization that she should look at the world through their eyes instead of trying to "be the killer" (the investigative innovation in *Red Dragon* and the FBI Behavioral Science Unit itself) is what breaks the case. It is in these details that you see how Harris outdid himself with this novel. He turned the whole investigative MacGuffin of *Red Dragon* (Will Graham sees the world through the killer's eyes) around in *The Silence of the Lambs* (Starling sees the world through the victims' eyes).

The force that makes Starling come to a true understanding of herself is also extraordinary. Which character forces her to accept herself for who she really is, "not one generation out of the mines," and drives her to this realization?

It's none other than the incarnation of evil…Hannibal Lecter. This is one of the reasons why the reader can't help but love Lecter. So much so that the reader even overlooks the fact that he's a cannibal. The reason why is that he's the only one who actually cares about Starling, wants her to find truth and live with it. Instead of living in lies and being a toady to a corrupt institution. Lecter may have not said this, but it's absolutely something he would agree with…a quote from John Milton's Lucifer in *Paradise Lost* "Better to reign in hell than serve in heaven."

MIDDLE BUILD

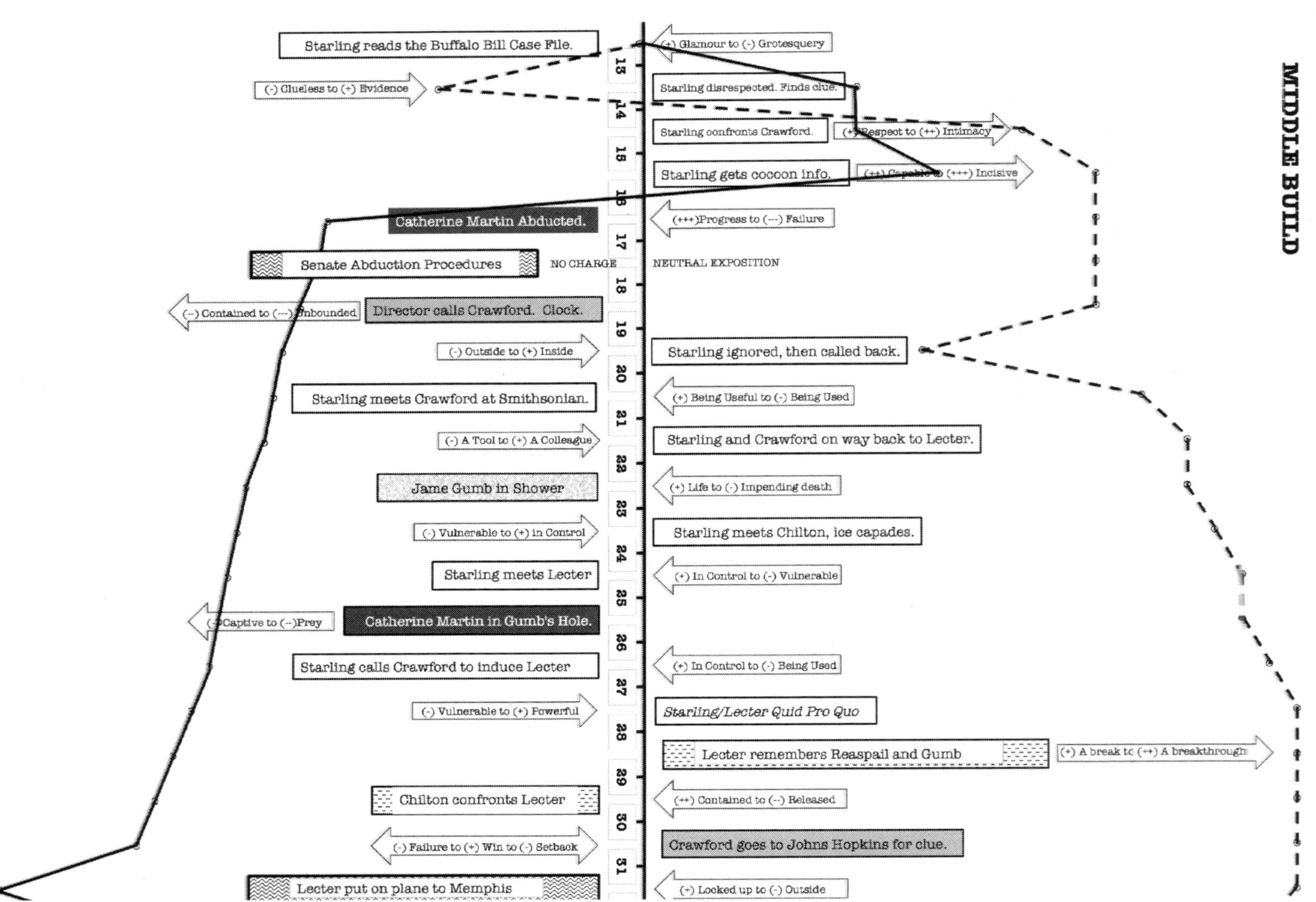

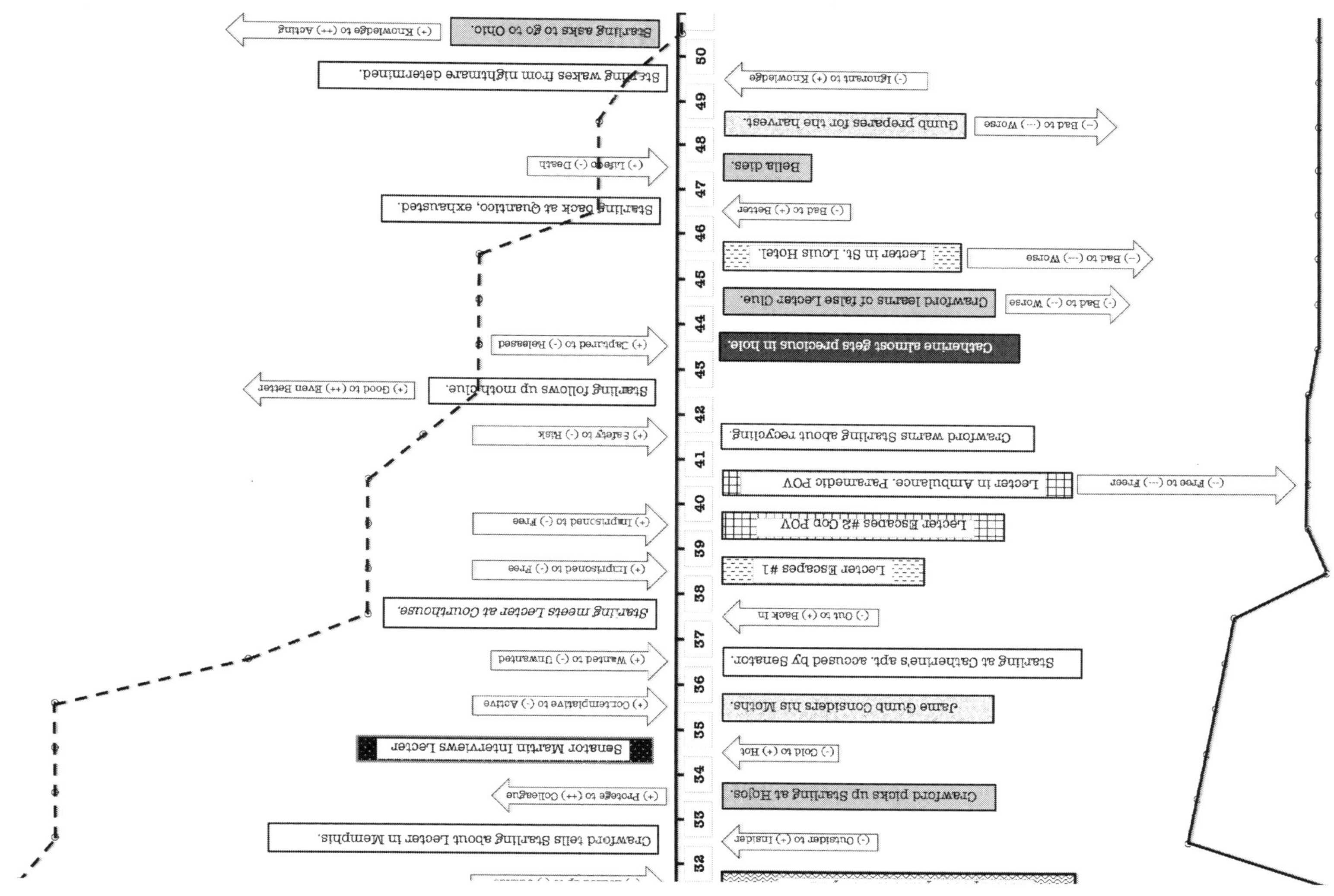
32
33
34
35
36
37
38
39
40
41
42
43
44
45
46
47
48
49
50
Crawford tells Starling about Lecter in Memphis.
(+) Protege to (++) Colleague
Senator Martin Interviews Lecter
(+) Contemplative to (-) Active
(+) Wanted to (-) Unwanted
Starling meets Lecter at Courthouse.
(+) Imprisoned to (-) Free
(+) Imprisoned to (-) Free
(+) Safety to (-) Risk
Starling follows up moth clue.
(+) Good to (++) Even Better
(+) Captured to (-) Released
Starling back at Quantico, exhausted.
(+) Life to (-) Death
Starling wakes from nightmare determined.
Starling asks to go to Ohio.
(+) Knowledge to (++) Acting
(-) Outsider to (+) Insider
Crawford picks up Starling at Hojos.
(-) Cold to (+) Hot
Jame Gumb Considers his Moths.
Starling at Catherine's apt. accused by Senator.
(-) Out to (+) Back In
Lecter Escapes #1
Lecter Escapes #2 Cop POV
Lecter in Ambulance. Paramedic POV
(--) Free to (---) Freer
Crawford warns Starling about recycling.
Catherine almost gets precious in hole.
Crawford learns of false Lecter Clue.
(-) Bad to (--) Worse
Lecter in St. Louis Hotel.
(--) Bad to (---) Worse
(-) Bad to (+) Better
Bella dies.
Gumb prepares for the harvest.
(--) Bad to (---) Worse
(-) Ignorant to (+) Knowledge

Harris has Lecter see through the bullshit around him and to not sit idly by. He acts and punishes the venal poseurs in life. And he's a real sucker for a regular Joe who has the courage to be comfortable in his own skin. Isn't that the kind of person we'd like to be too? Not only someone who can separate the noble from the political, but someone who has the nerve to take up arms against the wicked and help the naïve defend themselves? Without the whole cold-blooded murder and cannibalism element of course, to abide by the Lecter code would be admirable, no?

Another way Harris sets up Starling's disillusionment is in scene 20 (chapter 17). After the news that Buffalo Bill has kidnapped Catherine Martin becomes public, Starling assumes that Crawford will pull her out of class again and have her join the investigation.

But he doesn't.

You'll see on the graph that there is another dip to represent this disappointment, which again only makes the reader more empathetic to Starling.

She's gone to great lengths to be ready to join Crawford when she hears about Martin. She even jumps in the shower with another trainee to speed up her preparedness. But instead of being Crawford's first call, she is forgotten, ignored.

Crawford does not share her expectation that she's become indispensable to the investigation. Crawford needed a nice looking woman to goose Lecter into giving up some information and he needed someone familiar with the provincial nature of West Virginia who could also do fingerprinting. Starling happened to fit the bill for both of those errands, so he pulled her out of class. But now, she's an afterthought. For Crawford, she's done what he needed of her (getting Lecter to give information), so now she's disposable.

Harris is using Starling's disappointment as a way to reinforce the fact that all is not what it seems at the FBI. Jack Crawford is not the benevolent mentor that he seems to be. But Harris is not quite ready to make Starling give up on the institution. Instead he's raising the stakes again. Crawford disappointed her once and he made up for it. He's definitely disappointing her again when he ignores her.

How many more times will Starling need to be disappointed before she sees the truth?

As an aside, it's interesting to note how Harris is playing out this relationship. It's sort of like a high school romance. The girl lets a boy know she's interested in him, he responds, she then pushes him away, he's devastated until she comes back again and he's even more in love with her. Not unlike a dysfunctional parent/ child relationship either. This is a purposeful choice on Harris' part. No question.

Harris does have Crawford call for Starling at the very end of the scene 20 (chapter 17) to rejoin him in the investigation. But the reason Crawford does so is not because he feels he should, but because he needs to use Starling again. It's because the head that Starling found in the storage unit, through Lecter's intercession, also has a moth cocoon inserted into its throat. Just like the one she found in the body in West Virginia.

That information necessitates that whoever killed the man whose head was stuck in the storage unit probably killed the floater in West Virginia, the other body with a cocoon in its mouth. And both are probably the work of Buffalo Bill. So Starling, the only one to unearth the head in the jar and the only one to see the cocoon in the West Virginia body, has connected Buffalo Bill with Lecter. So Crawford pulls her back into the investigation based on merit, yes, but also because she's the catnip that will get Lecter to play along and give up more information. The complicated and political nature of the FBI is now coming into focus. For the reader. But not necessarily for Starling. She's too focused on her object of desire (to become a valued and celebrated agent in the FBI) to step back from her tenacious striving to see the real truth.

When Starling hears that Crawford's decision to bring her in was based on the discovery of the cocoon, her justified belief in the FBI is restored and is now almost sacrosanct to her. You can almost read her thoughts.

It is a meritocracy! Whew!

So when Crawford tells Starling that she has to go back and talk to Lecter again, she doesn't hesitate. She doesn't stop to think that Crawford's using her... Again! She thinks now, wholeheartedly, that she should do what she's told. And if she does that, and does it well, she'll get what she wants. Crawford will give it to her because she's earned it...

Meanwhile, while Starling's worldview grows ever positive, the Story's external life value, life/death, gets more negative. Onstage death (as opposed to the discovery of dead bodies) is becoming more and more inevitable. With the earlier establishment of the clock ticking after Buffalo Bill's abduction of the senator's daughter, it's clear that the FBI has no real clue who Buffalo Bill is or why he's doing what he's doing. It's so clueless, it's relying on a trainee to do the hard legwork in the case.

Harris makes this FBI cluelessness clear by giving Buffalo Bill (Jame Gumb) his own chapter (20, scene 23). This is Gumb's first appearance on stage and it's very strange and frightening, but what's remarkable is its specificity. This guy is off the reservation and no one has any idea who he is, let along where he is.

Back to Starling.

So, emboldened by her success finding the cocoon in West Virginia and getting the lead to the head in the jar from Lecter and her justified belief in the FBI, Starling goes back to see Lecter in scene 25 (chapter 22). She finds him about twenty steps ahead in what's going on.

Lecter schools Starling and warns her about how she's being played by Crawford and company. And he even tells her how she'll save her own life at the very end of the book (it has to do with the smell of goat). But Lecter won't tell Starling WHY Buffalo Bill is doing what he is doing **until she agrees to confide in him.**

Remember that the WHY? for the antagonist is a convention of the thriller. It's called the MacGuffin. What's so smart about Harris is that he understood, before anyone else, that the real life FBI Behavioral Science Unit itself was an effort to search for MacGuffins. The thinking is that if we know WHY killers kill, what they get out of it, we'll be better equipped to stop them. Obviously the pathology goes much deeper than the above the surface object of desire for a serial killer, but it's the first stage to getting into his internal object of the desire. Discovering the ways in which the killer acts out those desires leads to his comeuppance.

Back to the Story.

In order to get her external object of desire (to become a respected FBI agent), Starling must allow the most brilliant killer in the world into her mind. What's great about this demand beyond the fact that it is a masterstroke in "Best Bad Choice" crisis questions, is that Lecter spells out the quid pro quo directly. He doesn't manipulate Starling. He tells her what it's going to cost her right up front. Crawford and company, on the other hand, deceive her.

Because Starling has just experienced the rush of fulfilled ambition from what she sees as her own merit, she agrees. She tells Lecter her worst memory of childhood. The quid pro quo, a Faustian bargain that will become more explicit and meaningful in a later chapter. Lecter also knows that Starling's monomaniacal ambition (as well as the ambitions of the creepy head of the hospital, Frederick Chilton), will deliver him from captivity.

He's made plans from the very first meeting with Starling based on knowing what everyone will do before they actually do it.

Scene 25 (chapter 22) culminates with Lecter explaining the MacGuffin.

He tells Starling that Buffalo Bill wants a vest with "tits on it." Buffalo Bill believes he's a woman and is making his own woman suit out of the body parts of his victims. I love the way Harris has Lecter use profanity here. The subtext is that the killer sees women as objects with interchangeable body parts—just like the FBI views victims who aren't senators' daughters.

Lecter then sends Starling away to get him a deal, knowing full well that Dr. Chilton is monitoring everything he's saying. Lecter is setting up his own escape by admitting that he knows who Buffalo Bill is. But it is important to remember that Lecter never lies to Starling or plays her like Crawford does. He's giving her just enough of what she'll need to catch the killer if she has the courage to see through the bullshit. But not one bit more.

Harris breaks away from the investigation after the MacGuffin is revealed to give us the point of view of the human being who will provide Buffalo Bill's vest, Catherine Martin. We see what she's going through and it's horrifying. Every second the FBI wastes…death gets closer. Add the fact that she'll be flayed and her chest will be sewn into a suit worn and paraded around by some mad man is definitely in fate worse than death territory. And we're only midway through the novel!

This is masterful construction of Progressive Complications. Now you know why the MIDDLE is called BUILD. And the view from the pit humanizes a prurient detail. It's as if Harris is telling us not to forget that the vest with tits is a human being. And for all of our rooting for Starling and her ambitions to make the grade, there is a person about to be slaughtered for every second she and her fellow FBI agents waste.

To repeat, the peak of Starling's justified belief arrives in scene 28 (chapter 25). She throws herself all on the line and agrees to give Lecter what he wants, entree inside her mind to her deepest thoughts—a sexual metaphor if there ever was one. She does this because she believes unequivocally that the FBI and the senator are telling the truth. They're backing her up and they'll live up to their promises. She believes they will protect her from Hannibal the Cannibal.

But Lecter knows that the FBI and Crawford are lying to Starling and he will use that knowledge to escape, but he also can't help himself from falling for Starling. This is why he's decided to help her find the truth about herself. In exchange for his penetration into her mind, he'll help Starling find Buffalo Bill all by herself too. If she's as smart as she thinks she is. What she does when she finds Buffalo Bill, though, is up to her.

Lecter also decides to give her a critical piece of information…the information that will save her from Buffalo Bill. All she has to remember is that schizophrenics smell like goats. Remember this scene? Scene 25, chapter 22? Lecter explains to Starling why Sammie, his new cellmate after Miggs killed himself, smells like a goat. It is this explanation that will clue Starling in to the fact that Sammie and Buffalo Bill share the same affliction. So in the climax of the entire novel, she'll remember that little tidbit and save herself. If you also have any doubt that Lecter knew who Buffalo Bill was and in fact where Jame Gumb lives…just go to the very first meeting between Lecter and Starling and you'll notice that he's made a drawing of the Palazzo Vecchio and the Duomo in Florence, Italy. He makes a special point of letting Starling know that he's drawn the scene as it would look from the point of view of the Belvedere.

Buffalo Bill/Gumb lives in Belvedere, Ohio. Talk about setting up a clue and paying it off!

He's mocking the FBI with his artwork at the very beginning of the novel (and at the end too) and they don't even know it. The only one who comes to understand how important his artwork is? Starling.

Also in scene 25 (chapter 22) Lecter tells Starling that Buffalo Bill is all about "change." Buffalo Bill wants to change himself, but he's wrong about the course he's taking to do it. Lecter knows that this yearning for change mirrors Starling's. Starling wants to shed her West Virginia, white trash, coal country past and become an important person, a crack FBI agent. If she can do that, she'll also avenge her father's death, the murdered night watchman who died when she was just a little girl.

Jame Gumb, the man behind the Buffalo Bill robe, wants to don new skin too. But he wants to do it…literally.

Lecter knows that by giving Starling the clues to understand why the killer is doing what he's doing, she may come to understand that she is metaphorically doing the same thing. The irony Lecter is trying to convey to Starling is that the only way she will be able to catch the killer is by being true to who she is... especially the nobody West Virginia girl part.

Of course, Thomas Harris never spells this subtext out. It reveals itself to the reader upon reflection. And even if it doesn't, the specificity of the telling is enough to sit with the reader for years.

Back to the clues. In scene 28 (chapter 25), Lecter tells Starling to look for men who have applied for sex changes but who have been turned down for the operation. To look for one person who has been turned down at every clinic in the country. The work required to do this, Lecter knows, will take the FBI far longer than it will for Gumb to kill the senator's daughter. But it's righteous information nevertheless.

Lecter's counting on the delay in getting the sensitive sex change information to enable him to escape.

Scene 28 (chapter 25) represents the peak of the positive worldview for Starling. She believes in her role in the FBI so intently that she opens up her subconscious self to Lecter. From this point forward, Starling is going to get a deep lesson in the realities of the institution she's sacrificed for.

Back to the external value shift.

After the big break that Lecter gives Starling in scene 28 (chapter 25), Harris triples down on the forces of antagonism.

He takes us into Lecter's brain in scenes 29, 30 and 32 (chapters 26, 27 and 29) letting us know that he knows exactly what he's doing. He's going to use the ambition and venality of Dr. Chilton to get him out of Baltimore. Chilton is so stupid that he thinks he's going to pressure Lecter into giving up Buffalo Bill all on his own. And then in scene 31 (chapter 28), Crawford goes to Johns Hopkins to follow up on the clue that Lecter has given Starling, only to find that the doctor responsible for the list of sex change operation patients is refusing to give up any information. It's going to take far more than "please" to get the info they need to track down Buffalo Bill. In these scenes, Harris presents Lecter, Chilton, and the doctor at Johns Hopkins as additional forces of antagonism undermining the efforts to stop Buffalo Bill, the primary force of antagonism.

Which brings us to the midpoint of the entire novel, scene 33 (chapter 30), the "Point of No Return Moment."

In scene 33 (chapter 30), Crawford informs Starling of all the obstacles now in their path.

Her reaction is rage, something that Crawford can completely understand. He's been swallowing his rage for thirty years. It is in this moment (when getting Buffalo Bill seems impossible) that Crawford finally sees Starling as a human being. He relates to her because of her anger. He sees himself, at last, in her. She's just not some cute broad he needed to dangle in front of Lecter anymore.

She's a pro, just like him.

Crawford gives Starling some advice..."Freeze your anger."

He thinks this is good advice because it allowed him to navigate the difficult political landscape within the FBI and rise to the head of Behavioral Science. What he does not know is that Starling has already let Lecter into her mind. She's all in. If they do not get Buffalo Bill, she will have submitted to a lifetime of Lecter's voice inside her head...perpetual internal torment...for nothing. Starling has already passed the point of no return internally, now she faces it externally.

In scene 33 (chapter 30), Crawford finally starts to tell her the truth. He confides to her about the FBI's bureaucracy, tells her that if she stays on the case, she'll most likely be recycled at the Academy. She'll have to start all over again and he won't be able to do anything to help her.

In addition to it being the Point of No Return, the entire case is now completely *personal* to Starling. Yet another convention of the thriller Genre ticked off by Harris in a completely innovative way. Many writers abide this convention to "make it personal" in a thriller by concocting some beef the killer has with the investigator. But Buffalo Bill couldn't care less about Clarice Starling.

The way Harris makes the case personal to Starling, of course, is through Lecter and the FBI.

While Lecter's goosing Starling's subconscious mind to push her into understanding her psychological condition and how it must change in order for her to succeed, the FBI is goosing her externally through the direct possibility that everything she's worked for up until this point will be taken away from her if she stays on the case. Talk about a crisis! Starling has reached the point of no return internally and externally. She either keeps going or quits now. There is no turning back.

Harris has taken a rather tired convention "make it personal," turned it on its ear, and made it a seamless and inevitable progressive complication, incredibly powerful and compelling. This is how you innovate conventions and obligatory scenes. You look at them in a different way than just a checklist of things you have to cram into your Story. You look at them as opportunities to elevate your Story.

And then Harris makes things even worse for Starling.

Crawford sends Starling to Memphis to hang around in case Lecter wants someone to talk to. In scene 37 (chapter 34), she goes to Catherine Martin's apartment to do a personal reconnaissance, just to see life from the point of view of the victim. (For those of you who have read *Red Dragon,* you'll see that this trip is akin to the trips Will Graham makes to see the crime from the point of view of the killer.)

And then the senator, Catherine Martin's mother, arrives and accuses Starling of stealing...the worst possible accusation to someone from Starling's background. She's made to feel like a commoner, not worthy of touching the material goods of one higher on the social ladder. This episode is even more negative movement of the internal worldview value. Here Starling is putting her entire life on the line to help find this woman's daughter and the mother treats her like a common criminal. And then Starling's quickly dismissed, told to go back to Quantico by one of the senator's flunkies, someone capable of ruining her career. Someone with far more power than Jack Crawford.

But Starling decides to disobey the higher ups. She transitions into a hero in this critical moment.

Starling goes to see Lecter one last time before going back to the Academy. It's a Hail Mary act. A great crisis (you're fired!) matched with a compelling climax (I'm going to keep working anyway) sets up a doozy of a resolution scene.

Scene 38 (chapter 35) is the last meeting between Lecter and Starling and it's a stunner.

"People will say we're in love," is one of Lecter's opening remarks.

Starling suspects that the Chilton-derived help Lecter has been giving the FBI, his whole "Billy Rubin" business is a deception, a red herring (another convention of the thriller Harris has made interesting). She nudges Lecter into talking more about the imago metaphor (the last stage an insect reaches before metamorphosis) that he'd spoken of in their last meeting.

Lecter's game to talk. He plays with Starling by asking her direct questions that reveal Buffalo Bill's occupation *"Do you sew at all? Did you make that costume?"*

Lecter also lectures (interesting choice of name Harris made for Lecter...lecturn, lecture…) Starling about one of stoic philosopher Marcus Aurelius' first principles, simplicity. What is the causal nature of Buffalo Bill? He Covets. He wants what he sees everyday. This of course is the clue that will send Starling to Belvedere, Ohio. The end of the argument Lecter is making without directly saying it is that Buffalo Bill began killing because he saw the victim (the Bimmel girl) every day. After he killed her he branched outside of his home quarters…to be safe. But the first one was the beginning of his last stage before his metamorphosis.

And what of Starling's first principles? What is her causal nature? Lecter goes deep and probes her about her darkest memory. Quid pro quo.

"What happened to you and the horse and what you do with your anger?"

Lecter always comes back to "anger" with Starling. While her actions are not those one would perceive as those of an angry person, Lecter knows something that the reader does not. He's put together Starling's psychological profile and he's probing her past to see if his theory is accurate.

Lecter knows that Starling's abandonment in childhood is a recipe for acute anger and self-loathing. It's psychology 101. Her father's death led to her mother's overwork and eventually to the young Starling being sent away to her mother's cousin in Montana. This is a multi-ton weight of injustice and abandonment for a child to comprehend.

A child is incapable of making the cognitive leaps necessary to metabolize such tragic circumstances. Their brains just aren't developed enough at that point in time. So their minds immediately move to express anger (along with fear and primal sexual urge, baseline emotional fallback positions for humans under threat) with the only being available to them. Themselves. They are alone and have no one to "act out" on.

The anger is internalized and the child begins to attack herself. *If I weren't so difficult my mother would have been able to take care of me.* Such internalized anger creates pervasive self-loathing in a child that either expresses itself through a serious personality disorder (Jame Gumb) or it wedges itself deep inside the psyche and is repressed (Starling).

Those high achievers that we all know are often driven by this deeply wedged self-loathing. They work relentlessly to prove themselves worthy. Short of metamorphosis into another person entirely (Jame Gumb), though, their efforts will come up short. Again and again and again. What's also remarkable about the effect of abandonment is an acute sense of injustice within the abandoned. Perceived or real injustice is that thing that the abandoned child as an adult has difficulty understanding.

Or accepting as an inescapable part of life.

Rage and uncompromising/impossible personal standards within the adult are the result.

Lecter knows that Starling is driven by deeply repressed anger and self-loathing. As he's an emotional cannibal as well as a literal one, he feeds on this knowledge. Hence his appetite for Starling's deep psychological wounds.

This scene is brilliantly realized because Harris has delivered Starling to Lecter just after she'd been the victim of, to her, a serious injustice. She's been accused of stealing by a powerful senator and her anger/rage is boiling by the time she comes in to see Lecter. Lecter, the psychological GPS device par excellence, senses this vulnerability and thus is successful in getting her to spill the beans about her longing for *The Silence of the Lambs*. She tells Lecter her recurring nightmare about the slaughtering of lambs from her past. How she cannot stop their screams echoing in her subconscious.

It is this unveiling of deeply seated childhood trauma that allows Starling to change her investigative methods and release her true genius. Knowing the truth about yourself, even if there is no magic pill to solve your dilemma, is empowering.

Starling's confessions to Lecter actually enable her to get rid of her own self-infatuation (her anger and her obsession with injustice and self-improvement/ elevation). She is now capable of empathy, capable of recognizing the emotions others experience. It is this release that gives her the tools necessary to solve the case. She'll be able to see the world in the way that the "victims" saw it (the opposite of Will Graham in *Red Dragon*).

Like all great thrillers, the protagonist and the antagonist are polar expressions of a single archetype. What separates Buffalo Bill and Clarice Starling, both abandoned children with deep-seated anger, is the ability to confront their inner demons. Buffalo Bill is incapable of doing so. Instead he decides he must literally change himself. But Starling is capable of confronting her inner demons and she does so with Lecter (the epitome of darkness) as her guide.

The first ten times I read *The Silence of the Lambs*, I did not pick up the significance of Lecter's infatuation with Starling's anger. It wasn't until I did a deep dive into the psychological literature about how deeply rooted anger presents itself, that I came to the understanding that Starling is a classic borderline personality case study. Highly functioning of course. One of those people who are incredibly accomplished and seemingly steady and centered with a secret.

What's also fascinating about the chronically angry is that they are great magical thinkers. That is, their inner torment is so overwhelming that they internally reason with themselves. *If I can just get my Ph.D. then I won't feel so bad about myself...* Without knowing why they harbor such anger and how that anger is trumping their adult cognition, these magical thinkers keep pressing forward... with great ambition...to move up the old social hierarchy in the hopes that if the whole world sees them as valuable and worthy, then perhaps they will too. They believe that third party validation will envelop them and silence the inner voice that degrades and abuses them as unlovable and worthless.

But, of course, it never will.

> *"Do you think if you caught Buffalo Bill yourself and if you made Catherine all right, you could make the lambs stop screaming, do you think they'd be all right too and you wouldn't wake up again in the dark and hear the lambs screaming? Clarice?"*
>
> *"Yes. I don't know. Maybe."*
>
> *"Thank you, Clarice." Dr. Lecter seemed oddly at peace.*

Lecter is at peace because he has solved the crossword puzzle of Clarice Starling. His diagnosis is spot on. Starling is a classic highly functional borderline personality. Her deeply seated anger is her causal nature…what drives her ambition. Her belief that if she catches Buffalo Bill, she'll be able to quiet the voices inside her mind (the sound of sheep being slaughtered is the metaphor for her inner torment) is magical thinking par excellence.

Lecter, the emotional and literal cannibal, then hands Starling the case file and points her in the right direction to find Buffalo Bill…to Belvedere, Ohio. For fun, go to scene 3 (chapter 3) and read about the painting Lecter has on his wall in the very first meeting with Starling. After you've re-read it, you'll have little doubt that Lecter has orchestrated the plot of *The Silence of the Lambs.*

Why does Lecter have such an affinity for Starling?

I think it's because Lecter and Starling share the same malady. Lecter figured out his problem a long time ago and chose the life of an Uberman, a Nietzsche figure parsing out his own sense of justice, while tormenting the simpletons around him for sport. Lecter is chronically angry too. We never do learn what drives Lecter's behavior. Thankfully. Not knowing is so much better.

But Lecter has dispensed with magical thinking. He understands that his inner voices are unrelenting and therefore he considers himself "of them" as opposed to "apart from them." He's identified himself with the darkness inside and expresses that identity with aplomb.

Starling is his counterbalance. She believes that her inner light is stronger than her dark voices and that if her actions are "good" then those actions will compile into a record of "goodness" that will beat down her darker impulses. Lecter will leave Starling alone after his escape because it brings him great satisfaction to see someone else playing this game at the deepest psychological level. She's his protégé of sorts and he'll enjoy following her life and career from afar.

I think Lecter empathizes with Starling. And he teaches her how to empathize too with his coup de grace of psychological probing. The only way she'll find Buffalo Bill is to embrace the skin she wishes to shed, the West Virginia girl. If she understands what motivates that kind of girl and puts herself in that girl's shoes, it will lead her to the dark force that covets victims like "the Bimmel girl."

So scene 38 (chapter 35) represents her literal point of no return. Driven by deep-seated anger triggered by the senator's accusing her of theft, Starling has spilled her guts to Lecter. She's supposed to have gone back to Quantico, but instead disobeyed orders. Whatever happens now, she won't be able to turn back the clock. She's put herself on the shit list of high political powers, a tier she will never rise to, for the rest of her life.

She will never be treated "justly."

The stakes for Starling continue to rise in the next sequence of scenes.

Lecter escapes just after his heart to heart talk with her. It's as if Starling has given him the nourishment and the motive to do so.

In scene 38 (chapter 35) Harris also has Lecter grill Starling about the time clock her father had to use when he was a night patrolman for his small West Virginia town. This is the second clock introduced in the Story and I believe it is a metaphor for the imminent necessity for Starling to see the real truth behind the FBI. They are using her just as her childhood town used her father. Her father died serving a bunch of assholes that used him like a human watchdog. If Starling doesn't wise up about the people using her, her clock will run out too. You'll see that Starling's worldview takes precipitous dive in this scene 38 (chapter 35). Doubting the institution in which she's placed her faith in is now overwhelming.

In scene 50 (chapter 47), after we've had the escape chapters, Catherine Martin's attempt to kidnap Jame Gumb's dog Precious, and Jame Gumb's preparations for the slaughter, we're back to Starling in Quantico. She's running her list of grievances in her mind after she awakes from her perpetual "screaming lambs" nightmare. She's pleased to be full of anger and not fear. Starling now recognizes that anger is a great motivator and, like Lecter, embraces it...unlike Crawford who eats his.

Starling goes to the laundry room, the sounds subconsciously reminding her of the last time she was safe...in her mother's womb. She goes through the Buffalo Bill file that Lecter handed her on her way out of his holding cell. In the file, Lecter gives her the clue to go to the area where the first victim was found.

> *Clarice, doesn't this random scattering of sites seem overdone to you? ...Does it suggest to you the elaborations of a bad liar?*

I love how Harris has Lecter use the word "liar." Starling has been lied to the entire book. By the FBI and by herself. The only one who never lied to her was Lecter.

At the end of scene 50 (chapter 47), we reach the crisis question of the Middle Build. Should Starling keep going on the hunt for Buffalo Bill and lose her place at the FBI? Or should she stay at Quantico and finish out her FBI training and lament the death of Catherine Martin? It's a best bad choice dilemma.

She goes to Crawford to tell him her decision. The climax of the Middle Build is scene 51 (chapter 48). This scene arrives just after Crawford's wife Bella dies. Starling gets Crawford's blessing and his pocket money just outside of the funeral home. The resolution is that Crawford sees Starling as the hero he never quite became. It's a very moving scene, perfectly executed. And Harris shows it from Crawford's point of view, a great way of showing how Starling has become his equal.

Let's look at the external value.

Remember that the end of the line for the life value progresses from Life to Unconsciousness to Death to the fate worse than Death…Damnation.

The last major shift in the Life value came in scene 17 (chapter 15), when Buffalo Bill abducts Catherine Martin. Now, the intellectual exercise of trying to clarify who the killer is from the clues left from dead bodies becomes a race to stop not just death…but the fate worse than death…having a woman's body defiled and used as a suit.

From scene 17 though scene 42 (chapter 15 to chapter 39), no one dies. But by scene 51 (chapter 48), death is prevalent. Lecter has viciously killed two guards and Bella is dead. Three bodies by the end of scene 51 (chapter 48).

It's now evident that no one is going to stop death.

How does Harris escalate the stakes from death to damnation for Starling for the final chapters of the novel? He's already established that damnation has arrived with the escape of Lecter for the entire FBI. How does he put damnation in play for Starling specifically?

It is the crisis of the Middle Build for her that takes the value to the limits of human experience, damnation. If Starling does not act, if she does not put her ass on the line and sacrifice her global object of desire of becoming a big shot FBI agent, Catherine Martin will die. She won't just die either. Her body will be desecrated.

So if Starling doesn't act, Catherine Martin will haunt her in a way that makes those little lambs screaming in her nightmares child's play. Martin's death on Starling's conscience, especially when she knows that Lecter has absolutely given her the key to finding Buffalo Bill, would damn her to a fate worse than death…a living hell. Imagine the internal torment for Starling. Not only would she be self-hating for not have the courage to do something but that very lack of courage causes the death of another human being. To die is one thing, to cause death or standing idly by when someone else is facing death is damning.

So to save herself from damnation, Starling must save Martin.

What about the Internal Value?

Remember that Harris chose the Disillusionment plot for his internal content worldview plot. And disillusion moves from Illusion (Blind Belief), to Confirmation (Justified Belief) to Confusion (Doubt), to Disillusion to Dysthymia. Harris does not go to the end of the line with the disillusionment plot here because he's working in the thriller Genre. If he were working on a Mini-plot literary novel, perhaps he would. But to go to the end of the line with the internal content value as well as the external content value would be too much for the reader. So instead he moves Starling one level before chronic depression, disillusionment.

The climax of the Middle Build is also the transition point of Starling into disillusion.

She's now completely going against orders from on high (far higher than Crawford) and she's going solo, without any backup beyond Crawford's personal support. She's carrying a gun but technically she is no longer allowed to present herself as an authorized FBI agent. She understands at this point too that what she's doing will destroy her naïve "want" of becoming an agent and rising in the bureau. She's learned that the institution is not just inept, it's corrupt and not in any real way devoted to justice or safeguarding the public.

As someone born into an unjust world, it makes perfect sense for Starling to shit can her career to fight for what is right. It's why she wanted to be an FBI agent in the first place. Whether she knows it or not, it was Lecter who probed her deepest childhood horrors that enabled her to come to this conclusion subconsciously. She knows the truth about herself…because of the horrors of her childhood she's a vigilante for justice. That is what she does and will continue to do with her anger. Fight for justice.

Just for fun, before we dive into the Ending Payoff of *The Silence of the Lambs,* let's look at the math of the novel.

The Middle Build comprises 38 chapters and 55,238 words (57% of the book). Along with the Beginning Hook, we've traversed 76% of the novel. So the Ending Payoff will be 24%. A 19/57/24 distribution of Beginning Hook, Middle Build and Ending Payoff. This is absolutely in the realm of standard novel form.

I can promise you that this composition is not a coincidence. The 25/50/25 guideline is an extremely helpful piece of information that will save you a ton of heartache.

69

THE ENDING PAYOFF OF *THE SILENCE OF THE LAMBS*

At long last, we come to the Ending Payoff of the novel.

Whether or not the book "works" will all come down to the Ending Payoff. Just about any gaffe (with the exception of the Inciting Incident) in the Beginning Hook or Middle Build can be made up in the Ending Payoff. And obviously, no matter how great your Beginning Hook or Middle Build is, if the ending fizzles, you will not have a Story that compels readers to tell one another about it.

Using our *Foolscap Global Story Grid* and our *Story Grid Spreadsheet,* I'll do the exact same thing we did for the Beginning Hook and Middle Build of the book for the Ending Payoff. I'll boil down each scene event that I've written on my *Story Grid Spreadsheet* to the shortest possible phrase or sentence that tells us what's happened. I'll then write down the event above or below the horizontal line to designate the value shift of that particular scene. So if the scene moves from a positive to a negative value charge, I will put the label for that scene beneath the x-axis. If the scene moves from a negative to a positive charge, I will put the label for that scene above the x-axis.

I'll track the movement of the "Life" and "Worldview" values in the y-axis too. The "Life" value will grow ever more positive as the FBI, and by association Starling, gets closer to identifying and capturing Buffalo Bill. There will be a big dip in the penultimate end to reflect the false ending in the book and then it will end in the positive and linger at the very, very end in the negative. Let's not forget that an even worse killer than Buffalo Bill, Hannibal Lecter, is at large now.

As for the "Worldview" value, it will fall into disillusion from the very start of the Ending Payoff. Starling no longer has confidence in the FBI and by necessity has chosen to go it alone. At the end of the novel, in the resolution chapters after the death of Buffalo Bill, Starling's worldview settles in to rest in the negative.

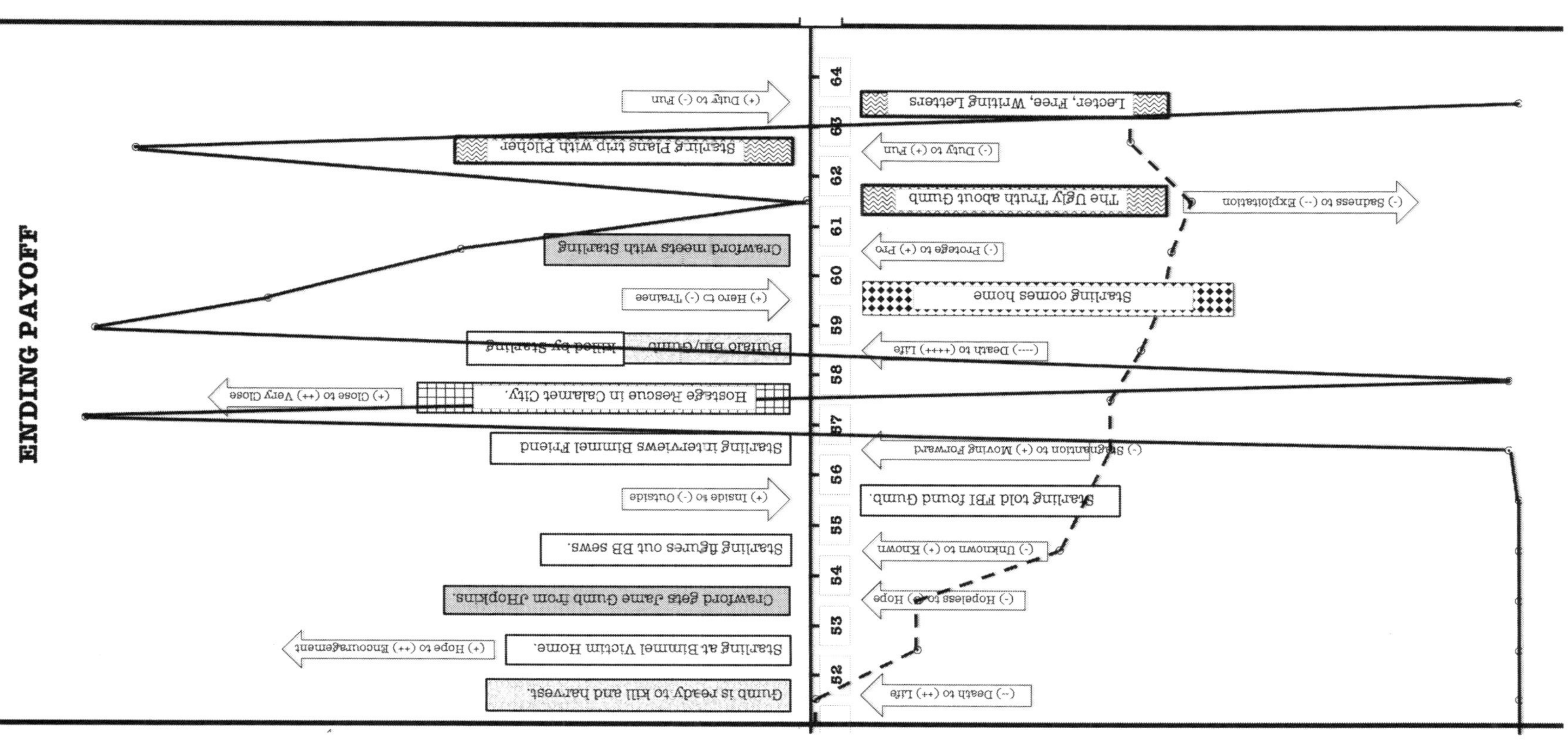
ENDING PAYOFF
Gumb is ready to kill and harvest.
Starling at Bimmel Victim Home.
(+) Hope to (++) Encouragement
Crawford gets Jame Gumb from JHopkins.
Starling figures out BB sews.
(+) Inside to (-) Outside
Starling interviews Bimmel Friend
Hostage Rescue in Calamet City.
(+) Close to (++) Very Close
Buffalo Bill/Gumb killed by Starling
(+) Hero to (-) Trainee
Crawford meets with Starling
Starling Plans trip with Pilcher
(+) Duty to (-) Fun
52
53
54
55
56
57
58
59
60
61
62
63
64
(--) Death to (++) Life
(-) Hopeless to (+) Hope
(-) Unknown to (+) Known
Starling told FBI found Gumb.
(-) Stagnation to (+) Moving Forward
(----) Death to (++++) Life
Starling comes home
(-) Protege to (+) Pro
The Ugly Truth about Gumb
(-) Sadness to (--) Exploitation
(-) Duty to (+) Fun
Lecter, Free, Writing Letters

Scene 52 (chapter 49) is the Inciting Incident of the Ending Payoff. Jame Gumb (Buffalo Bill) moves forward with his plans to harvest the hide of Catherine Martin. Harris writes it from Gumb's point of view. Scene 52 (chapter 49) is all about establishing Gumb's state of mind and how he actually does what it is he does... the technical aspects of creating a woman suit. As it is so clinical, the impact on the reader is chilling. This guy has not one reservation about killing a woman and cutting off her skin. She may as well be a tree he'd like to strip of bark.

Following up on Lecter's clue from the case file that Buffalo Bill's pattern of abduction is desperately random and that his causal being is to covet what he sees, scene 53 (chapter 50) shows us Starling's investigation into the life of Buffalo Bill's very first victim, Frederica Bimmel. She goes to Bimmel's room to suss out any clues about what men she may have known before her death. Her theory, based on Lecter's suggestion, is that whoever killed Bimmel was around her for some time...so much so that he coveted her skin.

Scene 54 (chapter 51) sets up the required False Ending convention of the thriller.

Crawford finally hears from the doctors at Johns Hopkins about the man who was turned down for a sex change operation. They give Crawford Buffalo Bill's real name, Jame Gumb. The reader knows that Crawford now has the right guy, but Starling does not. Giving the reader more information than the protagonist is a great way of ratcheting up narrative drive. Harris is a master at this.

Back to Starling in scene 55 (chapter 52). She's figured out that Buffalo Bill is a tailor. Obviously, if he is making a "woman suit," he knows how to sew. She recalls Lecter asking her if she knew how to sew too, which only confirms her conclusions.

In scene 56 (chapter 53), Starling tells the FBI's switchboard operator about her findings. But he's not all that interested. The operator tells Starling that they've tracked down Buffalo Bill and that the Hostage Rescue Team is on the way to break down his door and catch him red-handed. This information raises the irreconcilable goods crisis of the Ending Payoff.

Should Starling abort the rest of her investigation in Belvedere, Ohio? Or should she carry on? What's the point really? She's not going to be the big hero and obviously she's been misled. If she heads back to Quantico now, she may even save her spot in the trainee program. That would be good for her. But if she continues it could be good for the case.

But Lecter's influence keeps her on course. Starling considers the fact that if they get Buffalo Bill in handcuffs, they will need a ton of evidence to convict him. And besides, she's moved beyond her own inner trauma after her head-shrinking session with Lecter back before he escaped. She no longer operates under illusions. So she reminds herself of what she's supposed to do, what her gifts are as a human being and how she can use them to help others—Jame Gumb will be arrested. The FBI will have to make the case that he's the killer of Bimmel. Her investigation will help. So the Bimmel father would at least know what happened to his daughter and who was responsible.

> *"Her job, her duty, was to think about Fredrica and how Gumb might have gotten her. A criminal prosecution of Buffalo Bill would require all the facts. Think about Fredrica, stuck here all her young life. Where would she look for the exit? Did her longings resonate with Buffalo Bill's? Did that draw them together? Awful thought, that he might have understood her out of his own experience, empathized even, and still helped himself to her skin.*[8]

In scene 57 (chapter 54) Starling chooses to continue her investigation and talks with a friend of Frederica's who works at a bank. She gives Starling the information that will lead her to Gumb's house.

In scene 58 (chapter 55) the Hostage Rescue team breaks down the wrong guy's door. Here is our obligatory false ending scene. Simply brilliant and totally believable knowing what we know about the FBI now.

In scene 59 (chapter 56), Gumb resolves to kill Martin even if it threatens his dog Precious. He puts on his robe to begin the process. He's going to use infrared goggles and take a headshot in the dark to kill Martin so that he doesn't accidently ruin her torso skin. But then Starling arrives at his back door and we've now reached the climax of the entire novel.

The hero at the mercy of the villain scene is the most important scene in a thriller and Harris delivers his in a HUGE way.

After much toing and froing, Gumb has turned off the lights in the basement and is moving around with his night vision goggles. He's enjoying watching Starling struggle to find her way. But just as he's about to shoot her, Starling smells something.

Heavy in her nostrils the smell of the goat.[9]

The smell is the same one that Lecter told her schizophrenics emit…Buffalo Bill is a schizophrenic. Starling then hears the snick of his gun. She turns to the noise, fires and expertly kills him.

Great climax! Over the moon great. The set up for it probably took a ridiculous amount of thinking and work, but what a payoff!

---

8 Harris, Thomas. The Silence of the Lambs (p. 325). Macmillan. Kindle Edition.

9 Harris, Thomas. The Silence of the Lambs (p. 346). Macmillan. Kindle Edition.

Starling remembered the goat smell that Lecter had warned her about back in Baltimore, which told her that Gumb was in the room even though she couldn't see him.

She was blind until Lecter taught her to "see" with her nose!

Not just her nose, but her ears too!

Starling was prepared for him to shoot her so she was attuned to the noise of the cocking of a gun. She knows that noise because she's an expert shooter herself. See the great stuff at the very beginning of the novel when we see Starling as ace of her shooting class! Harris set up her expertise long ago in the Beginning Hook of the book.

She trusts her instincts and senses and kills Gumb before he can kill her.

This scene also mirrors the death of her father who was murdered in darkness when he confronted a criminal. Thematically, she's won back the family honor by facing down the same circumstance as her father and triumphing. Justice has been restored.

Starling's life is now at equilibrium. She's seriously changed, though.

Her object of desire (being an FBI agent) is no longer the magical trophy that will bring her inner peace. But she also understands that defending the weak is her destiny…it's what she needs to do to dissipate her anger.

The remaining scenes resolve the novel. They bring down the fever of the reader in a very believable and compelling way.

Starling even gets a little love from the FBI.

They haven't washed her out of Academy. Instead she's given a couple of extra days to pass her exams and her friend Ardelia Mapp as tutor. She passes. And she resolves her romance with the nerdy scientist at the Smithsonian too. She goes away for the weekend with him.

While Starling's found a modicum of peace, leaving the reader satisfied, Harris also leaves the ending open. Hannibal Lecter is still on the loose. One killer may be dead, but an ever more dangerous one is now loose.

Irony anyone?

70

THE FINAL TWEAKS

So, we've tracked the entire scene-to-scene movement of *The Silence of the Lambs* in terms of its external and internal values. And we've identified quite a number of places within its scenes where Thomas Harris has abided by the conventions and obligatory scenes of his chosen global Story—the serial killer thriller. We've also tracked the exact places where the Beginning Hook has transitioned into the Middle Build and where the Middle Build has transitioned into the Ending Payoff.

Let's now load all of that information into *The Story Grid* so that at a glance, we'll be able to remind ourselves where Harris did what. The real value of *The Story Grid* is in its immediate gratification. That is, in the years prior to creating *The Story Grid* infographic, every time I had a question like "*When did Thomas Harris drop in his clock?*" I had to go look at a pile of notes.

And I'd have to dig through it until I found the answer. I don't know about you, but once I found that answer I'd often forget the original question I was trying to answer!

But now with *The Story Grid*, all I have to do is look for the clock moment on the grid. Then I'll know it was in scene 19 (chapter 17), six scenes into the Middle Build. Similarly, when you map out your own *Story Grid* for your work in progress, you may see that you've jammed a whole bunch of stuff into one series of scenes, or your values are not dynamically moving in the way that they should. Seeing it visually as opposed to trying to piece it together in your brain intellectually will be extremely useful.

So our final *Story Grid* for *The Silence of the Lambs* with all of the crucial conventions and obligatory scenes marked as well as the BH, MB, and EP demarcations follows.

The Story Grid

The Silence of the Lambs by Thomas Harris

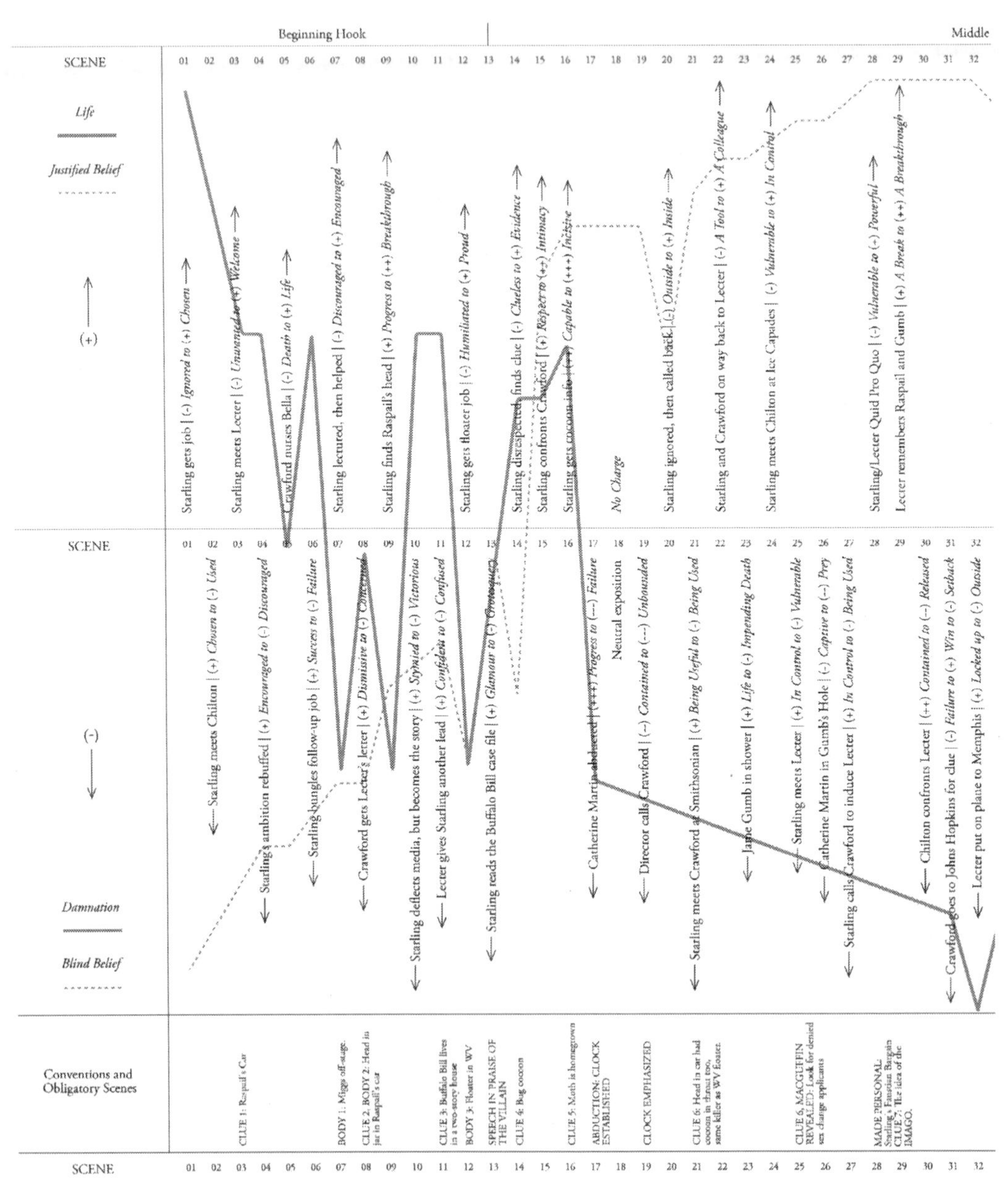

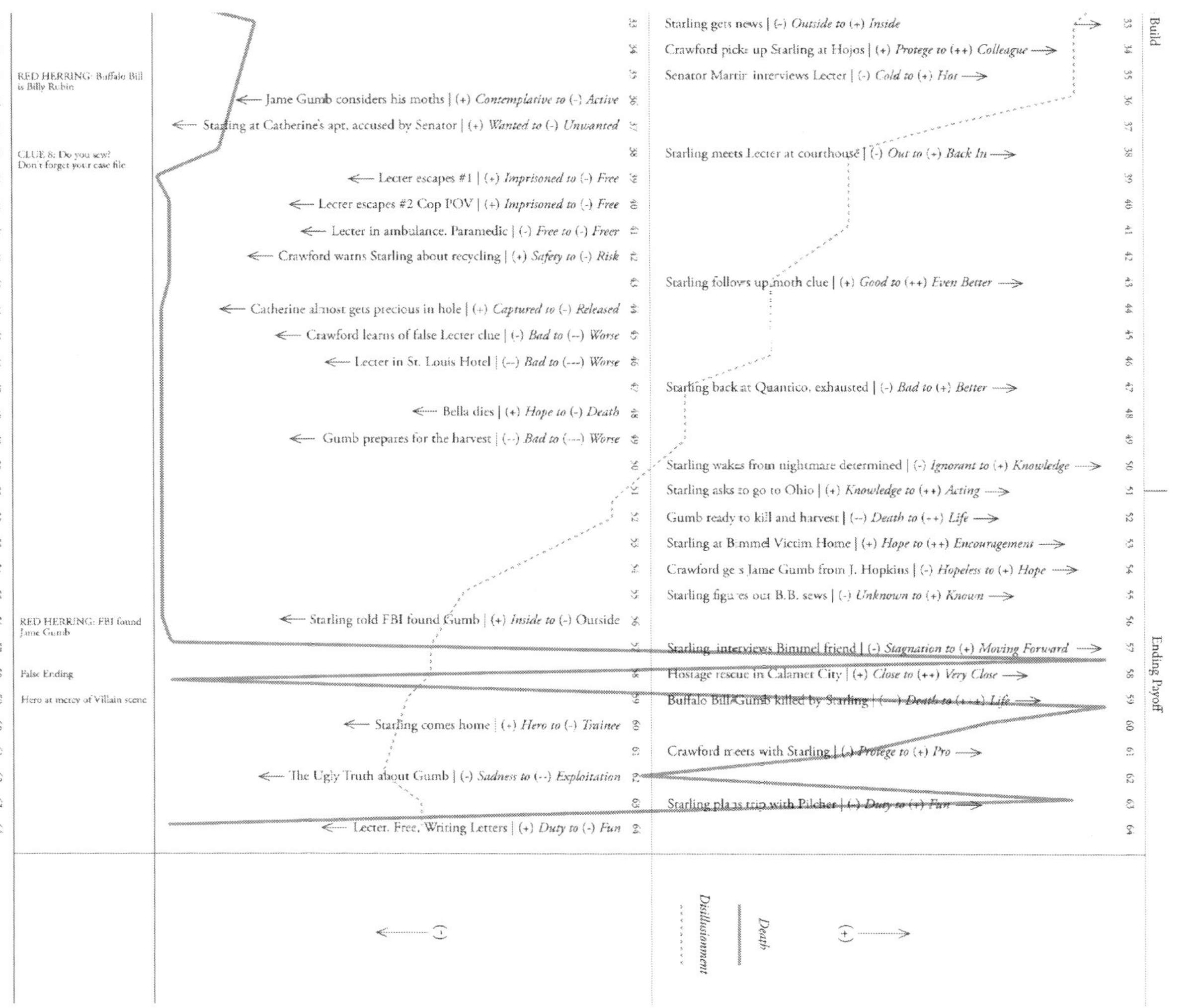
Build
Ending Payoff
33 34 35 36 37 38 39 40 41 42 43 44 45 46 47 48 49 50 51 52 53 54 55 56 57 58 59 60 61 62 63 64
Starling gets news | (-) Outside to (+) Inside
Crawford picks up Starling at Hojos | (+) Protege to (++) Colleague
Senator Martin interviews Lecter | (-) Cold to (+) Hot
Starling meets Lecter at courthouse | (-) Out to (+) Back In
Starling follows up moth clue | (+) Good to (++) Even Better
Starling back at Quantico, exhausted | (-) Bad to (+) Better
Starling wakes from nightmare determined | (-) Ignorant to (+) Knowledge
Starling asks to go to Ohio | (+) Knowledge to (++) Acting
Gumb ready to kill and harvest | (--) Death to (++) Life
Starling at Bimmel Victim Home | (+) Hope to (++) Encouragement
Crawford gets Jame Gumb from J. Hopkins | (-) Hopeless to (+) Hope
Starling figures out B.B. sews | (-) Unknown to (+) Known
Starling interviews Bimmel friend | (-) Stagnation to (+) Moving Forward
Hostage rescue in Calumet City | (+) Close to (++) Very Close
Buffalo Bill/Gumb killed by Starling | (--) Death to (++) Life
Crawford meets with Starling | (-) Protege to (+) Pro
Starling plans trip with Pilcher | (-) Duty to (+) Fun
Jame Gumb considers his moths | (+) Contemplative to (-) Active
Starling at Catherine's apt. accused by Senator | (+) Wanted to (-) Unwanted
Lecter escapes #1 | (+) Imprisoned to (-) Free
Lecter escapes #2 Cop POV | (+) Imprisoned to (-) Free
Lecter in ambulance. Paramedic | (-) Free to (-) Freer
Crawford warns Starling about recycling | (+) Safety to (-) Risk
Catherine almost gets precious in hole | (+) Captured to (-) Released
Crawford learns of false Lecter clue | (-) Bad to (--) Worse
Lecter in St. Louis Hotel | (--) Bad to (---) Worse
Bella dies | (+) Hope to (-) Death
Gumb prepares for the harvest | (--) Bad to (---) Worse
Starling told FBI found Gumb | (+) Inside to (-) Outside
Starling comes home | (+) Hero to (-) Trainee
The Ugly Truth about Gumb | (-) Sadness to (--) Exploitation
Lecter. Free. Writing Letters | (+) Duty to (-) Fun
RED HERRING: Buffalo Bill is Billy Rubin
CLUE 8: Do you sew? Don't forget your case file
RED HERRING: FBI found Jame Gumb
False Ending
Hero at mercy of Villain scene
(-)
(+)
Death
Disillusionment

But *The Story Grid* on the cover of the book and on the poster of *The Silence of the Lambs Story Grid* doesn't have all this information. What's up with that?

We stripped down the exhaustive information of the writer's version of *The Story Grid* to its essence for the infographic version for a simple reason. There's just too much INSIDE BASEBALL in the crazy detailed one. Whittling down the details, we came to the conclusion that the most important visual takeaway for *The Story Grid* is the movement of the external (the red line on the cover) and internal (the blue line of the cover) content values. To view our pretty infographic in richer detail and full color, just go to www.storygrid.com and check out the resources section of the website.

EPILOGUE

A TOOL, NOT A FORMULA!

One last big thing to remind you.

I think I've stated numerous times that *The Story Grid* is a tool. It is not a formula.

You cannot just plug a bunch of stuff into The *Foolscap Global Story Grid* or *The Story Grid Spreadsheet* and then diagram it out in the final *Story Grid* and voila have a terrific book come out at the end. If that were the case, I'd do it myself. *The Story Grid* is a tool, a method to check your work or to inspire a work. Nothing more.

I want to leave you with a few other thoughts.

It took me twenty-two years to figure out that *The Story Grid* was not something that any other book editor I knew used. After innumerable lunch and drink dates, I found out that they didn't create their own method to evaluate work by studying Story structure. And they thought I was kind of a nerd for doing that myself. Acquire it, tweak it, get it to market were their mantras. And sometimes that was mine too. Remember that editors don't work for writers. They work for publishers.

Now that I'm a grizzled vet and I understand the realities of the book publishing Business versus the desires of Art, I see *The Story Grid* as a tool to bridge the gap between commercial necessity and literary ambition.

First things first…commercial necessity. Rest assured, using *The Story Grid* will absolutely do no harm to your Story. It will not turn a book that works into a book that doesn't work. It will not botch up your best scene or convince you to cut your best secondary character.

Instead *The Story Grid* can make you learn a great deal about why you've written your Story in the first place. And that knowledge will be indispensable to making your work better. Not just a little bit, but to such an extent that you will find yourself re-energized to laser focus on what exactly your Story is and how you can make it the best it can possibly be.

The Story Grid is all about getting from "Doesn't Work" to "Works" to "Holy Moly This is Incredible!"

Remember, like a joke, if your Story has three major movements—a Beginning Hook, a Middle Build, and an Ending Payoff—for a simple, compelling premise, it works. But that doesn't mean a publisher will offer you a contract or that one million or even one person will buy it.

Now having something work is nice.

But we all know that some jokes are good and make us chuckle and some make us spit out our food. Same with Stories. Some are okay. Some change our lives.

If you want your Story to be great, you've got to hone it and edit it yourself. Even if you get a Big Five publisher to take it on...*especially if you get a Big Five publisher to take it on*. The publisher has bought your Story because they are confident that it will sell to a critical mass of readers "as is." That's their job. Whatever editorial commentary they provide after they've bought it will be first and foremost all about getting their investment back! So they're not going to ask you to take another look at your Lovers Kiss scene and make it less cheesy. A lot of people like cheesy...probably more than those who don't. Only you will care enough to really push yourself to take it from cheesy to heart wrenching.

Now, you may wish to have a greater impact in the world than just selling to ten thousand people (hitting that number is a huge success regardless). If that is the case, you need to know how to analyze and improve the work you've already done without killing the good stuff. This is what *The Story Grid* is for. It's for fixing flaws and bettering strengths.

If you write a better Lovers Kiss scene than the solid cheesy one you've written before, readers will recognize it. They want that better scene. They really do. And if you give it to them, they'll come back for more of your work in the future.

If you use *The Story Grid* tool rigorously and do not give in to the "good enoughs," it will definitely prove the difference between "nice work here, but it's not quite right for us" to "we're getting our numbers together to make you an offer."

It's my contention that most writers don't fear the work. They want to do the work. No one, though, has clearly laid out in practical terms exactly what that work is. I built *The Story Grid* methodology to do that.

Most amateur writers understand the general concepts of Story: that they need a compelling Inciting Incident and that they have to satisfy the expectations of their audience for the particular Genre they've chosen to write. But they have no idea where to begin and no idea of how to analyze their work after they've done some of it to make sure it can withstand the critical winds and turbulent external forces of nature. The problem that bedevils most novice writers (and even some seasoned pros) is that they fall in love with the glamorous aspects of the literary trade—the romance of "the creative process," the thrill of dashing off chapter after chapter in a white heat of inspiration, etc.—and they undervalue the blue-collar aspects of Story construction and inspection—understanding and mastering Genre, Story form, character, Story cast, and so forth.

They fail to learn how to edit.

The inescapable fact is that you need an editor who cares about making your book not just "work" but for it to transcend its Genre...to break new ground in such a way that it changes the way people see the world. And there is only one editor alive with that kind of commitment.

You.

ACKNOWLEDGMENTS

What started out as a hubris-laden declaration, *I'll just toss off some thoughts and we'll bang out a paperback*, for Steven Pressfield and my little publishing company soon turned into a monster.

Over the three years it took to write, *The Story Grid* became nothing less than the sum total of my life's professional work. To get that kind of stuff out of your frontal lobe requires a lot of help.

Without Steven Pressfield, I'd still be sulking in front of a computer screen with miles to go before I slept.

Steve and I have worked together for almost twenty years. On this project, we reversed roles. Steve took on the editor role and I took on the writer assignment. It could have been a disaster. But Steve was the nicest noodge ever. He never pressured me and I have no doubt he would not have damned me even if I'd never gotten this book onto paper. And that was a real possibility. His editorial notes were incisive and kind. They made a meandering mess of stuff cohere.

We've won some and we've lost some. But it's always been fun. Even in our darkest publishing hours, we've always found something to laugh about. Thanks, Pard!

My wife Bibb and my kids Bleecker, Waverly and Crosby had to hear hour after hour of blather about this book for far too long. They never made me feel bad about it. Instead they listened and helped me immeasurably to simplify things that could easily have ended up obtuse and didactic.

Callie Oettinger, the brains behind Black Irish Books, coordinates all of the production, sales and publicity for our titles. And she does it with a commitment and purpose that inspires.

Jeffrey Simon is our dear friend who makes video production, design and technology something that two old dogs can actually understand.

Derick Tsai at Magnus Rex is an absolute pleasure to work with. A designer par excellence with the tact of Norman Vincent Peale, Derick created all of the art for *The Story Grid* and got me through a major meltdown at the finish line.

Our copyeditor Amanda Brown is a Godsend.

Seth Godin gave me the subtitle. Thanks, Seth!

All of the subscribers to www.stevenpressfield.com and www.storygrid.com engage and care in a way that keeps us honest and focused on what we care most about.

Made in the USA
Lexington, KY
09 March 2018